Outpacing Change
in Pharma Operations

Editors
Martin Lösch
Ulf Schrader

Head of Global and European Pharmaceutical and Medical Products Operations Practice
Martin Lösch (Martin_Loesch@mckinsey.com)

Head of North American Pharmaceutical and Medical Products Operations Practice
David Keeling (David_Keeling@mckinsey.com)

Head of Asian Pharmaceutical and Medical Products Operations Practice
Vikas Bhadoria (Vikas_Bhadoria@mckinsey.com)

Global Pharmaceutical and Medical Products Operations Practice Coordinator
Vanya Telpis (Vanya_Telpis@mckinsey.com)

for more information please contact Vanya_Telpis@mckinsey.com ii

Contents

Delivering sustainable future state

Developing new strategies for new times

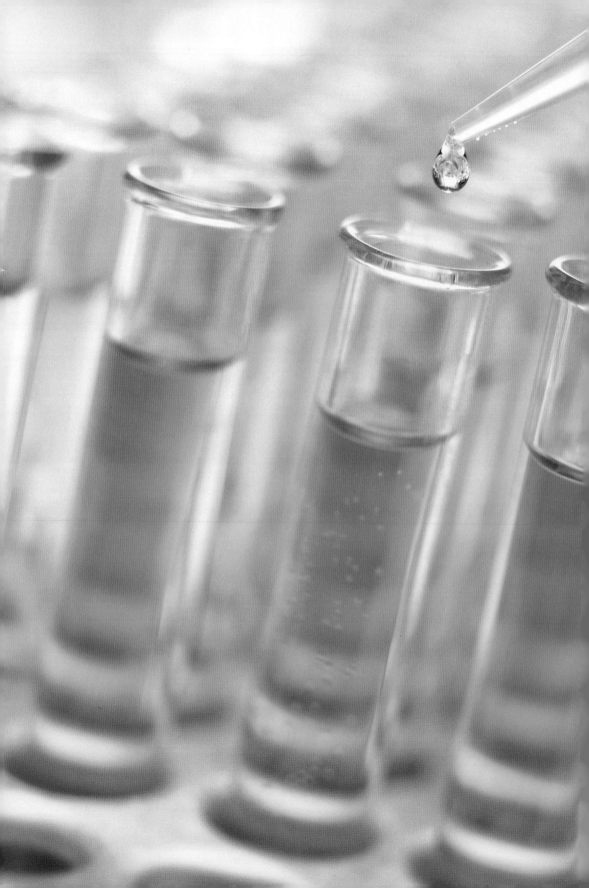

Introduction

Preface: Outpacing change

Martin Lösch, Ulf Schrader

Trends in pharma

Pharma continues to be an attractive industry. The EBIT margin is around 30% for the top 15 pharmacos and 20% for the top generics companies, compared to only about 13% for the S&P 500. Despite this overall positive picture, the industry is undergoing significant changes with implications for operations:

- **New consumers.** Most growth will come from new markets, such as Brazil, Russia, India and China. We expect overall pharma sales in emerging markets to grow by $100 billion between 2010 and 2015—which will require new and often different supply chain solutions to provide the right product to the right customer at the right cost and in the right way

- **An overburdened public sector.** Health care spending will grow 1.5% to 2.5% faster than GDP, imposing ever more severe financial challenges and causing governments to increase pressure on drug spending. In Germany and the UK, our research estimated that prices for the top 25 generic products dropped by 40% between 2005 and 2008, and we expect similar declines elsewhere

- **Generic competition.** Drugs worth about $250 billion in sales, or about 30% of today's global pharma market, will lose patent protection between 2010 and 2015. Production volume will shift from originators as generic companies become the largest drug manufacturers. Many originators, including Sanofi Aventis, GlaxoSmithKline and Novartis/Sandoz, are investing in generics—and building dedicated supply chains to support the growth

- **Product differentiation.** With R&D productivity lagging, pharmacos continue to look for product differentiations, including combination drugs, patient-specific packaging, drug/device combinations, and tiered product offerings. Operations will need to move beyond supplying product on time to driving innovation and exploring new technologies. Only a few pharmacos have those capabilities today, presenting new opportunities for contract manufacturers

- **Risk management.** Risks will continue to go up, driven by globalization, more external partners and a broader range of products and technologies. Regulatory requirements will also increase. American and European regulators are pushing for better processes and control, and emerging markets are establishing stricter regulations. Operations will need to help find relatively low-cost strategies to meet tougher standards.

In short, operations will need to deliver more at much lower cost, in a stricter regulatory environment, while capturing growth opportunities through geographic expansion and product innovation.

Operations as a key value driver

Every pharma company faces major new challenges, but many people see the business as an R&D and marketing game. They tend to underestimate the contribution from operations, often because they don't know enough about it.

Looking at key metrics with an unbiased view, we can see huge opportunities. The average unit cost in top-quartile pharmacos is 50-65% lower than the industry average. Solid technology production capacity is four times larger than demand requires. Despite great efforts, inventory levels have not come down in recent years—and are triple the comparable figures in packaged goods.

Industry-wide, we see an opportunity of $110 billion, corresponding to over half of today's COGS (Exhibit 1) and an EBIT increase of 45%. From a capital market perspective, assuming a typical EBIT multiple of 12, this would create a value of $1.3 trillion. It is therefore no surprise that senior strategists are looking more closely at operations.

But profits are not the only aim of operations improvements. Like quality performance, excellence in operations is now the ticket to play. For the

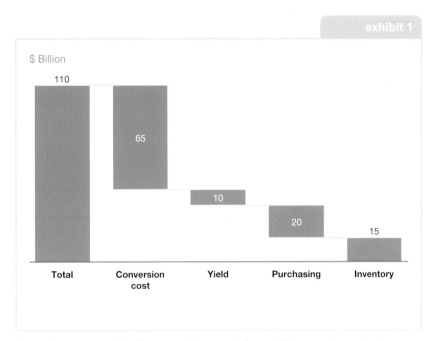

exhibit 1

$ Billion

110

65

10

20

15

| Total | Conversion cost | Yield | Purchasing | Inventory |

increasing commodity-like part of the portfolio, and for growing markets beyond Europe and the US, low costs are often essential to success.

Some pharmacos began operational excellence efforts more than 10 years ago, but many of those efforts failed, some due to lack of understanding, others because they were undertaken in a half-hearted way, underestimating the magnitude and breadth of change required. Making the necessary changes can be challenging due to the costs of restructuring a legacy production footprint. But the people challenge is even bigger. Many leadership teams still lack an understanding of what a lean company looks like and don't "walk the talk." Sustainable performance improvements are rooted in mindsets and skills, management structure and company culture. These cannot be changed overnight, and late starters are naïve to believe they can easily catch up.

In other industries, companies that embarked early on perfecting execution have built sturdy competitive advantages. Toyota opened its doors to visitors in the early 1990's, for example, but competitors have begun to come close to its performance only recently. To this day, only Toyota manages to produce compact cars, station wagons and vans on the same assembly line in an efficient manner.

Other first movers in operations excellence, such as Dell, Alcoa, Caterpillar, GE and Wal-Mart, have captured leadership positions in their industries through leadership in operations. They have proven people wrong who said they could catch up or that "value beats cost."

But what these winners really achieved was not simply operational improvement that lowered costs and lead times, but the institutional capability to outpace others in the *rate of improvement*—and that is what this book is about.

Outpacing change

Everybody is driving change, but not at the same speed. More than the improvements themselves, what matters is the institutional capability to improve. This requires the analytical ability to spot the right issues, management alignment on what success means, effective decision processes, open internal and external dialogue to develop creative solutions, and transparent monitoring mechanisms to ensure delivery. It also requires high "skill-will"—the capability to improve one's own performance and lead others to improve.

Operations can be improved in three areas:

- **Technical system.** Improvement can include better production processes, technical setup, machine layout, or workflow organizations

- **Management infrastructure.** Better organizational and management processes (controlling, reporting, decisions, reward and recognition, etc.) provide no direct improvements, but they improve focus and execution

- **Mindsets and behaviors.** People need the right mindsets and capabilities to tackle change.

Excellent companies show distinctiveness in all three areas. If one is missing, the improvement process often stalls. But if they are in place, the organization can move through repeated cycles of diagnosing situations, defining a future state, implementing it, sustaining it and then moving on to a new strategic focus for further improvements.

We have organized the book along this cycle of continuous improvement (Exhibit 2):

- Diagnosing the opportunity

- Delivering sustainable future state

- Developing new strategies for new times.

In each chapter, we offer our perspectives on outpacing competitors—how to make step changes that go far beyond typical improvements in the range of

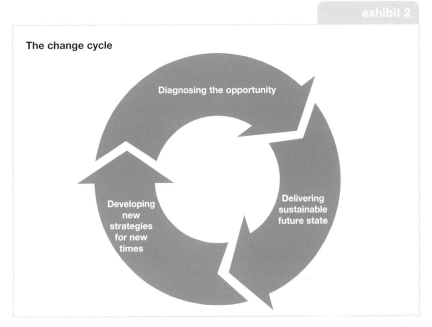

The change cycle

Diagnosing the opportunity

Delivering sustainable future state

Developing new strategies for new times

factor cost increases. Looking beyond successful projects, we aim to identify scalable and sustainable change that will improve institutions in areas such as purchasing, API and pharma production, distribution and quality, technical development, and supply chain management.

Our recommendations arise from our experience in over 600 engagements in pharma operations and supply chain over the past three years, and a wealth of proprietary research. As always, we hope to stimulate your thinking, and we look forward to your feedback.

Outlook on pharma operations

David Keeling, Martin Lösch, Ulf Schrader

The pressure is building for fundamental change.

Before we look into the future, what do we see if we look back? Overall, pharma operations have not changed much. Yes, companies have gradually cut costs and lead times, and the business is managed more professionally today. But pharmaceuticals are still made and distributed essentially the same way they were 20 years ago. That will have to change.

It's hard to make accurate predictions in a dynamic environment, but we can safely assume that today's challenges will become more severe. The industry and its stakeholders' efforts to resolve pressing issues will likely trigger fundamental changes. Companies that anticipate and adapt to these changes will thrive in the years ahead. Here are the opportunities we believe are most relevant:

Freeing up $25 billion in cash from inventory

On average, pharma underperforms on working capital management. The average pharmaco holds 180 days of finished goods inventory on hand, for example, with top performers at about 100 days. Their peers in the consumer goods industry hold only 60 days' inventory, based on McKinsey benchmarks.

Pharmacos may not want to cut inventory to 60 days, since their margins are higher and the lifesaving role of some drugs calls for higher service levels. But at current inventory values, pharma could free up $25 billion (all figures in US dollars) if it reduced inventories on hand to a realistic target of 80-100 days.

This huge opportunity is within reach, but only for companies that can align across functions and use their capabilities rigorously. Companies will need an increasingly powerful supply chain function, with broader and deeper involvement in planning, production, distribution, and purchasing processes. Data transparency will be necessary to operate an increasingly global supply chain. This will not require expensive new ERP systems, but it will demand a clear IT strategy.

Eliminating overcapacity of 50% or more

Today's 75% overcapacity in solid dose manufacturing[1] (see Exhibit 1) has arisen for a variety of reasons: volume shifts from originators to generic competitors (who often build highly cost-effective assets), "once-daily" and combination medications, shifts in technologies, deliberate over-investments to create safety buffers, and increasing productivity. A McKinsey study of over 30 global pharmacos shows average annual productivity increases of 7% over the past four years, which implies that productivity would double in a decade.

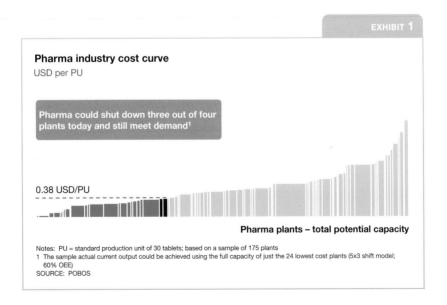

EXHIBIT 1

Pharma industry cost curve
USD per PU

Pharma could shut down three out of four plants today and still meet demand[1]

0.38 USD/PU

Pharma plants – total potential capacity

Notes: PU = standard production unit of 30 tablets; based on a sample of 175 plants
1 The sample actual current output could be achieved using the full capacity of just the 24 lowest cost plants (5x3 shift model; 60% OEE)
SOURCE: POBOS

---

1   This assumes a three-shift utilization of key equipment, average to good performance, and less than 40% downtime on the equipment.

Overcapacity in API production is even worse, thanks to high-potency molecules, improved synthesis routes, better productivity, and a major shift of production to low-cost countries, especially India and China.

Pharmacos must therefore continue and even accelerate network consolidations. These will have to happen gradually to balance the need for a competitive infrastructure with restructuring costs. But as the high-tech industry has painfully demonstrated, those who wait too long will get caught in a trap where the cost of restructuring overburdens their P&L and they start to tumble.

In the past, many pharmacos preferred to sell plants rather than close them. This was not cheaper, but it avoided the social unrest that goes along with closures. We expect it to become more difficult to find buyers, especially for plants without valuable know-how. It is clear that someone will have to carry the cost of downsizing.

Getting third parties under control

With few exceptions, pharmacos have moved away from the belief that they should produce products in-house by default. Today, the dominant model is a balance of in-house and contracted production, with most pharmaceutical production in-house and API outsourced. On average, a global pharmaco works with 100 to 200 contract manufacturing organizations (CMOs)— probably too many.

A more proactive approach to external partnerships is a powerful way to optimize utilization and reduce risk—and it can accelerate innovation. Partners can bring new formulations to the table, along with packaging ideas or devices. As breakthrough research becomes more difficult, these can become key differentiators.

Managing external partnerships requires shifting the focus from manufacturing towards supply. Making this shift involves new capabilities and governance mechanisms. Companies should conduct systematic screenings of high-value partnerships, design contracts to create win-win situations, and create supplier performance management mechanisms. In some cases, supplier development programs will make the best use of a pharmaco's knowledge. Managing a supplier network also requires the involvement of functions beyond Operations, especially Marketing, Quality, and Business Development, to ensure balanced decision-making that considers aspects from "total cost of ownership" and risk exposure to image and competitor strategy.

Making the supply chain more flexible

Capacity needs can change within months or even weeks, while capacity planning often takes a "one-year plus" perspective. This disconnect has to be resolved through a more flexible supply chain, because as today's vast overcapacity is brought down, the risk of backorders goes up. The right supply chain requires flexibility along five dimensions: assets, suppliers, people, processes and strategy.

Assets need to become more "fluid" to ramp volumes up or down quickly at a reasonable cost. Dynamic capacity management can include in-house production, contact manufacturing, buying, selling and mothballing plants, and creating overflow assets in low-cost regions. Leading pharmacos are contemplating trading capacity among themselves to help balance supply and demand and sharing knowledge and technologies. We estimate that the top 10 pharmacos could generate savings of $1-2 billion using these approaches

Pharmacos often focus too much on negotiating cost savings or ensuring compliance requirements, rather than improving total cost of ownership and value-creation through supplier flexibility. This takes more than rewriting a few contract terms: strategic sourcing planning and supplier integration, development and renewal can help a company gradually create a flexible supply base.

The increasingly global and complex pharma supply chains need highly skilled and internationally experienced talent who can drive supply chain innovation projects around the globe and sustain an edge on competitors. Pharmacos also need to manage demand fluctuations with existing employees by introducing flexible shift systems and shared labor pools.

Leading companies are starting to embed flexibility in their supply chain processes. Lean fulfillment and replenishment, fast-track processing for crucial launches, nimble S&OP processes and forecasting focused on major events help them outpace the competition.

And a coherent supply chain strategy based on segmentation can balance flexibility and cost across all elements and concentrate investments where they produce the biggest returns. Companies that segment their supply chains can reduce the need for flexibility in key products and markets, and standardizing processes reduces variability created in-house. Better information strategies can maximize foresight to allow balancing over time.

Learning the commodity business

In Germany, mutual insurance funds have started to tender drugs for their members, the most prominent example being AOK[2]. Despite legal challenges, they have lowered drug costs by 40-50%. While tendering models differ by country, they are increasingly important and now account for over 15% of the European generics market.

This reflects the increasing commoditization of drugs. Many innovator companies, including Sanofi Aventis, Pfizer, GlaxoSmithKline and Novartis/ Sandoz, have long relied on a hybrid of innovative products and generics, and these companies have made it a strategic priority to maximize the value of their commoditized portfolio. But they will succeed only if they create a new operating model to address the specifics and stand up against competitors like Teva and Dr. Reddy's.

The commodity market requires low production costs and flexibility in the entire organization to grasp emerging opportunities. To select a successful pricing strategy, a company must have a clear understanding of the COGS for a specific product. Coming from a value-based pricing, rather than a cost-plus system, many pharmacos lack the financial systems to know the real cost of products, and may add a disproportionate share of overhead to their commodity products.

While operational performance has improved significantly over the last decade, innovator companies still struggle to create the mindset of a generic company and radically drive down cost. Many "lean" efforts have captured only a fraction of the improvement potential.

Finding the next $20 to 30 billion in savings

On average, the pharma industry is still far from being lean. But there are some examples of operational excellence where further cost reductions are not obvious. How can sites tap into new opportunities to reduce their COGS? Based on McKinsey analyses, quality-by-design and design-to-cost could yield $20 to $30 billion industry-wide.

Few companies today design or tailor technology platforms, or even consider them early on in the development process, to avoid extra equipment, processing steps and rework. Why? First, no single owner in the organization drives platform strategies and simultaneous development. Responsibility for technical development typically lies with R&D, not Operations, and R&D does

---

2   Allgemeine Ortskrankenkassen

not have the incentives or knowledge to avoid cost during the market phase. We expect organizational changes in the future to address this and to be a major catalyst for savings. Second, platform strategy is by necessity a long-term effort, with payback periods of five years or more.

With a further portfolio fragmentation and a proliferation of technologies, quality-by-design and design-to-cost will become even more important. Portfolios will increasingly cover not only therapeutic drugs but also diagnostics, biomarkers, drug/device combinations, patient packs, and so on.

As companies explore new technologies and process design, they must also rethink technical development. For example, how can they (almost) eliminate changeover times through liquid API?   How can they avoid QC testing through process control, rather than the traditional trial and error approach? The opportunities are huge, but so are the investments. Companies will have to think through their strategies carefully.

Lifting the regulatory burden

For obvious reasons, quality will remain the top priority in pharma. But what is the best way to achieve it? Between 25 and 30% of conversion costs today are quality-related, based on McKinsey benchmarks, mostly because more global plants serve major markets. Harmonization efforts have been long underway, but it is hard to predict when they will succeed, especially as emerging markets create their own standards. Many countries are "averaging to the max"—adopting a combination of the strictest developed market standards. It is more difficult to comply with Brazil or Russia today than with the FDA, for example, even though the FDA has increased its scrutiny.

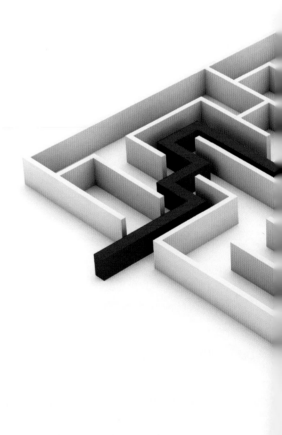

Companies will need to move away from mere "risk avoidance"—an impossible goal in any case—to a more structured risk assessment and prioritization of resources, not to cut costs but to focus more closely on what matters.

Since harmonizing global oversight is at least partly a political process, it is inherently unpredictable. But the industry's willingness to join forces on quality and compliance has already translated into the design of an industry-wide supplier auditing system. This could be a good starting point to engage more with regulators and accelerate harmonization, avoiding a further proliferation of compliance systems.

In the short term, companies can radically simplify their quality and compliance systems, making them cheaper, simpler and therefore safer. Most operational excellence efforts in quality and compliance have delivered unexpectedly high savings.

Catching the train to emerging markets

Emerging markets will be the growth engines of pharma. Seven out of ten people live in emerging markets today, and every year, over 100 million children are born there.

We expect pharma sales in emerging markets to grow from about $80 billion today to $180 billion by 2015 as companies struggle to serve about five billion people there. Life expectancy in these markets is among the lowest in the world and the healthcare infrastructure is poor. Now is the time to lay the groundwork for increasing market share.

While the opportunity is huge, so is the challenge, especially from an operations point of view. In India, for example, prices are 85 to 90% lower than in the US and they continue to fall. Some Indian companies produce tablets at a cost of $2 per thousand, compared to the roughly $60 that multinational corporations spend on average. This has major implications for business models, especially for pharmacos selling into markets with cost-plus pricing structures. Achieving low cost is not just a matter of raising margins— it is a prerequisite to entry.

The challenge of emerging markets goes beyond cost: it also includes innovation, flexibility, and distribution. In India, for instance, combination drugs are driving growth, and Indian companies are quick to launch these new formulations. The innovation model is designed "customer-back" rather than "science-forward." In distribution, models vary widely across countries and pose different challenges. In China, for example, companies face over 1,000 wholesalers in a multi-layer structure; in Mexico, retailers expect pharmacos to provide category management skills; and in other countries, pharmacos such as Sanofi Aventis in Brazil have forward-integrated to ensure distribution and create strategic advantages.

Serving emerging markets at large scale to capture growth requires a different model, not just adjustments. The diversity of these markets requires more flexibility, balanced with global synergies. This is true for the BRIC countries and for Africa, where no pharmaco has developed an effective distribution model. Why do mobile phones sell profitably in Nigeria, but drugs do not?

Nearly all pharmacos use the same strategy to capture growth in emerging markets. The difference will be in the quality of execution, especially in operations. In the years ahead, most pharmacos' output will be destined for emerging markets. Many of these markets will also require that production be local or in a low-cost region. The emerging market supply chain will therefore not be an annex—it will become the *core* of pharma operations.

Winning on talent

There are still huge opportunities in pharma operations. As we have outlined, this will require major changes in operating models, organization, technology, mindset, and geography. Pharmacos will have to consider if they are in a position to manage all these changes themselves or if they will partner with others. This decision depends largely on the talent they can attract, retain, and develop, not only to manage the day-to-day business, but also to lead the change.

But talent and skills matter beyond management. Navigating rising challenges requires that all employees, including operators and first-line managers, are developed and deployed to the maximum of their abilities. Quality space, standard work, JIT, and the other techniques of smart operations all require skilled and motivated staff.

Human Resources and Operations today tend to work side-by-side, not together, and have little understanding of the other's challenges or capabilities. Defining a joint agenda and leveraging training, coaching, career planning and incentives to develop the best people will be essential.

* * *

Operations used to be judged on the delivery of quality product to the market. Today, companies must deliver quality at low cost. While there are still many obvious opportunities to reduce cost further, companies also need to ask "what's next?" We believe that the time has come to rethink pharma operations and create a vision and strategy that go beyond cost reduction and capacity planning for next year's budget.

How can operations accelerate growth—in Africa, for instance? How can innovations in operations trigger new business models? How can a manufacturer organize the integrated and paperless distribution of drugs directly to patients?

Companies that can conceive and adopt a bolder strategy will create a strategic advantage. In the future, nobody in those companies will then dare to claim Operations is not core to business success.

Diagnosing
the opportunity

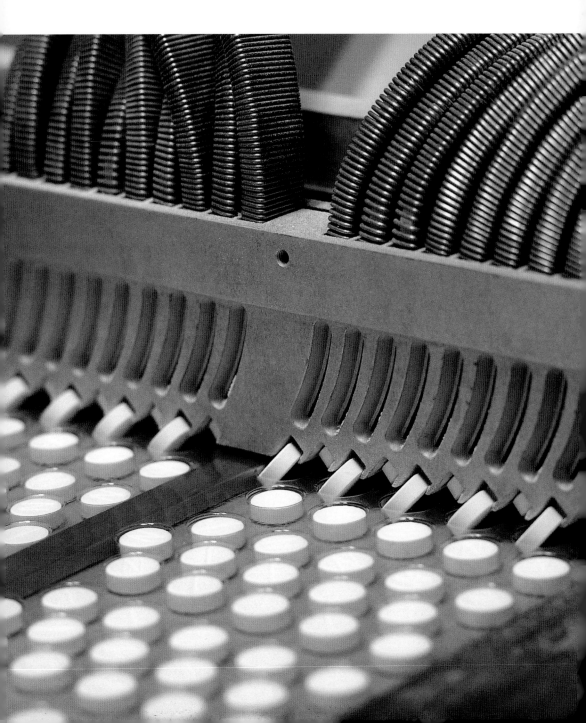

Driving a transformation in efficiency

Philipp Cremer, Martin Lösch, Ulf Schrader

Pharmaceutical companies risk being too cautious in their quest for productivity improvements. New research shows that the widespread adoption of the best practices in operations will deliver cost reductions of 50% for typical pharma firms.

The pharmaceutical industry is waking up to the fact that operational excellence is important. After decades in a world where patents protected revenues and regulatory concerns constrained operational change, companies now understand that they will need to be faster, more productive and more flexible to compete in tomorrow's industry. In response, most are embarking on operational improvements of one sort or another.

These efforts are essential, but many companies are insufficiently aggressive in setting targets for operational improvement. The average rate of productivity improvement across the industry is 7% per annum. A new benchmarking study of more than 30 global pharmaceutical manufacturers, however, reveals that top plants today are already more than twice as productive as their average counterparts. That gap will only widen if the majority of firms fail to mount an effective response: top performers in the survey are improving their performance by 20% every year.

The study, part of the POBOS benchmarking effort, included a detailed analysis of the financial data and operational performance of more than 2,500 work centers at 200 plants around the world. To ensure the comparability of data, we clustered the main technologies (solids, steriles, etc.) and normalized all results for factors such as differences in product technologies (coated versus uncoated tablets, for example), unit sizes (large versus small blister packs), value chain configurations, and levels of outsourcing.

No excuses

There appear to be few barriers preventing all plants from achieving the performance of the top quartile. Despite broad geographic differences—for instance, European plants are often more productive than those in North America—there are top players in every region we studied. This finding suggests that industry-wide improvement will offer substantial rewards: by matching the top players' total labor productivity (capital productivity shows comparable results), average drug makers would enjoy annual labor and unit-cost savings worth 5 to 6 percentage points of earnings before interest and taxes. At the industry level, the value of that opportunity exceeds $40-50 billion (see Exhibit 1).

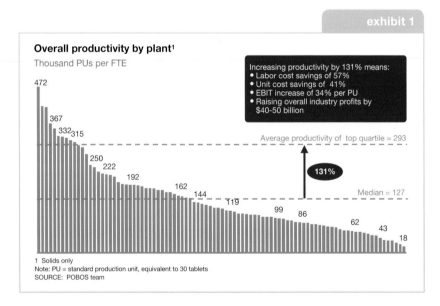

exhibit 1

Overall productivity by plant[1]
Thousand PUs per FTE

Increasing productivity by 131% means:
• Labor cost savings of 57%
• Unit cost savings of 41%
• EBIT increase of 34% per PU
• Raising overall industry profits by $40-50 billion

Average productivity of top quartile = 293

131%

Median = 127

472
367
332 315
250
222
192
162
144
119
99
86
62
43
18

1 Solids only
Note: PU = standard production unit, equivalent to 30 tablets
SOURCE: POBOS team

Not surprisingly, small plants, those producing fewer than about 1.5 billion tablets a year, are substantially less productive. But the benefits of scale tail off rapidly, and apparently do not extend to the largest plants—those exceeding about 3 billion tablets a year (Exhibit 2). Additional management complexity may sap their productivity.

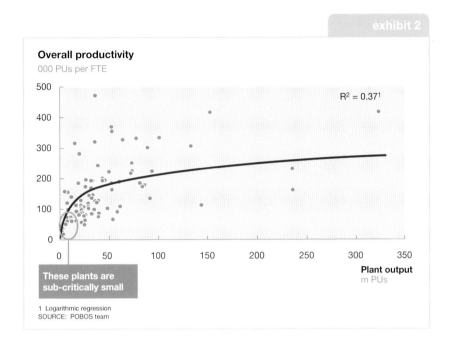

exhibit 2

Overall productivity
000 PUs per FTE

$R^2 = 0.37$[1]

These plants are sub-critically small

Plant output
m PUs

1 Logarithmic regression
SOURCE: POBOS team

The data also shows that the most productive plants are often among the most complex, with over 1000 SKUs and 300 different formulations. A typical packaging line handles more than 100 SKUs and a typical production line handles more than ten formulations.

Complexity has forced the top performers to define more rigorous process standards and apply them strictly. People understand their responsibilities and perform their tasks in highly effective ways. This finding is highly counterintuitive for most operations managers who have strived to produce in large batches and packaging campaigns. The reality is that the undisputable benefits from increased batch and lot sizes are small compared to the huge impact lean techniques can bring. Only in tailored production setups with (semi)dedicated equipment, we can see "simplicity" being a major driver of efficiency.

A similar logic applies for regulatory approvals: the data shows that the most productive plants are likely to be validated by FDA, in some cases also by EMEA and PMDA.

Nor are the high achievers buying their way to improved performance with expensive manufacturing equipment. High line speed alone does not correlate with higher productivity. We found some plants with low- to average-speed equipment—often sourced inexpensively from India, China and Korea at 15% of the cost in the US—that had achieved high productivity and low overall unit cost. The faster the equipment, the harder to change over and run with few stoppages.

Finally, the most productive plants in our survey achieved this performance without sacrificing either quality or service levels. In fact, higher productivity was correlated with better quality performance.[1] These findings should not seem counterintuitive: better plants boost quality by building it into their processes, not by catching problems downstream with more frequent inspections and consequent interruptions to production. In parallel, we see that the laboratories operate more efficiently. In top-performing labs, technicians test twice as many batches as those in an average lab.

Improving productivity requires looking carefully into the direct and indirect areas (maintenance, quality, administration), but for different reasons. Direct areas typically account for 60% of the headcount, but indirect areas are important because they represent the biggest performance spread. In particular, top-performing generics plants show half the indirect cost of top performers from innovator companies, while the advantage in direct areas is small.

Not only more productive

The most productive plants in our survey enjoy other advantages, too. They release 97% of their products to market without rework, compared with 92% for average companies. This is one of the major drivers of "hidden work" based on our analyses. The stable, standardized processes used by the best plants also drive up yields. The best companies we surveyed achieved yields of more than 99%, a gap of more than 5% over poor performers.

The best pharmaceutical manufacturers respond much more quickly to demand. Top-quartile players in our survey reach final delivery twice as fast as average manufacturers, and more than five times faster than bottom-quartile competitors (exhibit 3). More efficient supply chains play a big role: top companies, for example, are more likely to conduct weekly rather than monthly planning cycles and can therefore respond to customer needs faster.

---

1   For more on quality see article "Finding the keys to quality productivity and performance" on page 64

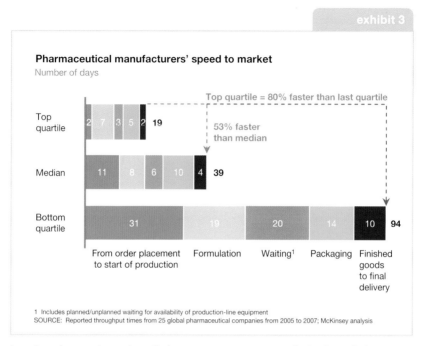

Pharmaceutical manufacturers' speed to market
Number of days

Top quartile = 80% faster than last quartile

Top quartile: 2 7 3 5 2 **19**

53% faster than median

Median: 11 8 6 10 4 **39**

Bottom quartile: 31 19 20 14 10 **94**

From order placement to start of production | Formulation | Waiting[1] | Packaging | Finished goods to final delivery

1 Includes planned/unplanned waiting for availability of production-line equipment
SOURCE: Reported throughput times from 25 global pharmaceutical companies from 2005 to 2007; McKinsey analysis

Leading drug makers also eliminate unnecessary complexity from their production-planning activities—for instance, by using fixed, repeatable, short-duration production schedules that increase flexibility and diminish the likelihood that they will be forced to change production plans for any given product. The financial benefits of speed include significantly lower inventory. For a bottom-quartile drug maker, reaching the throughput performance of top quartile companies would be worth 2% of EBIT.

Much more with much less

The advantages enjoyed by the best plants come from a fundamentally different approach to the way they manage and operate their facilities. They exhibit dramatic differences in the way they staff their lines and in efficient equipment use to achieve superior overall equipment effectiveness and utilization.

The top performers in our survey separate man and machine when staffing their lines. For example, they may assign one operator to manage two tablet presses, where their less efficient competitors use between two and four people to complete the same work. Leaders achieve this by using smart line balancing techniques to allocate tasks, ensuring that their staff spends more time adding value and less waiting for other processes to complete.

The operational-equipment effectiveness (OEE) of top performers is more than twice those of bottom-quartile plants, and when we looked closely, we found that process design, continuous optimization based on root-cause problem-solving and the resulting process stability accounted for two-thirds of the difference. Low performers, for instance, are less likely to standardize measurement or equipment control parameters, and therefore generate more than twice as much waste from line stoppages. Top performers have less than 10% OEE loss, and average performers about 20-25%.

Equipment utilization also shows considerable variation. High performers reach levels around 58%—corresponding to a three-shift setup that is effectively utilized at 80%—compared to an industry median of 30%. Average companies that could raise their utilization to 58% would increase EBIT by around one percentage point (Exhibit 4). This is another place where scale matters, since instability in production schedules and losses of production volumes have a smaller impact on utilization in large plants.

Getting there

For low- or average-performing pharma plants, the challenge is to create a new approach to operational improvement. The advantage enjoyed by leading plants is remarkable as much for what these plants have not done as for what they have. Little of their performance advantage can be attributed to automation, faster equipment or more sophisticated IT. The key differentiator is how effectively assets and people are deployed to increase OEE and reduce non-value-added time. Consequently, capital investments have less impact than time spent tacking waste, and training operators to apply new standards and tools.

Getting this right requires abandoning the all-too-common culture that focuses on fixing only the symptoms of underperformance: compensating for fluctuating demand by stockpiling inventory, compensating for low yields by overproducing, or running lines more slowly and with higher staffing to avoid stoppages, to offer three common examples.

Instead, companies must go to the core of the issues—bit by bit and with cross-functional collaboration. They must remove the root causes of stoppages, implement design-to-quality processes to avoid poor formulations and establish robust forecasting and demand management processes that minimize avoidable volume fluctuations. Doing this will deliver higher performance today—and help these companies accelerate and embed ongoing improvements, laying the foundations for sustainable competitive advantage.

* * *

Our research shows that doubling productivity can and should be a realistic
aspiration for many pharma companies. By striving for excellence in every
aspect of their operations, rather than taking last year's budget as a reference
point, these companies can take strides to close the performance gaps of
50% or 100% that exist today. Doing so could fundamentally change the
competitive landscape. A top-performing plant in Europe today, for example,
can serve its local market more cost effectively than the majority of plants in
India and China.

Research in brief:
Operational excellence in API

Kai Biller, Paul Rutten, Ulf Schrader

If pharma formulation and packaging plants face challenging times, API makers have it even harder. API production has been a primary target for new market entrants from India and China, resulting in intense price pressure. It is common for API prices to drop by 10-15% per year for more than six years after loss of exclusivity if there is competition from the Far East (see Exhibit 1). The factor cost advantage of India and China in API production is much bigger than in formulation and packaging. The reason is that the differences in automation of an average line are lower, so wage levels play a bigger role. In addition, capital assets, such as buildings and vessels, are built by local companies rather than sourced globally.

These factors help explain the relentless wave of site sales, restructuring, downsizing and downright outsourcing of all API production by pharma companies.

Despite this highly competitive environment, there may still be a significant opportunity for productivity improvement in existing API facilities. As part of the POBOS project, we looked at over 25 API sites. Productivity in these plants varied less than in formulation or packaging sites, but the best plants we studied were still three times more efficient than others. This is a surprisingly large productivity gap for such a mature and partly commoditized industry.

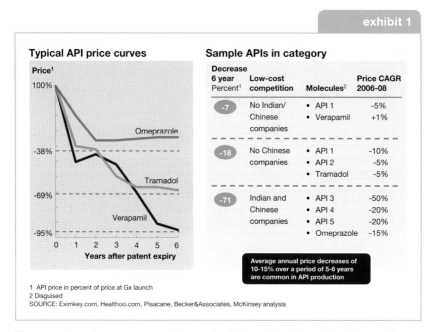

exhibit 1

Typical API price curves

Price[1]
100%

Omeprazole

-38%

Tramadol

-69%

Verapamil

-95%

0   1   2   3   4   5   6
Years after patent expiry

Sample APIs in category

Decrease 6 year Percent[1]	Low-cost competition	Molecules[2]	Price CAGR 2006-08
-7	No Indian/ Chinese companies	• API 1 • Verapamil	-5% +1%
-18	No Chinese companies	• API 1 • API 2 • Tramadol	-10% -5% -5%
-71	Indian and Chinese companies	• API 3 • API 4 • API 5 • Omeprazole	-50% -20% -20% -15%

Average annual price decreases of 10-15% over a period of 5-6 years are common in API production

1 API price in percent of price at Gx launch
2 Disguised
SOURCE: Eximkey.com, Healthoo.com, Pisacane, Becker&Associates, McKinsey analysis

Tracking down the sources of this productivity variability requires thorough analyses. Not all differences are performance-related, but some are driven by technological differences and production volumes. Our data also hints that some plants—particularly during the run-up to commercial launch—are operated in a manner that prioritizes flexibility over efficiency, making some overcapacity inevitable. However, our initial results also show that productivity in these plants does not have to suffer.

In many of the areas of productivity where formulation and packaging plants have big potential for improvement, API players are already performing well. They have an average utilization of above 80%, while the average in pharma is around 35% (see Exhibit 2). Overall equipment effectiveness (OEE) in formulation and packaging is typically around 45%, while in API it is over 70%. Meanwhile, QC labs are around 15% more productive than in formulation and packaging. Similar patterns can be found in maintenance productivity, QA productivity and overhead.

These good results should not be cause for complacency, however. Benchmarking results show that API plants could still make substantial reductions in line staffing, cut overhead further and continue to enhance their OEE. As in other pharma plants, standard work, performance transparency, willingness to challenge the status quo and building the right skills to improve production will be of high value to API makers.

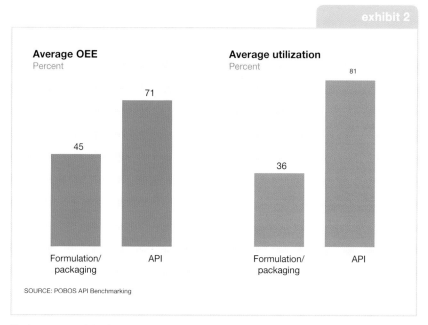

SOURCE: POBOS API Benchmarking

Perhaps surprisingly, we found that yield variability was a particularly important productivity lever at API plants. Across the industry, we have found yield variations up to 30% from batch to batch and campaign to campaign. Although yield measurement and yield control will never be perfect, the numbers indicate a substantial cost-saving potential. The API industry might make better use of its extensive in-process controls to eliminate variation and drive up yields.

Our conclusion from the benchmarking is that network rationalizations will continue to leverage factor cost advantages in Far East. At the same time, however, the significant variability in process controls and productivity means that Western plants will still be able to outcompete low-cost players on specific technologies or skills. All in all, the pull to the east should not distract from the substantial opportunities to improve efficiencies of the current footprint, which often are larger than expected.

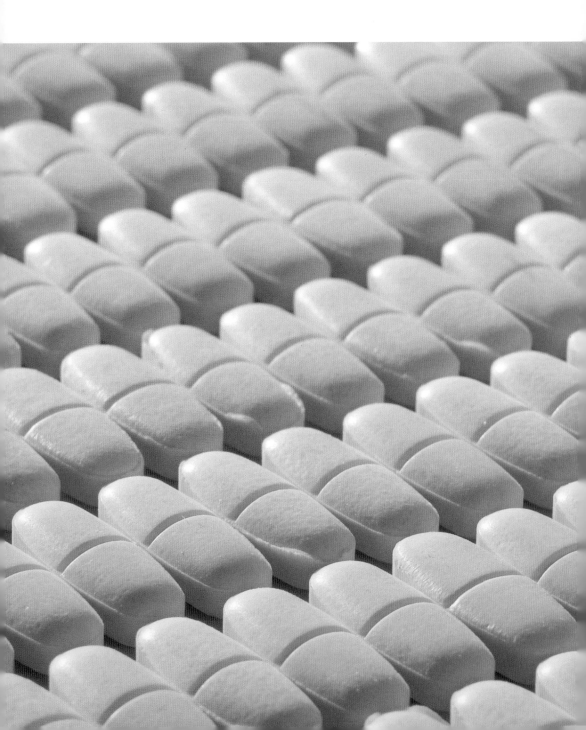

Holding the
diagnostic mirror

Vikas Bhadoria, Thibaut Dedeurwaerder, Jonathan Tilley

Pharma managers should learn to watch their operations differently, see opportunities for improvement on the shop floor, and learn from top-performing peers and leaders in other industries how to capture these opportunities. The company that succeeds in this effort will emerge as "the Toyota of the pharmaceutical industry."

The pharmaceutical industry is lagging other industries in operational efficiency, as indicated by OEE ranges of 10-60%, up to six-month lead times, and other measures. Few pharma managers understand shop-floor operations and their potential for improvement, and few learn from their industry peers, even those whose performance is far superior. But even the best-performing pharmaceutical plant is miles away from the efficiency achieved at the average Toyota plant. Only those pharma companies and plants with enough courage and imagination to learn and apply lessons from other industry leaders can hope to break from the pack.

Diagnosing by "Genchi Genbutsu"

When Taichi Ohno, Toyota's head of production engineering after the second world war, visited Ford's plants in Michigan, he may have been impressed by what he saw in the industry leader's facilities. But beyond understanding the manufacturing system, he found many areas for improvement on the production line, such as a leveled pace of production and a smaller work-in-progress inventory. His visit, and the knowledge he took back to Japan, show how looking at systems or processes with fresh eyes can reveal new insights at the most basic level. This is exactly what pharmaceutical companies need to do now to uncover opportunities for improvement in operations.

This type of visit offers several lessons. Years before Toyota codified its core manufacturing principles, Mr. Ohno had already found new approaches to looking at production processes. The principle was "Genchi Genbutsu"—go and see for yourself. Managers watch processes, in person, to understand the fundamentals of what adds value and what does not. This approach would later become one of Toyota's most famous slogans, and it is fundamental to production process diagnostics.

No matter how good their information, pharma managers rarely find inefficiencies in operations behind a desk. Yet all too often, managers accept the data in front of them without challenge. Anybody who wants to know what really goes on in manufacturing, including people's difficulties and daily worries, must go to the shop floor and look, listen, question and understand.

We find that many pharma managers get wrapped up in other areas and fail to understand how much value can be added. They spend too little time watching operations or meeting and talking with employees. People on the shop floor often tell us that managers seem uncomfortable during visits. Not sure how they should behave, what they should be looking for or asking, many managers are actually relieved when they can return to the safety of their offices.

What should they be learning?

Pharma managers need to "learn to see" waste and variability in familiar processes, rather than just the barriers to change. Managers must ask "what would it take" rather than simply report "why we can't do it." Looking for waste and variability, especially in your own operations, requires courage. It also requires observation. In more than 50 plant walks and diagnostics we have conducted, we have seen pharma executives gain tremendous insights and benefits.

When we brought pharma managers to the shop floor, we sometimes found that less than half the equipment was running, and that multiple weeks of work in progress (WIP) was stored in many different places. On other occasions, we found different operators working on the same equipment with no clear work descriptions, and saw for ourselves the heavy burdens of batch documentation.

Results from these diagnostics speak for themselves: Many plants can improve their productivity and throughput times by 30%, and some by 50%.

What are leading pharma plants' best practices?

Some pharma plants perform up to 20 times better than their lowest-performing peers, according to POBOS benchmarks for over 200 facilities. What distinguishes the top performers?

What we notice first when visiting top performing plants is the activity on the shop floor. Paradoxically, it is relatively low! Corridors are lonely, lines are populated sparingly, and people aren't running around. Multi-machine handling helps make this possible. But implementing this seemingly simple principle requires three enablers that distinguish top performers:

- **Machine effectiveness** at top-performing plants is significantly higher, with OEEs as high as 60%. Lines have fewer minor stops and breakdowns; product changeovers are executed efficiently; lines are run at a speed that meets the targeted output and quality. Underlying high machine effectiveness is a problem-solving approach where production operators, maintenance technicians and engineers collaborate in the pursuit of continuous improvement. Line performance is monitored systematically and continuously. Where a gap appears between planned and actual performance, the team responds immediately by looking for the root cause and implementing countermeasures.

- **Efficient workplace design** also plays a key role. Good plant layout enables multi-tasking. This includes a minimum of physical barriers on the shop floor to allow operators to flow between areas (e.g., automatic doors, same clean room classification throughout production). Line operators at top plants have all they need at arm's length, and work stations are close to each other to reduce walking and searching time.

- **Elimination of non-value-adding activities**. Obviously, high machine effectiveness and efficient workplace design help reduce non-value added activities like repairing, waiting and walking. But top performers push it further. For example, by adopting the "critical to quality" principle, they reduce documentation by limiting the number of inputs to the items that really matter for product quality. Beyond removing non-value adding tasks, they also try to simplify activities. Fewer and simpler tasks mean fewer mistakes. The number and frequency of in-process controls are reduced to what is appropriate based on the process need and knowledge, rather than habit or tradition.

Many top performers have also reduced non-value-adding activities by investing in automation, such as automatic weighing stations and guided vehicles, container-washing machines and electronic batch records. The distinctiveness here, however, lies not so much in the investments but in the way the automation and systems are selected and implemented.

Top performers understand that automation in itself does not guarantee performance or productivity. For any automation investment, they require a clear business case that is reviewed in a thorough capex approval process. Also, any process to be automated is optimized in depth before being automated to avoid "locking in" inefficiencies.

Another characteristic that distinguishes top-performing plants is the mindset of their leaders. Most recognize that pharma is no different from other industries that have applied lean concepts. A recurring challenge is the perception that lean principles are difficult to marry with pharmaceutical operations, because of the highly regulated nature of the industry.

But managers at high-performing plants find the lean journey does not expose them to undue risk—and can even offer the same kinds of benefits seen in other industries. On one hand, managers understand that productivity and efficiency do not have to compromise quality, and that simplified work processes can reduce complexity, non-value-added activity and opportunities for error. What's more, with quality being one of the main functions in pharma plants, managers also understand how lean principles can have tremendous benefits when applied in the quality department itself.

How Toyota would make pills

Given the huge spread in performance, pharma plants can learn a lot from each other about how to run operations efficiently. But even the best-performing plants can raise their aspirations by looking critically for waste and variability in their operations. A key purpose of a diagnostic is to find the technical limits of "what would we have to do" to improve. Each company should aspire to be the "Toyota of the pharma industry." Admittedly, cars are not pills or vaccines. But it is worth thinking about how Toyota might go about making pills; this insight guides how we look at a diagnostic.

When comparing a top-performing pharma plant with the production system at Toyota, questions immediately arise:

1. Why are line-OEEs below 90%?

2. Why is throughput time 10 to 30 times longer than actual process time?

3. Why don't all operators follow a standardized work pattern?

Pharma executives reply with rational-sounding explanations, such as that change-over times and campaign sizes limit the flow, they face quality constraints, and that unforeseeable events prevent further standardization of work.

These explanations for inefficiency sound like those of automotive executives of 30 to 40 years ago. Yet today the car industry produces an exceptional variety of a products in an ever more efficient way, with ever shorter delivery lead times and extremely high quality. Toyota assembles all the variants of more than one model on a single production line with a 97-99% run ratio (a kind of an OEE measurement), with virtually no buffer stocks, while achieving the best quality-performance in the industry, enabling them to offer five-year warranties in many markets.

It is reasonable to believe that Toyota would immediately address the poor OEE-levels of 10-60% in pharma. Just as automotive companies started improve equipment effectiveness decades ago, pharmaceutical companies should now follow suit.

Toyota would not accept a product's spending more than 30 days in a manufacturing facility. They aspire to get production down to pure processing time. Production would be controlled by pull to minimize work-in-process levels. Quality checks would be built into the process via error-proofing, and confirmation would be done in real time, leading to immediate release on receipt of any test needing incubation time.

Finally, by no means would Toyota allow non-standardized work execution. Standardized work is the basis of performance and improvement. Every process—be it a quality test, a changeover, or a line replenishment—would be torn down to its basic elements. These would be sequenced and put onto a timeline, and managers would meticulously verify adherence to standards.

When Mr. Toyoda, former president of Toyota Europe, grandson of the founder and now the head of Toyota, visited the assembly plant in France a couple of years ago, he complained that operators did not follow standardized work processes. Indeed, during the plant tour, he stopped on the line, opened the standardized work manual for the position, and verified second-by-second that the operator performed the job according to its specified elements.

In what other industry does the head of the corporation take the time to investigate how a process is executed on the factory floor? Or pause long enough to ask why an operator handled a bolt with his right hand instead of his left?

* * *

What nobody thought possible in the automotive industry 50 years ago came true as one leader emerged. Pharmaceutical executives should take a page from Toyota's playbook. They should aspire to excel on cost, service and quality and move away from the current "either-or" mindset.

Those with the courage to look firsthand at their operations—and the imagination to find the solutions to remove waste and variability from the processes and production system as a whole—will become leaders in their industry. They may earn the title, "the Toyota of pharma."

Unleashing the hidden value in maintenance

Kristoffer Dieter, Frank Scholz

More pharma companies are embracing lean operations, but too few see maintenance and engineering as a target for transformation. In fact, smart maintenance techniques can be a powerful driver of plant efficiency.

Cost pressures are driving many pharmaceutical companies to turn to classic lean techniques to sustainably reduce costs. While production and quality operations often play critical roles in lean transformations, maintenance and engineering services are often left untouched as companies pursue what they see as "low-hanging fruit."

A lean transformation in maintenance can have enormous benefits for pharma operations, however. Given the sheer size of the maintenance and engineering component of many pharma sites, a transformation in this area can greatly improve overall cost performance and productivity (Exhibit 1). Moreover, capturing opportunities in maintenance can be as straightforward as more traditional applications of lean.

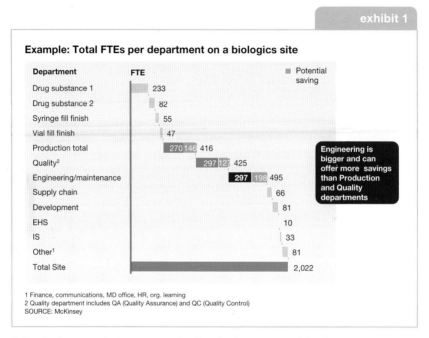

exhibit 1

Example: Total FTEs per department on a biologics site

Department	FTE	Potential saving
Drug substance 1	233	
Drug substance 2	82	
Syringe fill finish	55	
Vial fill finish	47	
Production total	270 146 416	
Quality[2]	297 127 425	
Engineering/maintenance	297 198 495	
Supply chain	66	
Development	81	
EHS	10	
IS	33	
Other[1]	81	
Total Site	2,022	

Engineering is bigger and can offer more savings than Production and Quality departments

1 Finance, communications, MD office, HR, org. learning
2 Quality department includes QA (Quality Assurance) and QC (Quality Control)
SOURCE: McKinsey

A few factors create huge opportunities for improvement in pharma maintenance:

- A heavy emphasis on compliance often drives sites to over-maintain equipment

- Managers see operations as the customer of maintenance, which breeds inefficiencies in the way maintenance is conducted

- Though maintenance costs per se may not have an obvious impact on the bottom line, good maintenance practices can greatly improve equipment availability and lower overall operating costs.

Transformations in maintenance typically cover three areas: efficiency, effectiveness, and planning/scheduling.

Maintenance efficiency

In maintenance, efficiency encompasses the speed and use of resources to complete routine (preventive) and non-routine (corrective) tasks. The usual efficiency metric is wrench time—what portion of a maintenance worker's day is spent repairing equipment. For most operations, we find initial wrench times between 20 and 30%. In a world-class operation that uses lean techniques, wrench time can be as high as 60%. Where equipment reliability is generally good, this can mean cutting maintenance costs by as much as half.

The key to improving wrench time is understanding the host of activities that fill the gap between average and world-class maintenance organizations. They typically fall into one of two categories: incidental tasks and pure waste. Incidental tasks, while not contributing directly to the repair or preservation of a piece of equipment, must be completed for work to be performed. They include reading task cards, troubleshooting, or completing required QA paperwork. Waste, on the other hand, includes activities that should not need to occur, or should occur less frequently. Examples include searching for parts and tools and repeatedly gowning and de-gowning to enter and leave suites. Waiting for equipment to become available is the biggest waste of time we find in pharma environments—it can account for 20% or more of maintenance technician idle time.

Measuring wrench time requires direct observation. For the most detailed analysis, observers attach themselves to maintenance teams and describe each activity in writing for later categorization. For spot checks, maintenance supervisors may take random walks through their spaces, note the activities of personnel and extrapolate to get a snapshot of wrench time (e.g., three of ten workers engaged in value-adding work would suggest a wrench time of 30%). (Exhibit 2)

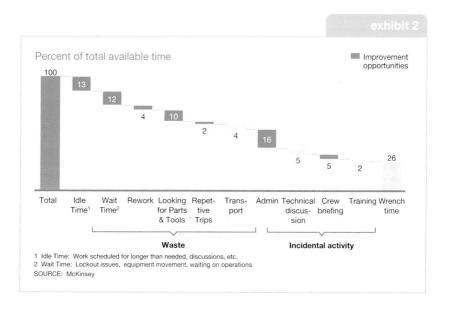

exhibit 2

Percent of total available time

■ Improvement opportunities

1 Idle Time: Work scheduled for longer than needed, discussions, etc.
2 Wait Time: Lockout issues, equipment movement, waiting on operations
SOURCE: McKinsey

In improving wrench time, a maintenance organization's goal should be to minimize incidental tasks and, to the greatest extent practicable, completely eliminate non-value adding activities. As an initial goal, most sites undergoing a maintenance transformation aim for a 40 to 50% wrench time improvement through the application of workplace organization (5S), improved storage and retrieval of parts and tools, and the application of standard work.

Workplace organization refers simply to the layout of the work area. This can include maintenance shop areas, toolboxes, and in some situations, the area surrounding work performed on equipment in situ. Simplification and organization of the workplace minimizes the time wasted on needless motion, searching for parts or tools, and generally "de-cluttering" to allow work to be performed.

As an added benefit, workplace organization allows elegant visual management: items out of place or missing are easily identifiable and can trigger immediate corrective action before precipitating any negative impact on wrench time. As an added benefit, emphasis on organization can also reinforce a greater sense of "compliance culture" within maintenance organizations that can otherwise feel somewhat external to the good manufacturing practices central to production or quality workers.

Achieving improved workplace organization begins by introducing one of the simplest of lean tools, 5S. Though the exact definition of each "S" can vary by company, the mnemonic most commonly refers to each element critical to creating and maintaining an organized workplace: Sort, Straighten, Sanitize, Standardize, and Sustain. (Some companies opt to adopt an additional "S," Safety.) 5S begins with sorting the materials found in the workplace and eliminating those that are infrequently or never used. The large rolling toolboxes maintenance technicians drag around large pharma facilities can contain an amazing assortment of fittings, fasteners, sockets, and general effluvia that only to add to the weight of the toolbox and make it hard to find anything useful.

In straightening the workplace, maintenance technicians will identify a specific location for each part or tool to allow for quick location and signal when something is out of place. The workplace is then sanitized (cleaned), with an emphasis on eliminating non-value-adding activities not required to maintain a clean workplace. Norms for organizing and cleaning the workplace are then standardized through checklists and SOPs. For sustaining the newly organized workplace, audits compare the current state of organization against the established standards and enforce 5S as the new culture of the maintenance organization.

The basic principles of workplace organization can also be applied to the storage and retrieval of parts and tools. Tool rooms can be reorganized to ensure that the tools most often used are readily available and easy to find. Frequently used parts and tools can also be located near their actual point of use to eliminate the need to fetch them at all. For example, some materials may be stored within GMP areas to reduce the need to de-gown and re-gown should additional parts or tools be required. Pre-kitting of parts and tools using detailed work orders allows needed material to be delivered to the worksite or can at least minimize collection time for maintenance technicians preparing to perform work. Finally, aligning part replenishment levels with measured usage rates will reduce the likelihood of a stockout and can dramatically reduce wasted time in performing maintenance.

While workplace organization and improved parts and tools management can systematically improve wrench time performance, there may be opportunities to improve the execution of individual maintenance tasks. Particularly for tasks that are performed frequently, process steps can be optimized and standardized to ensure the closest approximation of "best practice" each time the task is executed. Specifically, adoption of standardized work details exactly which steps must be taken to complete a given maintenance procedure, how long each task should take, what parts and tools will be required, and any other amplifying information that will aid the technician in completing his task quickly and efficiently. Any relevant quality checks can similarly be incorporated into the maintenance procedure.

Standardizing work for most maintenance organizations is among the most daunting tasks faced in a holistic maintenance transformation. High-frequency jobs must first be identified and prioritized, and collecting best practice techniques can be difficult. Nevertheless, standardizing tasks can also be among the most powerful tools in continuing to improve wrench time once more systematic improvements are already in place. For maintenance organizations, standardized work becomes the single biggest enabler of effective performance management: it encourages comparison of each job event against its allotted time, points to areas where new best practices are emerging and can be captured in revised procedures, and facilitates root-cause problem-solving when jobs take longer than expected. Moreover, it can help supervisors schedule technicians with greater ease, accuracy, and most important, utilization. Whereas a pre-lean maintenance organization may schedule a technician's work in daily or half-day blocks, leading to significant "white space" and idle time, more detailed scheduling can make better use of maintenance resources throughout the day.

Maintenance effectiveness

While a good maintenance program can reduce a pharma plant's labor requirements for a given level of planned downtime, an effective program can even more dramatically reduce costs by reducing unplanned downtime and unnecessary preventive maintenance burden. For example, an effective maintenance program could improve the OEE (operating equipment effectiveness) of a packaging line, increasing throughput while reducing overtime or extra shifts required to catch up for lost time. Furthermore, an effective maintenance program could reduce the labor and downtime devoted to maintenance tasks that do not substantively contribute to the reliability of a piece of equipment or the OEE of its line (e.g., replacing a light bulb used for ambient lighting before the bulb has actually blown).

Excellence in maintenance effectiveness is often best achieved through a reliability-centered maintenance program (RCM). RCM is based on the premise that an effective maintenance program minimizes the likelihood of injury or lost revenue due to the failure of a critical piece of equipment. While a particularly risk-averse organization may tend to over-maintain equipment, an organization that follows RCM will seek to identify which pieces of equipment are most critical to operation or safety, then strive to prevent plausible and costly failures. RCM leverages two elements for building the most effective maintenance: failure modes and effects analysis (FMEA) and equipment strategy.

Using FMEA, a pharma plant can identify safety- and operation-critical equipment and the biggest sources of lost production time, understand the drivers of possible equipment failure, and begin to design corrective actions that will inform the creation of an effective equipment strategy. FMEA begins with attributing a level of criticality to each piece of equipment, elucidates the functions of these pieces of equipment, brainstorms possible equipment failures that could restrict performance of these functions, analyzes the root causes of each of the most likely and/or costly failures, and finally, assigns corrective actions.

As a first step, we often advise sites embarking on FMEA to select an equipment system or production line that appears to be their most troublesome, and begin to analyze the underlying drivers of OEE on the line. This exercise begins with operators collecting information on equipment downtime, then comparing these results against historical records on where the most time (or expense) has been attributed to the chosen line.

The result will be a Pareto diagram of "bad actors" within the line that shows which pieces of equipment are the most critical. A combined team of operators, maintenance technicians and engineers then describe the function of each piece of equipment and the ways it could fail. For example, a labeling machine on a bottling line would have the function of applying a label to each bottle at a specified rate, and could functionally fail by misapplying labels, applying at less than rated speed, or simply not labeling bottles at all.

Once these failures have been identified, the cross-functional team describes the possible modes of failure that could lead to reduced capacity. It is useful at this stage to limit thinking to failure modes that have historically been observed or seem likely to occur (e.g., an electric motor in a packaging hall is more likely to fail due to a burned fuse or faulty electrical connection than because of flash flooding). The team should also be mindful of the potential effects of this failure, at least qualitatively: lost production time, personnel hazard, costly repair, or in some cases, minor or no inconvenience. Where available, operators and technicians may use supplier information, equipment history, or personal experience to attribute the likelihood and cost of failure to each component.

With failure modes and effects identified, the team may consider root causes. Two simple root-cause identification techniques are the Five Whys and fishbone or Ishikawa diagrams. In the Five Whys, the FMEA facilitator asks for the "first level" reason a failure could occur, then probes more deeply (generally but not always to the "fifth level") to uncover the fundamental reason a failure occurred. For the example of the electric motor, one could ask why the fuse burned. Overcurrent, perhaps. What led to the overcurrent condition? An electrical fault elsewhere, or a fuse that is not rated to handle the motor starting current. Why was the rating insufficient? The wrong fuse was installed. Why was the wrong fuse installed? The required fuse rating was not updated on the equipment work order. Why the was the work is incorrect? Engineering did not communicate the specification change to planning, and so forth.

To develop an effective equipment strategy, a site takes the insights developed through FMEA and operationalizes them into a series of explicit decisions on how and when equipment will be maintained. Based on the nature, likelihood, and consequences of various failure modes, the site can intelligently choose which equipment to focus on with preventive and predictive/condition-based maintenance, and which components should be allowed to run to failure. A two-by-two matrix, mapping the relative importance of a failure (lost production, safety hazard, repair expense) against its likelihood, can guide the maintenance organization towards the appropriate strategy.

Once the team has selected the general maintenance strategy for a component or piece of equipment, they can use the specific failure modes and root causes to select the right type of preventive or predictive, condition-based maintenance. Preventive measures may be undertaken based on usage (hours used), frequency, or observed conditions (vibration analysis, thermal spectrometry, chemical sampling, etc.).

A plan can include regular servicing of equipment, such as basic lubrication and cleaning. Maintenance should be meticulously planned to support efficient completion of each required, predictable tasks. For failures that will require corrective maintenance, the team can recommend which recovery actions will be planned in advance. For equipment intentionally run to failure, or situations where equipment fails unexpectedly despite preventive maintenance, repairs and replacements are generally planned; completely unanticipated failures are left unplanned, and thus leave the site open to the most risk.

PM rationalization is a special interest in heavily regulated industries like pharma, particularly given the emphasis on demonstrating a compliance culture—which often leads to over-maintaining equipment. In pharma, this can mean maintaining some equipment as Good Manufacturing Practice (GMP) controlled when not required, or performing too-frequent or unnecessary calibrations. Using a risk-based, fact-driven approach, calibrations can be reduced dramatically across entire pharma sites; production-related calibrations can be reduced in some cases by over a third, and indirect-function calibrations by nearly half. (Exhibit 3)

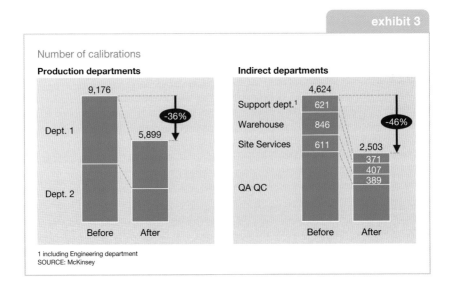

exhibit 3

Number of calibrations

Production departments

9,176

Dept. 1

-36%

5,899

Dept. 2

Before   After

Indirect departments

4,624

Support dept.[1]   621

Warehouse   846

Site Services   611

-46%

2,503

371
407
389

QA QC

Before   After

1 including Engineering department
SOURCE: McKinsey

Planning and scheduling

Beyond any other elements of maintenance, planning and scheduling are the most important in driving efficiency and effectiveness. Done well, planning and scheduling can enable performance management, facilitate capture and spread of best practices, minimize planned and unplanned equipment downtime, and directly improve maintenance technician wrench time. Planning and scheduling functions (often combined in many organizations) must promote risk-based prioritization of maintenance work, provide a channel for feedback on tasks performed, and manage relationships between operations and maintenance.

Risk-based work prioritization uses concepts similar to those in equipment strategy; where in equipment strategy the overall approach to maintenance of a piece of equipment is a function of the likelihood and severity of the consequences of not doing it, in risk-based prioritization, the allocation of precious maintenance resources is allocated using similar logic. Most traditional prioritization schemes rank jobs strictly according to equipment criticality, often resulting in needless "break-ins" to the agreed maintenance schedule and all of the waste (waiting, searching, rework) attending such last-minute changes of plan.

In risk-based prioritization, only those jobs for which the risk of not performing the maintenance immediately is unacceptable can disrupt the schedule. All other tasks are ranked and worked in reverse order of the acceptability of their risk. A pharma site adopting a risk-based prioritization approach should create its own definitions of likelihood and consequences based on experience and the relative criticality of each of its processes. (Exhibit 4)

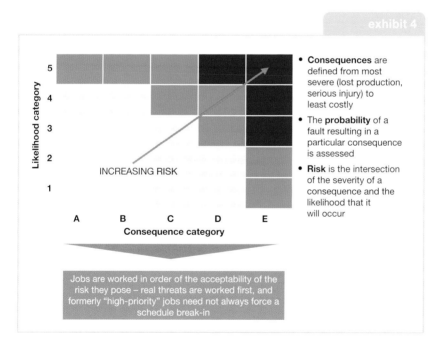

exhibit 4

- **Consequences** are defined from most severe (lost production, serious injury) to least costly
- The **probability** of a fault resulting in a particular consequence is assessed
- **Risk** is the intersection of the severity of a consequence and the likelihood that it will occur

Jobs are worked in order of the acceptability of the risk they pose – real threats are worked first, and formerly "high-priority" jobs need not always force a schedule break-in

As noted earlier, a significant driver of maintenance efficiency is the quality of the work plans. Good plans state explicitly the steps involved in a maintenance task, accurately estimate time required to complete each step, note any necessary safety precautions, list all necessary parts and tools, and act as a general repository of information regarding best practices with respect to the given job.

Critical to achieving this level of quality in planning is the incorporation of feedback from tasks already completed into plans for the same or similar maintenance tasks. At the most basic level, this feedback should include a qualitative assessment of the accuracy of the process steps and sequencing as well as the time estimates for each. Within the context of a continuous improvement culture, this feedback will also address ideas for better methods to complete the maintenance or perhaps even possible equipment or equipment strategy modifications that could eliminate the need for performing this particular task at all. This process of continuous iteration of job plans becomes a partnership between the maintenance technician and planner and can be achieved through a variety of methods: mandatory feedback requirements to close every work order, inclusion of planners in maintenance shop daily huddles and problem-solving sessions, and periodic convening of "best practice" workshops to discuss high-frequency or high-cost maintenance tasks.

While feedback can be the most powerful lever in improving planning quality, establishing and maintaining a cooperative relationship between maintenance and production operations through scheduling can have an equally dramatic effect. Ask any shop-floor maintenance technician or supervisor about the single biggest driver of wasted time, and he or she is almost bound to answer, "Waiting to get equipment released from operations."

The idea that operations is the customer of maintenance is basically sound, since it helps to drive a value-stream mentality through to best serving the end customer—the patients. Unfortunately, it can also lead to costly inefficiencies. It is therefore crucial that maintenance and operations collaborate to build a schedule, often in a daily meeting, and that the maintenance organization becomes agile enough to respond to changes in plan without needlessly idling technicians.

In one biotech site, for example, operations and maintenance agreed to a pact in which operations would release equipment within one hour of the scheduled time or provide at least a one shift notice that they would be unable to comply; maintenance, in turn, vowed to deploy their newfound maintenance efficiency techniques to complete work within the shift allotted or inform operations one shift in advance that they would be unable to complete the work.

High-quality plans play an enormous role in improving the harmony between operations and maintenance and reducing technician idle time; with better estimates of times necessary to complete tasks, and pre-kitting parts and tools for upcoming jobs, schedulers and supervisors are able arrange technicians' days at a much greater level of granularity and flexibility.

While many maintenance organizations simply hand out a stack of work orders to be completed each day, often with the expectation that many will be left unfinished, more detailed scheduling allows for an hour-by-hour assignment of work and therefore considerably greater capacity for handling last-minute requests or perturbations of the production schedule while fully employing maintenance technicians.

* * *

By understanding the interdependencies among maintenance efficiency, effectiveness, and planning and scheduling, a pharma site can lower maintenance costs, including labor, materials, and lost revenue due to unplanned downtime, by 30% or more.

While many of the techniques required to unlock this value can be deceptively simple, capturing full value sustainably requires a wholesale change in the way that many pharma sites view the overall maintenance function. Instead of seeing operations as the customer of maintenance, a lean organization needs to foster a sense of collaboration across all functions and a site-wide orientation towards support of holistic, cross-functional value streams. Savings found in a maintenance transformation are ultimately sustained only with new mindsets. To foster new ways of thinking, site leadership must get involved in the transformation, participating in problem-solving, engaging shop-floor maintenance technicians, and establishing meaningful metrics (PM-CM ratio, maintenance costs, equipment availability and the like) that track progress and encourage continuous improvement.

The changing biotech landscape and the drive for operational excellence

Amit Jain, Chris Paulson, Ric Phillips, Jatan Shah

The biotech industry is still growing fast, but a confluence of trends, led by the rapid expansion of the biosimilars market, will raise operational excellence on the biotech firm's agenda.

Biotechnology is one of the most attractive areas in the pharmaceutical landscape, with historically stronger performance than companies focused on synthetic small-molecule compounds (see Exhibit 1). Biologic therapies also offer strong growth potential: they already comprise nine of the top 20 drugs, and we expect them to comprise 20 to 30% of sales by 2012. This opportunity in biologic therapies has enticed many traditional drug companies to invest heavily in the field through internal expansion, joint ventures or acquisitions.

Until recently, many biotechs enjoyed high margins and concentrated on revenue growth. But several forces today are raising uncertainty and driving changes in the industry that spur biotechs to focus more on operations:

- **Price pressure on drugs:** Drugs are facing increasing pricing pressure as payors and government look to control costs. These

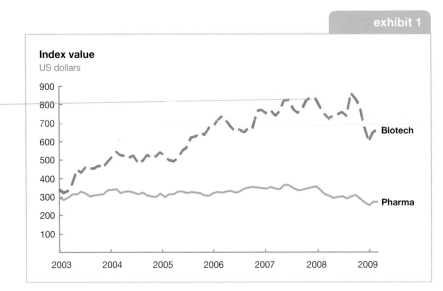

exhibit 1

Index value
US dollars

(chart shows two index-value series from 2003 to 2009: "Biotech" rising from about 300 to above 800, and "Pharma" remaining near 300)

pressures could substantially reduce margins for some large molecules with extremely high development and manufacturing costs.

- **The complexity of manufacturing-related regulatory requirements:** Manufacturing-related requirements are changing, both in terms of content and inspection frequency. Content changes have emphasized quality control and standard harmonization. The changing regulatory environment may increase the need for biologics manufacturers to track regulations more carefully and make operational changes faster.

- **High R&D costs:** Developing a drug can easily cost billions of dollars due in part to increasingly complex research and development, including clinical trials, many of which now require larger patient populations, longer studies, or active references to show statistical significance or improved outcomes.

- **Increasing activity in the biosimilars field:** In some markets, the mere possibility of biosimilar entry will lower the price of biological medicines, and multiple biotech drugs will come off patent in 2012 and 2013. Given manufacturing costs' impact on overall margins, lean manufacturing and supply chain dynamics will become increasingly important as new players enter the market. With COGS at 70 to 80% of the total costs incurred for biosimilars, compared to 15 to 20% for biologics, the next wave of biosimilars will compete increasingly on cost-effective manufacturing.

Given these trends, biotechs will need to improve operations to remain competitive. In addition, the biotech industry is likely to see overcapacity in the next few years thanks to recent investments and process development improvements, such as standardization and platforming of processes to accommodate new products in existing plants, yield improvements with advances in technology, and greater column capacities. This will also force biotechs toward the lower end of the cost curve.

Put simply, pharmaceutical firms that want to succeed in biotech must be extremely proficient at managing biotech's much higher technical and operational complexity while maintaining superiority in research and development. We believe biotech firms will need to excel in four critical operations areas:

1. Develop a sophisticated strategy for production capacity based on biotech portfolio size, pipeline risk and installed capacity

2. Stay at the forefront of operational technology and process innovations

3. Get the basics right: Improve operations and drive sustained excellence in existing facilities

4. Create a high-performing operations organization by enabling a culture of continuous improvement to sustain performance in each of these areas.

These steps will help biotechs start down the road of operational excellence—a capability they will need to remain competitive and prosper in the years ahead.

A. DEVELOP A SOPHISTICATED STRATEGY FOR CAPACITY

Companies must answer significant strategic questions as they set their biologics manufacturing strategy. Manufacturing capacity is highly concentrated today—the top ten biologics companies have over 70% of industry mammalian capacity, while the top five biologics CMOs hold 87% of total CMO mammalian capacity.

Building manufacturing capacity is extremely costly and challenging: creating a large-scale operation takes four to five years and $200-$500 million or more, compared to a similar small-molecule facility that might cost just $30-100 million. Also, biologics manufacturers face strict and rising regulatory scrutiny in the US and EU. Given the capital requirements, effective utilization of new capacity and ongoing cost management become critical.

Manufacturing of biologics also requires process excellence to minimize rejections and ensure productive utilization. The facility must have enough capacity to accommodate rejected batches. Depending on their capabilities, companies are building biotech capacity in-house, through contract manufacturers and acquisitions.

Building in-house manufacturing

Integrated pharmaceutical and biopharmaceutical companies view manufacturing as part of their core business. Many believe in-house production protects IP, often a key differentiator in this business. It also allows better control over timelines and product quality, which can define financial success. In-house capacity offers flexibility to adjust to sudden shifts in demand.

In-house manufacturing may also allow faster scale-up for pharmacos with experience, and lead to smoother registration for those with established regulatory processes. It also provides support during clinical trials and may offer cost advantages with lower operational risk.

Biotech firms' focus on research and development, however, has caused many to lag other industries in manufacturing. Company valuations are based largely on core assets on the market and in the product pipeline rather than operational metrics—which explains how non-product pipeline-related investments, such as manufacturing expansion, can lower share prices. Also, there is a race to make R&D investments.

Many firms that have built in-house expertise are expanding manufacturing capacity in tax-advantaged regions like Puerto Rico and Ireland, where they intend to transfer technical expertise while benefiting from the lower operating costs. The biotech sector has so far been conservative in moving operations to emerging markets, but those markets are becoming more attractive as they improve intellectual property protection, provide more capabilities and talent, and advance regulatory policies. In addition, countries trying to promote this industry may further subsidize low-cost, local competitors in these areas.

The key to in-house manufacturing is the ability to attract and retain talent in manufacturing, including process development scientists, validation engineers, QA, QC and regulatory experts. Companies are taking multiple approaches to finding these increasingly scarce people, including leveraging relationships with academia, looking outside the region, and hiring industry leaders for their expertise and their ability to attract additional talent.

Leveraging CMOs for capacity (including innovative sharing strategies)

More companies are acknowledging the value of CMOs for biologics manufacturing. Large CMOs, such as Boehringer Ingelheim and Lonza, with in-house capacity of 20 KL or more, focus on manufacturing late-stage clinical and marketed products, and typically offer mammalian and microbial systems. Smaller CMOs, such as DSM, Akzo Nobel and Cambrex Biosciences, focus on compounds in early-stage clinical trials, with a strategy to expand capacity and capabilities and shift toward later-stage and commercial products.

Many small biologic players lack the capital to invest in their own production facilities, and they face risks if they have no experience in scale-up or commercial-scale manufacturing—especially if they have few biologics in their portfolios. Some companies have time limitations, such as short- to mid-term supply needs, and it is too late to build their own production facilities.

Contract manufacturing can be an effective risk-mitigation strategy when a contract manufacturer can help meet overflow demand. Some firms are signing long-term agreements and co-investing in new capacity to offset financial risk. Some are avoiding setting up their own facilities, preferring to secure additional capacity through long-term relationships with leading CMOs.

In some instances, contract manufacturers have purchased plants from biotech companies, and vice-versa. For example, when Genentech no longer needed its Spanish plant capacity, Lonza purchased the plant and operated it as their CMO. Later, when Genentech needed capacity, Lonza built a facility in Singapore and allocated contracted volumes to Genentech. As a part of this arrangement, Genentech also had an option to buy the entire Singapore plant if capacity requirements became big enough. Genetech recently exercised that right and bought the facility from Lonza. Sharing capacity across multiple manufacturers to mitigate the risk of uncertain capacity needs is gaining credence in the field, and can significantly lower the risk of an expansion.

Depending on CMOs can present some risks. Despite current overcapacity in the market, for example, some customers may have difficulty getting access to adequate production capacity in time to meet demand, given long lead times for scale-up and production facility customization. In addition, it is possible that overcapacity among CMOs today may be replaced by undercapacity by 2015-2020.

Acquisition-based capacity-building

Many large pharmacos are gaining biologics manufacturing capacity through acquisitions. Roche acquired the remaining 44% of Genentech for $46.8 billion to expand its biologics portfolio and solidify leadership in oncology. Pfizer acquired Wyeth to expand its pipeline and obtain Wyeth's biologics and vaccine capabilities. GSK acquired Stiefel to expand capabilities in specialty dermatological products. And AstraZenecca recently acquired Celltech.

While acquisitions can certainly add capacity and speed products to market, they often come at a high price—both in terms of upfront costs and the time and effort required to integrate the companies' expertise and culture.

To summarize, companies need to continue to adapt to changes and refine their strategies for capacity based on biotech portfolio size, pipeline risk and evaluation of their internal capabilities.

B. STAY AT THE FOREFRONT OF PROCESS AND TECHNOLOGICAL INNOVATIONS

Innovation in process and technology will continue to provide companies with competitive advantages. The benefits will include lower COGS and increased output and productivity.

Several companies are focusing on improving process development:

Titre improvements: Higher titers have the potential to reduce COGS significantly: a 5x improvement in titer could reduce COGS by over 25%. Contributors to higher titers include genetic engineering of cells to increase secretion of proteins, improved growth media that reduce contamination, and advanced sensors to better monitor and control process. A few companies are exploring the genetic modification of cell lines with an order of magnitude titre improvement potential. DSM/Crucell, for example, achieved a record titer of 27 g/L using the PER.C6 ® system; Lonza is using a proprietary GS gene expression system to optimize cell lines to increase output. An increased titer due to a modified cell line will not impact biological plant design but will require additional trials for comparability (for existing drugs).

Expressions systems: While microbial and mammalian technologies are the key

for current and future pipelines, companies are evaluating other expression systems. Many are still in their infancy, and questions remain about scientific feasibility and regulatory approval.

Antibody fragment: Though the market remains relatively new, companies are exploring antibody fragment-based products. Instead of using a whole antibody, researchers are using fragments to produce drugs. Antibody fragments can be produced in simpler bacterial cells and may offer the potential for more product through smaller-scale microbial production.

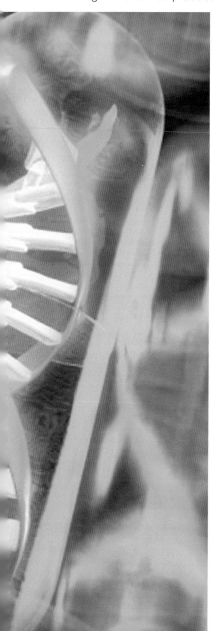

Other companies are focusing their efforts on different manufacturing techniques. These include:

Flexible plants and disposable technologies: Disposable, single-use components are increasingly used in the manufacturing process, especially for first-process steps, such as smaller-scale reactors. The benefits can include lower labor costs, faster changeovers with less need for cleaning, more process flexibility, lower upfront capex requirements, and the elimination of validation time. Companies with large facilities, however, will need to weigh these benefits against the costs of making the changes.

Purification improvements: By improving resins to have more dynamic binding capacity, some companies can increase yields to 93% and lower COGS, since resins constitute about 80% of variable costs. Key enhancements include better resins to purify more solution with the same amount of raw material (e.g., increasing die binding capacity of resins) and new "recipes" to increase yield by modifying process parameters, such as flow rates and bed height.

Some other companies are adopting a range of different systems and tools, including:

Process stabilization: Moving to more stable and well-defined fermentation media, using process analyzers, such as spectrometers, to monitor material in real time, and automating process control can reduce cross-contamination and failures, increase plant output and improve batch success to as high as 95%.

Electronic batch records: Companies are using ERP-like systems to manage creation and submission of batch records, and some are exploring MES systems to automatically generate batch records. Benefits include: faster collection and review of paper documents; fewer record errors with a structured approach to data collection, system time and date-stamping; lower compliance costs; and shorter time-to-market by speeding the scale-up to commercial production. This will lower overall COGS with less labor and documentation and easier quality assurance and control.

Quality by design/process analytical technology: This FDA initiative gives manufacturers flexibility in defining process parameters while filing for approval, allowing to improve processes continuously within a defined space. Batch success rates in some cases have gone up by about 30%

C. GET THE BASICS RIGHT: IMPROVE CURRENT OPERATIONS AND DRIVE SUSTAINED EXCELLENCE

To be successful, biotech companies will need to drive sustained operational excellence, focusing on end-to-end operations. The sector could benefit by bringing its performance closer to the levels of the high-tech, automotive and consumer packaged goods industries. For example, overall equipment efficiency (OEE) in the biotech sector is about 10-50%, compared to 65-80% in semiconductors. Similarly, yields in biotech are at best 70% compared to yields of 95% or more in semiconductors. Although it is unrealistic to expect biotech firms to close the gap completely, they have real opportunities in yield, cycle time, inventory, equipment and labor effectiveness. Better performing companies are able to drive value with a variety of approaches:

Increase commercial and clinical capacity through better planning and asset utilization

Falling margins and scarcer capital will continue to raise asset productivity requirements for biotech companies. As a result, increasing commercial and clinical production capacity through better asset utilization and planning has become a significant source of value.

Increase overall equipment effectiveness and reduce losses by using standard work techniques. This approach focuses on four areas: (i) speeding changeover (e.g., buffer preparation, equilibration); (ii) eliminating slack from non-biological process steps, such as avoiding complicated processes in third-shift or inflexible staffing; (iii) minimizing small stops, such as waiting for operator interaction; and (iv) maximizing equipment reliability with preventative maintenance and other means. Critical path analysis to identify these opportunities can substantially reduce cycle time.

Reduce time between lot starts by evaluating potential to nest lots. GMP regulations rightly emphasize segregation between lots to eliminate issues of contamination. In several instances, limited segregation between process steps, such as between inclusion bodies' recovery and purification, prevents parallel processing of lots. But physically segregating lots between suites or within a suite can yield significant benefits that often outweigh the costs involved.

Increase plant uptime. Scheduled maintenance and upgrades often contribute greatly to plant downtime. Evaluating and streamlining these efforts can help, including performing certain activities when the plant is running, or implementing phased shutdowns. Companies that manage the process well can reduce annual downtimes to two to three weeks.

Optimize clinical planning horizon. Clinical production is often associated with high scrap due to the uncertainties of clinical trials and the success of the drug. To compound the problem, a company may begin planning and manufacturing cycles before gaining accurate insights into demand. Optimizing planning cycle horizons to when demand signals are more accurate can reduce waste.

Reduce operating cost across manufacturing, process development and quality by methodologically eliminating waste

To substantially increase equipment and labor effectiveness year over year, biotech companies must identify and reduce sources of waste throughout the value chain. Three opportunities can be good places to start:

Eliminate waste from critical path production activities. Understanding the activities that take the most time along the critical path, such as buffer preparation for fermentation, and eliminating waste there can significantly increase productivity and reduce cost. The Toyota "7 wastes" approach can improve unit operations by reducing overproduction, waiting time, excess inventory, excess operator motion, unnecessary material transportation, re-work, and over-processing.

Use creative shift structures. Creative sharing of staff and cross-training can help reduce costs and raise productivity. Depending on the environment, companies should evaluate product-based versus process-based staffing and shift structures. Examples include sharing crews between processes, such as cell culture and purification; across products, such as quality labs for different products, with dedicated setup and cleanup crews; and within a process, such as across multiple fill lines. Implementing the optimal approach can help reduce inherent inefficiencies at ramp-up, ramp-down, and between lots.

Increase productivity in quality control. McKinsey recently conducted a survey to understand what drives quality productivity and performance in pharma and biotech companies[1]. We found that high-quality productivity and performance go hand-in-hand. Quality productivity varied widely across sites and activities, and, perhaps more important, even the most productive plants had meaningful room for improvement. Major levers for raising productivity include: reducing the variability in requirements and times for standard tests; optimizing environmental monitoring program testing to meet GMP requirements; evaluating which tests can be performed on the floor instead of in the lab; and executing non-critical-path tests in batches.

Lower inventory and working capital by right-sizing inventory targets and implementing a consumption-based pull model

Supply and demand planning for biotech companies can be complex, especially for those with diverse product portfolios that cover a wide asset base. High gross margins can drive companies to produce too much as they try to avoid shortfalls and missed revenue—which can lead to excess inventory. The shorter shelf life of many biotech products may exacerbate this issue and increase the amount of "scrap" even further. Three steps can start to rectify this problem:

Right-size inventory targets. While inventory reductions are not the only way to reduce working capital, they are a good starting point for many biotech companies. They should set inventory targets based on the safety stock levels needed to handle supply/demand variability and risks.

Eliminate overproduction by implementing a consumption-based (replenishment) operating approach. In situations with higher volatility and uncertain demand, a pull-based model can be effective in fill-finish and packaging, where cycle times last two to five days and process steps are stable.

---

1   For more on quality see article "Finding the keys to quality productivity and performance" on page 64

Align and simplify the sales and operations planning (S&OP) process.
A common source of concern at biotech manufacturing plants is the variability in the production signal, even for products with relatively stable demand. Companies can reduce this variability and achieve more stable and cost-effective operations by standardizing information flow and decision rights, and improving alignment on forecasting across sales and planning.

Speed the launch of pipeline molecules with faster technology transfers and process characterization

Improvements in process development (and hence reduction in time to market) require tactical and strategic adjustments, including streamlining key processes, such as commercial process development (CPD) or technology transfer; and making strategic decisions about when process development activities should occur.

Reduce time for technology transfer. The 18 to 32 months it takes to transfer the technology for a new molecule affects not only its market entry, but associated costs, risks, and decision options. Firms wanting to speed the process and lower costs can map their value stream and perform a lean analysis of technology transfer, identifying redundancies by defining the purpose of each step.

Reduce waste in process development. Speeding process development activities often reveals strategic opportunities. For example, if the CPD cycle time can be improved enough, a company could delay CPD until phase II results are clear, avoiding unnecessary investment. Factors to consider include: an activity's cycle time; the potential for molecule failures prior to phase II results; delaying product launches if the activities are performed later; and additional regulations that require companies to demonstrate knowledge of process control early in the development cycle.

While no one answer fits every situation, companies should evaluate which options provide the biggest strategic benefits. For instance, as they gain experience with product platforms such as monoclonal antibodies, they will reduce the variability of cycle times and increase their knowledge of molecule feasibility earlier in the development process. Both will also reduce their investment risk in process development activities.

D. CREATE A HIGH-PERFORMING OPERATIONS ORGANIZATION

To maintain and embed operational improvements into an organization, managers often have to make substantial changes to the company's structure and performance management systems. There is no "one size fits all" prescription, but most successful plants share a few attributes: clear cost transparency with strong accountability and incentives that align to the vision. They underline these traits with an ongoing effort to build the new culture into day-to-day business. Specifics include:

Ensuring cost transparency through activity-based tracking. Cost transparency at a granular level of detail, such as cost per non-conformance and corrective and preventive action, is a critical element of activity-based tracking that helps companies measure true allocation costs and assess integrated productivity[2]. This understanding of costs and productivity changes allows the organization to link changes to margin improvements.

Enabling process or product-based cost accountability. Accountability is essential to sustainable success. Companies drive it by creating process- or product-based "cells" that can "buy" services from support functions, including process development, facilities and engineering. But companies must strike the right balance between cost and service levels to ensure product delivery when using this approach.

Incentivizing best-practice sharing and increased productivity: Shared KPIs that tie to well-designed incentives can build a sustained mindset of operations excellence and ensure best-practice sharing across functions and sites, which can lead to significant improvements by ensuring each site and function achieves internal best-in-class performance. For example, companies can track NCs closed within 20 days to incentivize rapid issue resolutions, or regulatory release time to incent immediate feedback to the process. Only with these in place will operations excellence become part of everyday business instead of a one-time event.

Institutionalize change management. The transition to the new operational mindset should receive the attention it deserves, or improvements will be short-lived. One proven approach is having an operational improvement office manage the transition, including training, management tools, metrics and staffing. Credible leaders from other areas of the plant should staff this office, along with trained industrial engineers who can rotate on a six-month basis.

---

2   More details see article "Integrated productivity management" on page 182

***

Emerging trends in biologics, including more activity in biosimilars and options to grow manufacturing capacity, mean that biotech firms need to focus more closely on operations. Biotechnology and pharmaceutical companies that have strength in research and development, and can manage the technical and operational complexities of their business, will be in a strong position to become the leaders of tomorrow's healthcare sector. They will have the creative and managerial savvy needed to make the right choices—to meet their goals and deliver high-quality products to the market on time and at the right cost.

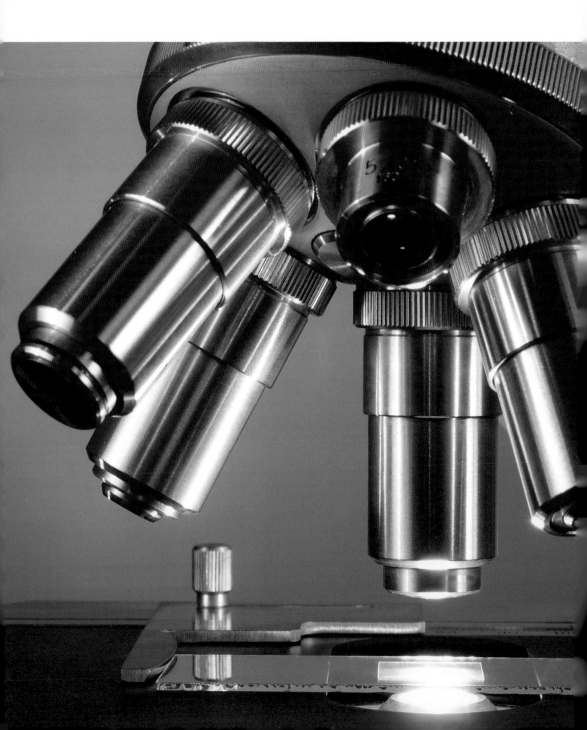

Finding the keys to
quality productivity and performance

Katy George, Andrew Gonce, Ric Phillips, Vanya Telpis

How can companies meet the challenges of a rapidly changing quality and compliance environment while cutting costs? The journey starts with understanding baseline quality productivity and performance, and the factors that influence them. In this article, we share insights gained by benchmarking multiple pharma plants.

Pharma companies may need to fundamentally rethink the way they organize their quality processes. As regulatory agencies shift their focus from adulterated products and deficient procedures to plant- and network-wide quality systems, companies need to build quality more tightly into every step of their product development and manufacturing processes, rather than relying on ever more frequent inspections—and they need to do it inexpensively. Quality functions at many companies are facing increasing demands to become more productive as the whole industry reacts to rising cost pressures.

In the face of these evolving challenges, pharmacos are exploring different quality productivity improvement programs and initiatives, and looking for new tools to help them navigate uncharted waters. The answers to some critical questions are far from obvious:

- What is the real cost of quality to the organization? How should quality productivity be measured?

- Will reducing quality cost mean sacrificing quality levels and incurring compliance risk?

- Which factors really drive quality productivity? How important is scale? Culture? Organizational structure?

- What improvement initiatives will make a real difference in quality productivity and performance?

Understanding the real cost of quality

Many pharma companies still rely on relatively crude metrics of quality productivity and cost. They may use ratios of quality to manufacturing personnel, for example, focus only on the quality control lab, or consider only the budget of the quality organization. As responsibility for quality becomes more tightly integrated into the wider organization, however, quality processes increasingly become the responsibility of staff in other functions, such as manufacturing, engineering or supply chain management. This integration calls for a more sophisticated approach to the measurement of quality, one that can track quality costs wherever they are incurred.

Over the past five years, McKinsey has been running the pharma operations benchmarking known as POBOS that now includes detailed analyses of quality processes at around 50 plants in eight pharma companies, together with selected quality metrics for more than 150 other plants.

The POBOS metrics have been designed to offer a unique insight into the efficiency and effectiveness of the new generation of pharma quality systems. Critically, POBOS measures quality productivity at the activity level, allowing performance comparisons across plants regardless of how they structure or staff their quality processes.

The insights from POBOS allow us to answer some of pharma quality executives' basic questions. The benchmarking has also helped identify some practices that correlate most strongly with improved quality productivity and performance.

Productivity doesn't sacrifice performance

The POBOS results show that one of the pharma CEO's biggest concerns— that high-quality efficiency would come at the expense of lower quality performance—is unfounded. Rather than sacrificing product quality, compliance or cycle time, productivity improvements are actually correlated with quality performance. The most productive plants in the benchmarking sample scored as high or higher than their less-productive peers on measures such as complaints per unit and investigations per batch (see Exhibit 1). In addition, all were in good standing with regulatory agencies, without warning letters or consent decrees.

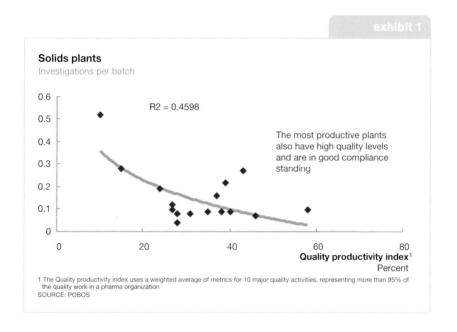

exhibit 1

Solids plants
Investigations per batch

R2 = 0.4598

The most productive plants also have high quality levels and are in good compliance standing

Quality productivity index[1]
Percent

1 The Quality productivity index uses a weighted average of metrics for 10 major quality activities, representing more than 95% of the quality work in a pharma organization
SOURCE: POBOS

The implication is that productive, high-performing sites operate in a fundamentally different way: rather than making a trade-off between cost and sustained quality, they find ways to complement lower costs with improved quality performance.

Structural barriers are low

Another common argument pharma quality leaders and plant managers put forward is that unique characteristics of their plants, processes or product range make it difficult to improve quality productivity. The POBOS findings should give these executives food for thought. The survey shows that, while structural factors do have an impact on productivity, they are not a barrier to superior performance (see Exhibit 2).

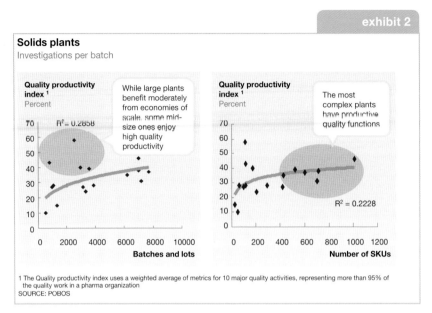

exhibit 2

Solids plants
Investigations per batch

Quality productivity index [1]
Percent

$R^2 = 0.2858$

While large plants benefit moderately from economies of scale, some mid-size ones enjoy high quality productivity

Batches and lots

Quality productivity index [1]
Percent

The most complex plants have productive quality functions

$R^2 = 0.2228$

Number of SKUs

1 The Quality productivity index uses a weighted average of metrics for 10 major quality activities, representing more than 95% of the quality work in a pharma organization
SOURCE: POBOS

Scale, for example, is not a critical factor for productivity in solids plants, which represent the largest part of the industry base. There are exceptions, of course: in sterile plants, scale is a somewhat stronger factor. These sites dedicate more quality resources to activities such as validation, equipment maintenance and environmental management, which benefit from economies of scale in larger facilities.

Complexity is an important factor in quality work, but higher complexity is not a barrier to productivity or performance. Highly complex plants can run with few complaints or investigations when adopting the right approach to quality. And such plants can even capture some slight economies of scope in activities, such as quality systems support, regulatory interaction and validation, although the correlation is weak.

The *regulatory environment* correlates most strongly with quality productivity (see Exhibit 3). The more tightly regulated the site, the lower its productivity. Plants that produce for non-U.S. and non-E.U. markets scored consistently higher on the relative productivity index.[1] The reasons for the difference may include local agencies' less-stringent regulatory requirements and a less-demanding consumer base that makes fewer complaints.

We found a similarly strong correlation for plants manufacturing over-the-counter products—they also show higher productivity compared to Rx peers,

---

1   The Quality productivity index uses a weighted average of metrics for 10 major quality activities, representing more than 95% of the quality work in a pharma organization

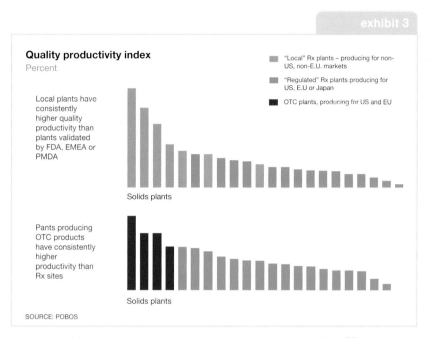

Quality productivity index
Percent

"Local" Rx plants – producing for non-US, non-E.U. markets

"Regulated" Rx plants producing for US, E.U or Japan

OTC plants, producing for US and EU

Local plants have consistently higher quality productivity than plants validated by FDA, EMEA or PMDA

Solids plants

Pants producing OTC products have consistently higher productivity than Rx sites

Solids plants

SOURCE: POBOS

exhibit 3

most probably due to fewer regulatory requirements even within FDA and EMEA. Within the regulated plant sample, however, we found significant variations in productivity, implying big improvement opportunities even for best-in-class plants.

Successful quality organizations don't all look the same

Organizational design choices, such as the relative size of the Quality organization within the plant, or the degree of centralization of the Quality organization, have no impact on productivity per se, because quality activities are carried out in all parts of the organization. Greater centralization, for example, enables faster implementation of standard methods and processes, although it sacrifices at least some of the proximity of quality to operational tasks and the speed and quality of problem-solving that comes with such proximity.

A variety of organizational structures—with different reporting lines between quality and operations units, site management and corporate quality—could work well if they fit the company culture and enable consistent application of best practices.

Hallmarks of successful quality organizations are their behaviors, practices, mindsets and cultures, rather than the structure of the roles. Clear lines of ownership, clear metrics and escalation procedures, and a common sense of purpose to target both performance and productivity are attributes associated with stronger organizations.   Less successful quality organizations often have adversarial relationships with production teams and revert to "checking" rather than collaborating and building quality into processes.

Best practices

The benchmarking project also delivered some important insights into the practices that drive better quality productivity and performance at pharma companies. In our in-depth analysis of quality processes, we assessed the quantitative impact of nine quality practices to understand their correlation with improved quality productivity and performance. We confirmed the importance of five of these improvement levers—high-performing plants across our survey applied them consistently.

Standardization

All of the most productive quality departments in our study adopted best practices that borrow substantially from lean operations. Standard procedures for activities are required for regulatory reasons. But many sites choose not to develop target times for these standard tasks to guide the quality teams. The lack of target times is often rationalized as "risky" or "too much information" in regards to regulatory concerns.

One site created standard times to help manage analyst schedules and speed releases. The standard times were based on actual analyst data, collected over months, showing that test durations varied by 400%. The site discovered that it could reduce average test time by 30 to 40% by standardizing the target time. Another site standardized best practices for integration techniques on one test, saving 1700 analyst hours per year. A third site was able to identify 9000 hours of potential savings through standardized SOPs and MBR review procedures.

Simplification

Unnecessary complexity causes redundancy, bureaucracy and confusion, significantly reducing the effectiveness and productivity of most quality activities. Benchmarked plants with a high number of SOPs were found to have lower productivity, more investigations and longer release times. Simple complexity reduction measures can immediately improve productivity and performance. The three best plants in the survey required an average of 3.3 people for CAPA approval, for example, while the three lowest-performing plants required, on average, nine people for the same process. The impact of simpler CAPA process was seen both in cycle time – top-quartile plants were able to process a CAPA in 17 days on average compared to 45 days for the bottom quartile, and in efficiency—top quartile plants processed 250 investigations per FTE annually, twice as many as the median.and three times as many as the bottom quartile.

Other examples of simplification include reducing the number and length of SOPs to improve understanding and compliance, eliminating unnecessary tests, and applying risk-based segmentation when selecting the right validation or quality training level. Senior management's visible support and involvement is critical to achieving the simplification mindset.

A company that recently launched an overall Quality systems simplification initiative estimated that simpler, clear, flexible and transparent Quality systems would reduce time spent reading SOPs by 30 to 50% and increase everyone's efficiency.

A site that simplified its validation process was able to decrease resources by 10% and cycle time by 50%. It standardized validation reports and protocol templates, implemented a site-wide validation master plan that tracked all projects across functional areas, adopted a risk-based approach that considered impact on product quality (using the ISPE guidelines), and increased its use of statistical tools such as SPC.

Reducing complexity through well-considered simplification efforts can do more than raise productivity and performance—it can also help enable the other best practices discussed here. Automating an overly complex process, for example, will not achieve the savings and impact available unless the process is streamlined first.

Automation

Automation significantly improves many key quality processes, including validation, batch record review, CAPA, training, environmental management, and stability testing. Some processes, such as CAPA, are typically highly automated; 83% of the benchmarked plants had electronic CAPA, providing such features as electronic documentation workflow, automatic milestone monitoring and personalized queries. Other processes, such as validation and batch record review, are still mostly manual in pharma plants.

The benefits of automation are particularly obvious for batch record review. The benchmarked plants with automated batch records were able to process many more batches than peers with manual records—4-5 times more for sterile plants. Automation increased productivity and improved quality in four ways: shortening cycle time by reviewing exceptions only; reducing errors; trending deviations better; and offering more accurate status reports. One plant that recently automated its batch records processed 24% more records with the same number of people and decreased packaging deviations from 7% to zero.

One site quality leader found the means to improve both performance and productivity by combining automation with processes standardization. "Because there are so many fewer places where individual operators have to transfer information by hand," she said, "there are fewer places where mistakes can be made."

Adopting and implementing automation requires careful planning and dedicated execution. Pharmacos must rigorously weigh the benefits and costs of each potential process. For example, for complex processes like lyophilization or those with decontamination cycles, investment in electronic batch records might not be justified.

Successful execution also requires a substantial commitment of time and energy to change behaviors and train operators. As just one example, companies that shift to automated batch review must also start focusing on error-proof design of the master batch record, rather than detailed batch review. As one pharma quality manager observed: "If you design in a signature for line clearance, but don't train on it, the line will stop."

Continuous improvement

Continuous improvement is a familiar but challenging topic in pharma quality, as most companies have employed such initiatives for years but with mixed results. Using lean techniques turns out to be one of the best ways to establish the culture, mindsets, and skills needed for ongoing performance.

Quality Control labs have traditionally been the first area to apply such techniques. A lab transformation approach will usually include standard tools such as visual aids for performance tracking, first-in, first-out processing, shared metrics and shared services across sites. The benchmarked plant with the highest QC testing productivity had reduced its QC lab cycle by over 60%—from 16 to 6 days. It accomplished this by redesigning its lab flow and applying multiple lean techniques: 5S helped reorganize samples handling, a spaghetti diagram improved lab floor workflows, non-value-added steps were identified and removed, log books were error-proofed, and a new cell concept increased ownership.

Validation still offers great potential for lean improvements. The plant with the most productive validation process in the benchmarking sample adopted basic continuous improvement tools, using them to change teams' mindsets and increase employee involvement in decision-making. As a result, validation lead time plummeted from 45 to 4 hours per month—a 90% drop. The plant saved $600,000 and reduced validation-related staffing by 40%.

Another site adopted a continuous requalification process whereby every run met the qualification requirements, eliminating the need for separate "qualification runs" and saving nearly 6000 hours per year. Byproducts of this practice included immediate detection of deviations, fewer invasions into the isolator chamber, and fewer shutdown days, increasing effective capacity of the line.

Benchmarked plants with high transparency of scheduling and batch flow between the quality control lab and the shop floor more than doubled the batch release testing productivity and shortened batch release cycle times. This level of transparency is usually achieved through shared information systems, visual communication boards or other collaborative solutions.

Prevention

Prevention is another important performance lever for pharmacos. It can include clear identification and focus on critical-to-quality (CTQ) parameters throughout the production process. By outlining the key elements of the process in which CTQs are impacted, leading companies align their testing with those elements, identify potential quality issues early, avoid additional processing, and reduce the time and effort required to investigate and address those issues later on. In our study, plants that specifically identified CTQ parameters enjoyed significantly higher quality productivity, with more than 40% more batch inspections per FTE than those that did not.

Over time, such focus on CTQs helps to eliminate overall process variability and raises performance. In addition, this focus aids productivity, since tests that are not aligned with CTQs are redundant, and those that detect little or no variability can sometimes be eliminated or reduced. This can free resources to improve efficiency or invest in more value-added efforts.

Another key to prevention is ensuring that managers conduct root-cause problem-solving for all identified issues. Understanding and solving those issues helps companies eliminate recurring problems that are a drain on resources and overall quality performance.

* * *

The path towards improving quality starts with good understanding of the baseline quality cost and performance. Companies can improve on this baseline by applying the right improvement levers to close the gap relative to their peers in each quality activity. Structural factors impose few limitations and achieving top quality performance is within the reach of most pharma sites.

How supply chain excellence can improve the bottom line

Peter De Boeck, Thomas Ebel, Sanjay Ramaswamy

Pharmaceutical companies are under increasing pressure to strengthen operational performance, but their efforts in the last few years have not measurably improved key performance indicators. In particular, working capital performance is low compared to other industries. By empowering their supply chain functions and focusing on end-to-end throughput time, many pharmaceutical companies can free up cash for new product development and improve their returns on invested capital while also boosting sales and service levels.

Times are changing in the pharma industry: growth in developed countries is slowing, and generic competition is increasingly fueled by blockbusters coming off-patent. Governments are curbing healthcare spending and increasing pressure on price. Many of the big global pharmacos are being forced to take severe measures to counter the rising pressure on their operating profits.

In the last couple of years, more than half of the top 20 global pharmacos have announced plans to lay off up to 15% of their global workforce. Many pharmacos are also restructuring their manufacturing networks to reduce the cost of goods sold—either by increasing the utilization of their remaining plants or shifting production, especially that of active pharma ingredients and bulk solids, to low-cost locations in Asia and Eastern Europe.

How can leading pharma companies leverage supply chain excellence to secure their business model and profitability levels? And how can they enhance both cost efficiency and customer service to improve their competitive position? Many launched improvement initiatives that focused on cost, throughput time and working capital. Despite all efforts, however, the supply chain performance of the top 20 Rx companies has failed to improve significantly (see Exhibit 1):

- A lack of improvement in material productivity is indicated by costs of goods rising at the same rate as sales, stabilizing at around 23% of sales in the last few years

- Sales, general and administrative expenses (SG&A) have grown at a rate slightly below sales. (The share of SG&A in sales fell from about 34% in 2000 to 30% in 2008)

- Although many pharmacos continued to outsource large parts of their value chain, which can lead to a significant working capital reduction, inventory reach remained fairly stable—200 days on average—from 2000 to 2008, indicating that they made almost no progress in reducing working capital.

exhibit 1

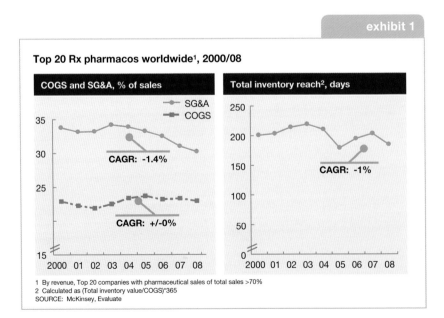

Top 20 Rx pharmacos worldwide[1], 2000/08

COGS and SG&A, % of sales

SG&A
COGS

CAGR: -1.4%

CAGR: +/-0%

2000 01 02 03 04 05 06 07 08

Total inventory reach[2], days

CAGR: -1%

2000 01 02 03 04 05 06 07 08

1 By revenue, Top 20 companies with pharmaceutical sales of total sales >70%
2 Calculated as (Total inventory value/COGS)*365
SOURCE: McKinsey, Evaluate

Traditionally, pharma companies have focused closely on product availability, drug quality and safety, and regulatory compliance, and less on optimizing their supply chain, such as by reducing inventories. Especially in the area of working capital, the value at stake is often regarded as too low to warrant substantial efforts. But the figures show that investing in inventory reduction can pay off handsomely.

Consider a $10 billion pharmaco with an inventory worth $1.4 billion—at an industry average of 200 days' reach. Reducing overall inventory by 40% would free up about $500 million in cash and cut holding and obsolescence costs by up to $100 million. This substantial sum could go into new product development, mergers & acquisitions or the bottom line. Beyond the immediate impact on P&L, a working capital program can shorten time-to-market and supply chain reaction time to speed market penetration.

McKinsey and the Georgia Tech Institute's survey of over 60 global companies underlines as well that supply chain excellence can drive value. The results of this survey, and our own project experience, show that EBITDA and supply chain excellence go hand-in-hand, and that there is still much room for improvement (see Exhibit 2).

exhibit 2

Dimension	KPI	Average performance		KPI definition
Service	Service level Percent	~96	~94	OTIF: percent of orders delivered in full on the original commitment date
Cost	COGS Percent of sales	~23	~57	Direct expenses incurred in producing a particular good for sale
	Distribution and logistics cost Percent of COGS	~5	~9	Total distribution and logistics costs including outbound transport/warehousing and inbound (supplier-end) logistics
Capital	Total inventory reach[1] Days	~200	~70	(Total inventory value/COGS) x 365. Total inventory value contains finished goods, work-in-progress and raw materials
	Inventory reach finished goods[1] Days	~80	~35	(Inventory value finished goods/COGS) x 365
	Share WIP of total inventory Percent	~35	~5	Inventory value work-in-progress/total inventory value
		Pharma	**Consumer goods**	

1 Average reach; Pharma Top 20 companies with pharmaceutical sales of total sales >70%; Consumer goods: Top 20 consumer packaged goods companies
SOURCE: Supply chain best practices survey, McKinsey, Georgiatech, Evaluate, Bloomberg

A comparison with the consumer goods industry illustrates opportunities available for pharma. While both industries have similar manufacturing setups (as opposed to typical assembly industries) and global sales reach, they differ in important ways: the consumer industry is a strong innovator in marketing and distribution, leading to shorter product lifecycles, high-impact of promotions, and dynamic channel strategies. Supply and distribution in the pharma industry is far more regulated: registration and approval processes, strict manufacturing and distribution requirements (GMP, GDP) and gapless documentation impose high costs and burden productivity improvement efforts. In addition, cost structures differ fundamentally, such as in value density—one pallet of patented drugs can be worth 10 to 50 times more than a pallet of consumer packaged goods.

What about the differences in supply chain performance? The good news is that 96% of pharma deliveries were on time and in full (OTIF) versus 94% in consumer goods. Pharmaceuticals also have a clear cost advantage over their consumer goods peers, with distribution and logistics costs amounting for just 5% of COGS as opposed to 9% for consumer goods. This reflects the high value density inherent in the pharma value chain mentioned above.

Pharma companies are much slower than their consumer goods peers in moving inventories, however. Total and finished pharma goods inventories are more than double those maintained by consumer goods companies. Moreover, the high share of work-in-progress inventory shows that pharmacos are suffering from long throughput times. Long production runs and quality release times, and a lack of synchronization between multi-step production processes, are the main contributors to this problem.

But is it valid to compare the pharmaceutical and consumer goods industries?

And is it possible for pharmacos to reduce inventory reach by more than half, to match their consumer goods peers? To answer these questions, it's necessary to develop a deeper understanding of the pharma value chain and the key drivers of inventory reach and throughput time—from raw materials to finished goods.

For the average pharmaco, the inventory value sitting in all value chain steps equals 200 days of sales at cost price. The finished product awaiting delivery (mainly in national distribution warehouses) represents nearly 2.5 months of sales. These inventories tie up capital and incur considerable carrying costs.

The end-to-end throughput time measures how long it takes a product to travel through all value chain steps sequentially—from the raw material in the factory to the finished pack dispatched to the wholesaler from the distribution warehouse. On average, the end-to-end throughput time in pharma companies is approximately 400 days. Exhibit 3 shows the biggest drivers of throughput time in a typical pharmaceutical company:

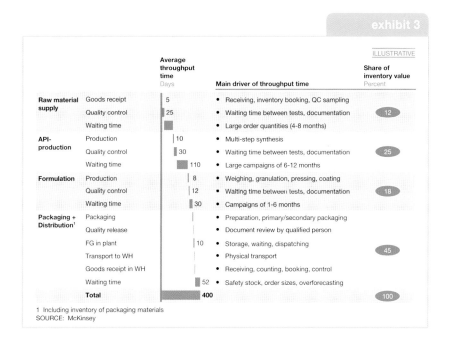

exhibit 3

ILLUSTRATIVE

		Average throughput time Days	Main driver of throughput time	Share of inventory value Percent
Raw material supply	Goods receipt	5	• Receiving, inventory booking, QC sampling	
	Quality control	25	• Waiting time between tests, documentation	12
	Waiting time		• Large order quantities (4-8 months)	
API-production	Production	10	• Multi-step synthesis	
	Quality control	30	• Waiting time between tests, documentation	25
	Waiting time	110	• Large campaigns of 6-12 months	
Formulation	Production	8	• Weighing, granulation, pressing, coating	
	Quality control	12	• Waiting time between tests, documentation	18
	Waiting time	30	• Campaigns of 1-6 months	
Packaging + Distribution[1]	Packaging		• Preparation, primary/secondary packaging	
	Quality release		• Document review by qualified person	
	FG in plant	10	• Storage, waiting, dispatching	45
	Transport to WH		• Physical transport	
	Goods receipt in WH		• Receiving, counting, booking, control	
	Waiting time	52	• Safety stock, order sizes, overforecasting	
	Total	**400**		100

1 Including inventory of packaging materials
SOURCE: McKinsey

- Raw material supply and API-production (waiting time included) emerge as the biggest drivers of throughput time. Big order sizes or production campaigns that cover 6 to 12 months of consumption are the main cause

- Production itself—the time needed for weighing, granulation, tabletting and coating during formulation—is notably one of the less time-consuming processes, accounting for only about 5% of total time

- Quality control is also important, accounting for about 20% of time, or 72 days. This means that about 20% of pharmaco inventory stays in quality control or quality release and is not freely available for further processing (this signifies only the quality control between the value chain steps and not the in-process control)

- Overall, waiting and freely available inventory takes up as much as 230 days or over 50% of throughput time.

Is there a real chance for pharmacos to reduce their throughput time?

Industry benchmarks, and our experience with operational improvement projects in pharmaceutical companies of all sizes, show there is.

Due to the specific demands of the pharmaceutical supply chain, such as good manufacturing practice requirements, quality controls and chemical production with long cleaning and set-up times, it will be difficult for pharmacos to reach consumer goods inventory levels while maintaining service levels. This said, there's still a lot to be gained through focused initiatives.

By implementing some targeted measures, pharmacos can decrease their average throughput time and inventory value by as much as 35% and 40-50%, respectively (Exhibit 4). This translates to a total inventory reach of just 120 days, which begins to close in on consumer goods, which clock in at around 70 days.

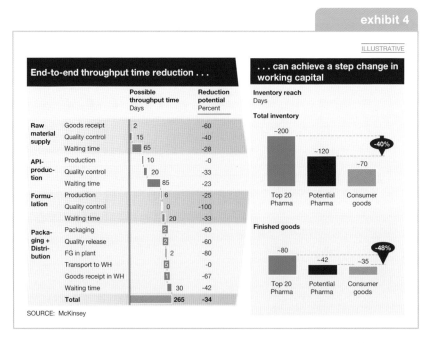

exhibit 4

ILLUSTRATIVE

End-to-end throughput time reduction . . .

. . . can achieve a step change in working capital

		Possible throughput time Days	Reduction potential Percent
Raw material supply	Goods receipt	2	-60
	Quality control	15	-40
	Waiting time	65	-28
API-produc-tion	Production	10	-0
	Quality control	20	-33
	Waiting time	85	-23
Formu-lation	Production	6	-25
	Quality control	0	-100
	Waiting time	20	-33
Packa-ging + Distri-bution	Packaging	2	-60
	Quality release	2	-60
	FG in plant	2	-80
	Transport to WH	5	-0
	Goods receipt in WH	1	-67
	Waiting time	30	-42
	Total	265	-34

Inventory reach
Days

Total inventory

~200   ~120   ~70   -40%

Top 20 Pharma   Potential Pharma   Consumer goods

Finished goods

~80   ~42   ~35   -48%

Top 20 Pharma   Potential Pharma   Consumer goods

SOURCE: McKinsey

Pharmacos can reduce their finished goods inventory by about 50% by:

a. eliminating stock in production sites by shipping immediately after production

b. Speeding quality release processes

c. Introducing optimal stock levels and replenishment rules for sales warehouses, and

d. Establishing more frequent deliveries based on smaller economic order quantities.

Pharma companies might also reduce inventory in the area of formulation by approximately 50%. One of the key drivers is reducing optimal campaign sizes. To do this economically, managers need to focus on reducing changeover times, for example, by using the SMED-approach, machine stops and speed losses through performance management on the shop floor. Pharmaceuticals should also optimize their multi-step production planning, among others, by implementing kanban to improve synchronization of process steps. A second driver is to reduce stock blocked through quality processes by speeding up the quality lead time or, if necessary, packaging under quarantine.

Moreover, pharmacos could reduce the time they need for processing raw materials and API production by about 30% by speeding quality processes and enabling smaller production campaigns.

What do top-performing companies do differently?

What matters and what doesn't? The joint survey analyzed supply chain practices and performance of more than 60 companies. Six important factors emerged. Supply chain leaders typically:

a. Explicitly link supply chain strategy to the corporate strategy and set clear, well-understood aspirations

b. Use segmentation to embrace the complexity that matters

c. Design and build forward-looking networks that balance cost and service

d. Create a lean, end-to-end value chain using strong cross-functional processes, and force trade-offs across functions

e. Strictly adhere to world-class demand and production planning processes

f. Get the right talent on board and hold them accountable.

Equally important is identifying factors that do not make a difference. The survey reveals that large investments in formalized IT systems do not pay off, as the complexity of such systems often requires unrealistically advanced user skills. Simple systems often foster better understanding and lead to better decisions. That said, end-to-end supply chain transparency still requires an integrated IT strategy.

A second strategy that often fails to bring the expected return is reorganization. In fact, no one organizational structure is obviously superior. Here the three archetypes of supply chain organizations:

- In a **centralized SCM organization**, supply chain management is located at the first management tier—reporting directly to the board—and has full responsibility for strategic and operative SCM activities across all business units

- In a **hybrid SCM organization**, the global or regional headquarters is responsible for selected service functions to the business units, for strategic tasks and for cross-business unit initiatives. Thus, global or regional headquarters serve as a center of competence and ensure the rollout of best practices across plants and countries. Operative tasks are performed by decentralized SCM organizations in the business units

- In a **decentralized SCM organization**, business units perform both strategic and operative SCM activities independently. An SCM coordination committee is often responsible for the coordination of cross-business-unit activities.

All three models work and can help companies manage cross-functional trade-offs and achieve operational supply chain excellence. The only model guaranteed to fail is the one in which the SCM organization is not closely linked to the corporate strategy. Most pharma companies operate under the hybrid model.

What steps should pharmacos take to improve their supply chain?

Many companies already have the knowledge and tools they need to significantly reduce their working capital—changeover time reduction, including inventory management, value-added time analysis, and kanban to synchronize different work centers. Having the knowledge and resources to apply these techniques is not enough, however. Reducing working capital requirements and achieving and sustaining excellent throughput times require a range of enablers.

Reducing working capital involves many stakeholders—sourcing, production, logistics, and sales—across the organization. SCM improvement teams should be deployed to help catalyze change. They can provide the methodology, coach sub-teams to implement best practice processes, set the right aspirations and ensure that the trade-offs are managed from an end-to-end perspective. Survey results show that a disciplined implementation of best-practice planning processes can significantly drive performance, reducing inventory and improving delivery fulfillment.

Speeding the supply chain often requires new mindsets for stakeholders along the value chain. Production departments need to shift their paradigm from the classical material requirements planning to pull systems. Pull systems stabilize order patterns across the chain and reduce excess buffer stocks. Managers looking to optimize finished goods distribution should reorganize the responsibilities between SCM and commercial units. Demand planners in the sales subsidiaries should focus on sales forecasting while the SCM function take responsibility for inventory targets, net demand planning and sales and operations planning. Incentives should be aligned accordingly.

In their journey to supply chain excellence, pharmacos should implement a rigorous supply chain performance management. They should choose and track KPIs around service (including lead time), cost and capital for each key value chain step. A KPI review board should track performance, identify issues and decide on corrective action on a monthly basis.

***

Today's highly competitive environment is challenging the pharma business model—and offering opportunities to identify untapped potential in operations.

Leveraging supply chain excellence to reduce throughput time can help pharmacos improve profitability and maintain their business models. Companies should look to implement a focused end-to-end improvement initiative to boost performance. This may require fundamental changes in the planning paradigm and shifts in responsibility between sales, production, and supply chain.

By focusing on reducing the throughput-time—from raw materials to finished goods distribution—pharmacos can reduce inventory by around 40% and more than halve the gap to their consumer goods peers. This can help them significantly improve profitability and ROIC and free up cash needed for new drug development. Being faster to market and reacting to customers more quickly will help boost sales and service levels. And removing hidden inefficiencies will also benefit the pharma supply chain by driving the process of continuous improvement.

Lean and mean:
How does your supply chain shape up?

Knut Alicke, Martin Lösch

Up to half the cost of many supply chains lurks ignored and unmanaged in outbound logistics and behind the closed doors of distribution centers. Much of that cost can be eliminated by applying lean manufacturing techniques.

For all the effort and ingenuity that pharma companies are putting into streamlining sales and operations planning, forecasting, inventory management and logistics, major opportunities remain in the outbound supply chain, from packaging to final delivery.

The typical pharma company operates a historically grown network with one or many warehouses in each country, different contracting terms and diverse transportation companies. Pharma logistics represent about 2% of sales, or 7-8% of the cost of goods sold, less than what we find in other industries (see Exhibit 1), and the outbound supply chain is often outsourced.

Under these circumstances, optimizing outbound logistics has not been a strategic priority for pharma companies. We think it should be—especially in the light of current industry cost and performance pressures. Distribution is the logistical interface with the customer. Inefficient or unreliable warehouse operations and transportation

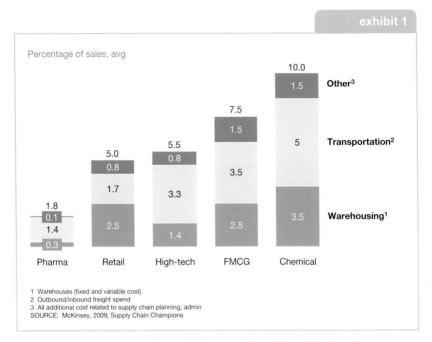

1 Warehouses (fixed and variable cost)
2 Outbound/inbound freight spend
3 All additional cost related to supply chain planning, admin
SOURCE: McKinsey, 2009, Supply Chain Champions

cost more than money—delivery delays can do quick and lasting damage to a company's reputation with customers. One pharmaco had to hold a CEO-level meeting to safeguard the relationship with a large retailer

Companies have made significant improvements to manufacturing, service and maintenance operations through lean techniques: eliminating waste, inflexibility and variability in their systems and reducing costs by up to 50% in the process. Yet few apply the same lean techniques in warehouse operations or transportation, even though they can have a dramatic effect. These operations represent 95% of the pharma logistics costs and, in our experience, companies can save 20-50% in warehousing and up to 40% in transportation.

Companies that run successful lean programs not only save money in warehouse operations but enjoy more flexibility and much better service, without significant capital investment. Logistics providers stand to gain, too. With contract logistics margins under pressure, developing truly lean warehouse operating systems dramatically reduces costs. Even more important, it serves as a powerful value proposition to customers in a market where providers struggle to differentiate their offerings.

A pharma company recently saved between 15% and 50% per warehouse in the negotiation phase with the service providers.

As in warehouse operations, companies that focus on transportation cost drivers gain on two fronts: they can control cost overruns or reduce current costs, and they can improve customer service and satisfaction by tailoring services, such as lead times and delivery frequencies, to customer needs and offering special services where they matter most. In a recent example, a pharma company reduced 25-30% of total transportation costs on the countries inspected.

WAREHOUSING

Understanding the baseline

The first challenge in optimizing warehouse operations is that there is no "standard"—they tend to be as diverse as the products they store. A multi-client facility, for example, with a huge number of SKUs and diverse inventory turnover, looks vastly different from a small-volume operation with a few SKUs. As a consequence, it has been difficult to identify best practices or apply them across a broad variety of settings. Warehouse managers struggle with special circumstances as they try to improve lackluster performance.

We have developed a comprehensive approach to performance measurement across all types of warehouse, providing supply chain managers with a tool to rate warehouse efficiency. We begin by calculating the clean-sheet cost, space and capital that an "ideal" warehouse would need to handle the given volume. We then adjust for site-specific circumstances, such as multiple floors and high labor costs. We add logistic service provider margins, if the warehouse is outsourced. The results reveal the warehouse's theoretical and realistic performance gaps.

A wide gap...

We have used the model to evaluate more than 40 diverse facilities worldwide. Most are operating 20 to 50% less efficiently than the clean-sheet reference. In one European warehouse, our clean-sheet model showed a performance gap of more than 50%.

The gap arose not because the warehouse lacked technology or suffered from the structural disadvantages of the goods it handles. Instead, we found that it is the cumulative effect of dozens of slightly sub-optimal processes and the lack of lean mindset. A few fundamental changes in the way these facilities

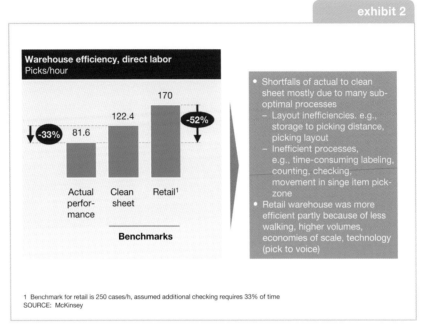

exhibit 2

Warehouse efficiency, direct labor
Picks/hour

Actual performance — 81.6   -33%
Clean sheet — 122.4
Retail[1] — 170   -52%

Benchmarks

- Shortfalls of actual to clean sheet mostly due to many suboptimal processes
  - Layout inefficiencies. e.g., storage to picking distance, picking layout
  - Inefficient processes, e.g., time-consuming labeling, counting, checking, movement in singe item pick-zone
- Retail warehouse was more efficient partly because of less walking, higher volumes, economies of scale, technology (pick to voice)

1 Benchmark for retail is 250 cases/h, assumed additional checking requires 33% of time
SOURCE: McKinsey

are organized and managed could immediately close at least half of the gap between current performance and the benchmark (see Exhibit 2).

Some warehouses simply suffer from lack of attention. Designed for one purpose a decade ago, their managers make only minor modifications to cope with dramatic business changes such as increasing product and delivery complexity, a merger or acquisition, or new technologies or supply chain structures.

Some solutions intended to improve performance often have exactly the opposite effect. Technology-heavy approaches, such as automated storage areas, sorting technology or classical transaction-based ERP systems, have a strong tendency to reduce flexibility, particularly short-notice flexibility, which is exactly what many modern supply chains demand. The payback on such systems is poor, with the capital cost being many multiples of the savings achieved by reducing relatively low-cost labor.

Outsourcing is a common practice in pharma, but it often fails to remedy bad warehouse practice. Managers may be tempted to outsource their operations to leverage factor cost advantages, for example, but outsourcing inefficient processes simply offers service providers higher margins. And since warehouse inefficiencies can arise externally, such as volatile demand patterns or undisciplined ordering, providers are often unable to create real cost advantage. Meanwhile, companies rarely use effective performance-based contracts to encourage service providers to optimize processes.

... Easy to bridge

At the heart of transforming warehouse operations is the rigorous and relentless application of lean and six sigma techniques to eliminate sources of waste, variability and inflexibility. Most are simple, pragmatic activities that require little or no financial investment—they rest on six building blocks of performance: processes, people, performance management, interaction with third-parties, layout and ownership (see Exhibit 3). The examples below are typical of projects worldwide.

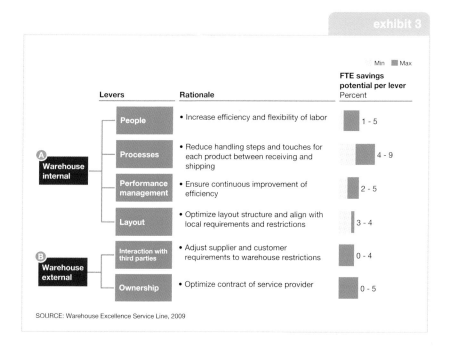

exhibit 3

	Min ▪ Max

Levers	Rationale	FTE savings potential per lever
		Percent
People	• Increase efficiency and flexibility of labor	1 - 5
Processes	• Reduce handling steps and touches for each product between receiving and shipping	4 - 9
Performance management	• Ensure continuous improvement of efficiency	2 - 5
Layout	• Optimize layout structure and align with local requirements and restrictions	3 - 4
Interaction with third parties	• Adjust supplier and customer requirements to warehouse restrictions	0 - 4
Ownership	• Optimize contract of service provider	0 - 5

A **Warehouse internal**

B **Warehouse external**

SOURCE: Warehouse Excellence Service Line, 2009

Better processes

The same sources of waste that the lean approach seeks to eliminate in the manufacturing context, such as unnecessary motion or double-handling, account for many unnecessary warehousing costs and introduce critical inflexibility. A tendency to stick with established processes and resist change also drives down efficiency.

For many orders, picking and packing processes can be combined, reducing handling steps, motion, transportation and space requirements.

Receiving processes often include labor-intensive breakdown of pallets, which is rarely well-organized or coordinated. By optimizing the sequence of actions for pallet breakdown and organizing workplaces to make the process easier, effort can be cut by half.

Pickers in one facility were spending two minutes between picks waiting for new lists to be printed. By introducing an automated system that produced a new list each time one was taken, pickers could always expect their next pick list to be available. In other faculties, simply ensuring that picking pallets were always available reduced expensive operator idle time.

In one pharma warehouse, the pickers had to put labels on all products delivered to hospitals. That required retrieving the products, putting a label on each package and putting it back in its original location. By attaching the label beforehand, this step could be completely eliminated, saving 50% of the pallet picking time (see Exhibit 4).

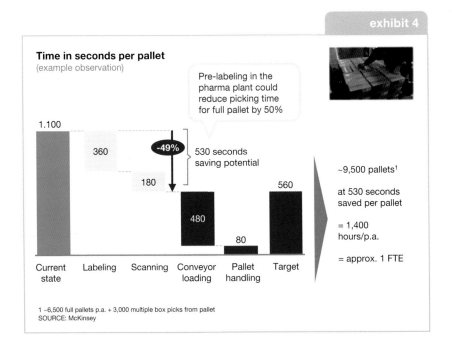

exhibit 4

Time in seconds per pallet
(example observation)

Pre-labeling in the pharma plant could reduce picking time for full pallet by 50%

1.100

360

-49%

530 seconds saving potential

180

560

480

80

| Current state | Labeling | Scanning | Conveyor loading | Pallet handling | Target |

~9,500 pallets[1]

at 530 seconds saved per pallet

= 1,400 hours/p.a.

= approx. 1 FTE

1 ~6,500 full pallets p.a. + 3,000 multiple box picks from pallet
SOURCE: McKinsey

Documentation and standardization are hugely powerful in process improvement. Once managers have identified and developed best practices, clear standard operating procedures help ensure that all staff use optimized processes.

Trained people

Workload requirements in warehouse facilities can vary by as much as 50% day to day. Around half of this variation can be predicted in many facilities based on historical data, but conventional approaches to workforce flexibility—either none at all or based on notice periods of several weeks—simply cannot respond to these rapid changes in demand. As a result, facilities are often substantially overstaffed to guarantee performance.

By reducing the notice period for shift schedules to one or two days, facilities can more closely match on-site staffing to demand, raising efficiency by up to 15%. Some facilities have achieved even better results using a super-flex temporary workforce, often students. They can respond to SMS messages with only a few hours' notice, allowing the facility to respond on the same day to unexpected demand peaks.

Given warehouse workers' relatively low skills and high turnover, many employers minimize recruitment and training investment to keep costs down. In our experience, however, improved training can boost productivity by 5 to 10%. Training must be regular and continuous and focus on specific aspects of each employee's performance, encouraging them adopt established best practices.

Some facilities have dramatically reduced staff turnover through straightforward refinements to their recruitment processes, such as aptitude tests on the shop floor. Applicants pick for one hour under observation. Those that do not show signs of significant performance improvement during that hour are not hired.

Performance management

Most modern warehouses collect detailed data on the performance of individual employees automatically as part of standard management systems. Unfortunately, few exploit this data effectively to motivate and improve employee performance. Just demonstrating ongoing performance in a clear, accessible way can deliver immediate improvements. A notice board showing the relative performance of pick teams, for example, can create competition and drive performance.

High-performing facilities supplement visible performance metrics with daily discussion of historical performance and upcoming expectations. A five-minute discussion at the beginning of each shift reinforces the importance of good performance and helps staff concentrate on key aspects of their own activities.

The biggest productivity improvements—of as much as 20%—come from linking pay to performance. Such systems must be set up with care to ensure that they reward quality as well as speed. Some facilities reinforce the impact of performance-related pay with near real-time feedback, using pick-by-voice technology, for example, to let staff know how well they are doing.

Measuring and rewarding the "softer" aspects of performance can deliver powerful long-term benefits too. A visible, rewarded, "employee of the month" scheme, for example, can have a positive impact on staff satisfaction. Measuring such activities as the number of improvement ideas implemented in a month, or the effectiveness of suggestions, can help foster a mindset of continuous improvement.

Interaction with third parties

Warehouses are not islands. To operate efficiently, a facility must interact effectively with three main external groups: upstream with suppliers, downstream with internal and external customers, and sideways with the wider organization. But not every warehouse operating model is designed to reflect the service requirements of internal or external customers. Warehouses are often unable to flex their operations in response to predictable fluctuations in customer demand, leaving them overstaffed or underperforming.

Improving supplier relationships can straightforward. Bad delivery accuracy can lead to congestion in the receiving area during peak times, for example. By assigning time-windows for delivery and clear consequences for missing the window (not receiving the truck, for example), volume flow can be leveled and the workforce utilized better.

Working with suppliers can also ensure that goods arrive in the right order and in the right form of packaging for direct storage, reducing labor required to receive goods. Optimum loading bay configuration for the types of vehicle used for delivery reduces double-handling as trucks are unloaded.

While it is not always possible to dictate delivery schedules or strategies to customers, leading facilities are beginning to exploit cooperative working methods to develop mutually beneficial least-cost approaches. Improved delivery performance and high customer confidence help to build the trust essential for this kind of activity. On this platform, some facilities are introducing variable pricing and service levels to encourage customers to order at the most cost-effective quantities and delivery frequencies, with higher levels of service available for a price premium.

Trust is also a key to better relationships with the wider organization. Some simple process changes can offer performance improvements, such as providing the warehouse with forthcoming delivery information as soon as it is available internally, for example. Others require cultural changes. One

facility suffered from administrative overhead because sales staff called to
check on the progress of express orders. By bringing the sales staff to the
facility and demonstrating the express picking and distribution process, facility
management gave the sales teams confidence that the system would work
without their intervention.

Improved flexibility

Many facilities opt for a "one size fits all" approach to layout, rather than
segmenting assets according to product types and customer requirements.
Many managers are also unwilling to alter facility layouts as demand patterns
change, eroding performance over time. A pharma warehouse was able
to reduce process time by 20% simply by eliminating picking from the
highest shelves (see Exhibit 5). Sometimes this problem is compounded by
investments in costly and highly inflexible automation equipment.

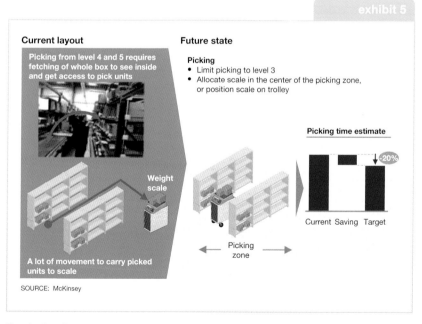

exhibit 5

Current layout

Picking from level 4 and 5 requires fetching of whole box to see inside and get access to pick units

Weight scale

A lot of movement to carry picked units to scale

Future state

Picking
• Limit picking to level 3
• Allocate scale in the center of the picking zone, or position scale on trolley

Picking time estimate

↓ -20%

Current Saving Target

← Picking zone →

SOURCE: McKinsey

Replacing fixed equipment with flexible, reconfigurable systems can have big
benefits, while the penalties of inflexibility can be severe. One retailer made
big investments in automating a warehouse before changes in business needs
created spare capacity. The retailer tried to resell this capacity to third parties,
but its system was so inflexible that it was unable to fulfill the requirements of
any of the interested organizations.

A common way to benefit from flexibility is to reorganize the facility layout to position items according to pick frequency. By placing fast and super-fast moving items right by the loading dock, walking distances and pick times can be reduced dramatically. Such implementations must be carried out with care, however. To avoid congestion at the pick face it is useful to mix the fastest-moving items with some slower movers.

The strategy for reviewing and revising slotting strategy should also suit wider business needs. Warehouses with high seasonal variability might review and re-slot every three months, for example, based on historical picking data, while some facilities might find it useful to re-slot on a monthly or even a weekly basis.

Ownership impact

The outsourcing of warehouses to third-party operators is a common strategy for companies that do not consider warehousing to be a core competence. But many such deals simply transfer inefficient processes to a new owner, while cost-plus contract terms seldom create an imperative for improvement on the part of the service provider. Outsourced warehouses are viewed as black boxes, leaving major opportunities for collaboration between suppliers, plants and customers on the table. Moreover, companies that have developed their own lean manufacturing system miss the opportunity to apply their expertise to these outsourced warehouse operations.

Change of ownership usually falls outside the scope of an improvement project. But this optimization approach can be applied just as well by a warehouse operator, creating competitive advantage from its ability to operate at lower cost and at higher flexibility.

TRANSPORTATION

Understanding the baseline

While pharmaceutical companies can save as much in transportation as they can in warehouse operations, delivering those savings requires a different approach. If companies have historically ignored their warehouse operations, at least they began with a good idea of the size and location of their facilities. Transportation costs, by contrast, come from many hundreds of thousands of widely distributed individual operations every year.

Complexity is what makes transportation difficult to improve. Many pharmaceutical companies have tremendous variability in their transport operations, with different customers demanding different service levels and a multitude of transport providers delivering services in different ways.

Companies can cut through this complexity, however. By building a full picture of their transportation operations, they can see, often for the first time, exactly where to find the primary drivers of transportation cost. Armed with this information, they can identify and exploit opportunities and save up to 20 or even 30% of transportation costs.

One large pharma player began optimizing transportation by analyzing historical transport data for a full year. It collected information and analyzed each delivery (e.g., shipment types, sizes, modes of transport, provider, customer, region, type of service and cost) to understand the real drivers of transportation costs. The analysis revealed that three critical service categories that had a disproportionate effect on transportation costs:

- **Temperature-controlled distribution.** While 98% of product by weight passed through the firm's ambient distribution chain, the 2% that had to be shipped in refrigerated vehicles accounted for a quarter of all shipments— and nearly half total transportation costs

- **Special delivery services.** Express shipping guaranteed by 10 AM the next day can cost two to five times more than conventional 24-hour delivery. These special deliveries represented only 1% of the shipments but accounted for most of the excess cost

- **Shipment size.** The vast majority of shipments weighed less than five kilos, but these small shipments cost the company around six times as much per kilogram as larger shipments. Even where the company did

manage to consolidate deliveries into larger shipments, it usually failed to capture all the available savings; by weight, a quarter of product was shipped in the lowest cost bracket, but nearly half fell into the next price bracket up.

Opportunities for action

Once they understand their cost drivers, companies can embark on a systematic approach to reduce transportation costs. They can look broadly at four main levers (see Exhibit 6). First, they can check compliance with freight contracts and minimize surcharges. They can challenge the rates provided by the freight forwarders. They can improve contract terms and conditions to share risks and benefits with their freight forwarding partners. And finally, companies can do much to understand customer breakpoints and incentivize customers to choose cost-effective options.

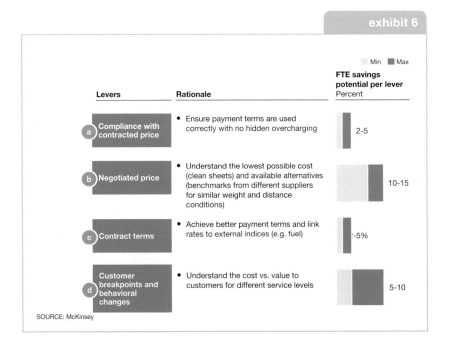

exhibit 6

Min   Max

FTE savings potential per lever
Percent

Levers	Rationale	
a Compliance with contracted price	• Ensure payment terms are used correctly with no hidden overcharging	2-5
b Negotiated price	• Understand the lowest possible cost (clean sheets) and available alternatives (benchmarks from different suppliers for similar weight and distance conditions)	10-15
c Contract terms	• Achieve better payment terms and link rates to external indices (e.g. fuel)	?-5%
d Customer breakpoints and behavioral changes	• Understand the cost vs. value to customers for different service levels	5-10

SOURCE: McKinsey

Compliance auditing

A simple auditing of monthly invoices will reveal the surcharges a company is paying due to special terms. It can check contract compliance by modeling the expected cost of shipments under the contract terms, and compare these with the actual bills from service providers. Significant deviation between the two can then be investigated and brought under control.

For example, some companies find that they are paying significant fuel surcharges or charges for waiting time or late payments. Where these charges are large, they can improve practices to minimize them—by ensuring vehicles are loaded rapidly on arrival at distribution centers, for example. Incorporating some exceptions into standard conditions can minimize the overcharges paid by the company and help its logistics partner to improve planning and scheduling.

Rates improvement

A comparison of freight tariffs offered by suppliers on similar routes will provide an independent benchmark. Some companies go even further, using clean-sheet cost-modeling to provide bottom-up estimates of a freight forwarder's cost of operation, fixed costs and profit.

Clean-sheet models use the best available combination of vehicle, fuel, labor and other running costs to calculate the lowest possible cost of providing an agreed service level (See example estimate in Exhibit 7). This cost is then used as a starting point in discussions with service providers. When pharma companies understand the causes of inefficiency in their suppliers' operations, they can challenge them to provide better tariffs. In the case of the company described above, clean-sheet cost modeling indicated significant savings potential even after accounting for inefficiencies like partial utilization of trucks and the supplier's failure to use its vehicles for back-haul operations.

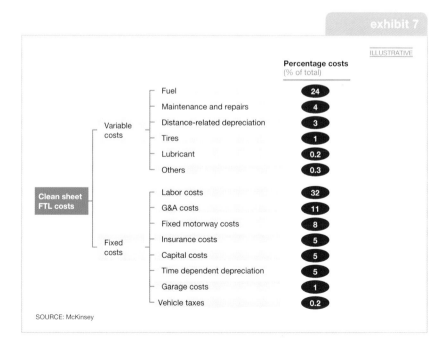

exhibit 7

ILLUSTRATIVE

Percentage costs
(% of total)

Clean sheet FTL costs

Variable costs
- Fuel — 24
- Maintenance and repairs — 4
- Distance-related depreciation — 3
- Tires — 1
- Lubricant — 0.2
- Others — 0.3

Fixed costs
- Labor costs — 32
- G&A costs — 11
- Fixed motorway costs — 8
- Insurance costs — 5
- Capital costs — 5
- Time dependent depreciation — 5
- Garage costs — 1
- Vehicle taxes — 0.2

SOURCE: McKinsey

Improving contract terms

The volatility of fuel prices has increased interest in contract terms that share risks and rewards. High fuel costs were painful for many logistics service providers. To protect themselves against further losses, many have increased their prices or introduced fuel surcharges. While fixed prices work in favor of pharma companies when fuel costs are high and rising, they create unnecessarily high bills when oil is cheaper.

A more effective approach for both parties is agreement that includes a variable portion of total cost associated with the fuel index. Such terms can do much to bring transportation costs closer to the true cost of delivering services (See example methodology in Exhibit 8).

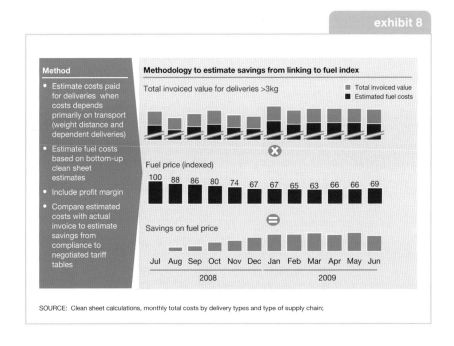

SOURCE: Clean sheet calculations, monthly total costs by delivery types and type of supply chain;

Understanding customer breakpoints

By changing the way the run their internal processes and incentivizing customers to select more cost-effective delivery options, pharma companies can cut costs and improve asset utilization.

Many outbound pharma supply chains operate at high service levels. For example, wholesalers may receive deliveries every day of the week or every two days. Working with wholesalers to reduce delivery frequencies to twice per week, for example, could cut transportation costs significantly (see Exhibit 9).

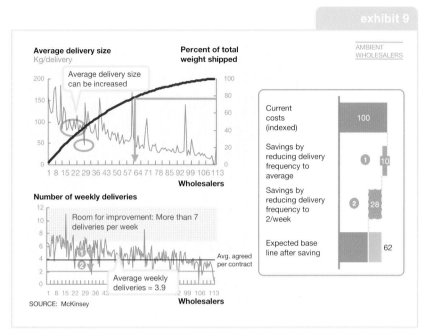

End customers enjoy high service levels too, with pharmacies and hospitals receiving off-hours or short-notice shipments, often at no extra cost. By eliminating high-cost delivery options, or introducing a nominal surcharge for urgent deliveries, even one that doesn't cover the full costs, companies can help change consumer behavior. In one example we investigated, pharmacies often requested deliveries before 10 AM the next day, assuming they would receive the shipment by noon. The cost of a 10 AM delivery, however, was 20% higher than a noon delivery, which was 20% higher than standard 24-hour delivery.

* * *

Logistics and distribution operations deserve more attention from pharmaceutical companies. They account for a significant share of overall supply chain cost, and optimized logistics performance can greatly improve the customer's experience of the supply chain.

The ability to deliver the products customers want, when they want them, in cost-effective ways could move logistics from expensive overhead to significant competitive differentiator. And achieving this kind of change does not require major capital investments or long lead times. With careful management of design, processes and personnel, most organizations could achieve double-digit performance improvements quickly and sustainably.

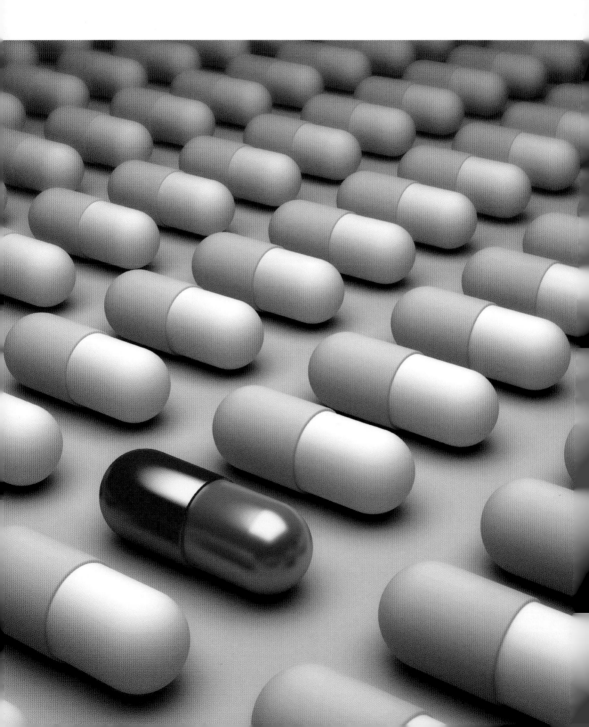

Supercharging pharmaceutical technical development

Doane Chilcoat, Ted Fuhr, Michele Holcomb, Jatan Shah

Smart companies are turning the technical development of new products from a source of delay, expense and frustration to a driver of competitive advantage. Taking a holistic, programmatic approach rather than making piecemeal changes can lead to step function improvements in lifecycle costs and product quality.

Imagine a world where the transition from R&D to manufacturing is seamless and swift, processes are easily scalable, and all the materials needed are manufacturing-safety-ready. In this world, the manufacturing process adds strength to the product's IP, and the formulation enhances market value. Instead of conducting multiple rounds of process development, all changes are combined, reducing total cost and comparability issues.

Now imagine another world in which the move to manufacturing is fraught with challenges—in the process and the organization. Scale-up requires major rework, and R&D materials and parameters are not easily transferable to manufacturing. Formulation is unable to meet the marketing specs, leading to delays. For biologics, half of early development cost is in process development, and companies routinely invest this money in programs that fail in phases 1 and 2. Companies launch with processes they know are mediocre and have to ration supply due to lack of capacity, despite investing $150 million in improvements—to a process that only cost $20 million to develop.

Is your experience closer to the first world or the second? While the results are much different, seemingly small changes are all that is required to move from one to the next. Like the flap of the butterfly's wing from chaos theory, a decision made early in R&D may have dramatic implications downstream. In the high-performing first world we describe, operations success is driven not only by the high-performers in the heart of manufacturing group, but also by excellence in Technical Development, the interface group between R&D and Operations. In this article, we explore what it takes to be a distinctive performer in Technical Development and the impact that creates for stronger, faster and better operations downstream.

Most industries recognize that a product's ultimate cost and quality are determined in the early stages of development and manufacturing process design (Exhibit 1). The pharmaceutical and biotechnology industries, by contrast, have traditionally "locked in" an early manufacturing process that worked in R&D and relied on it through scale-up and launch. As regulatory and economic environments become more demanding, pharmacos will need to take new approaches that reduce costs, use capital more effectively and improve process efficiency and stability.

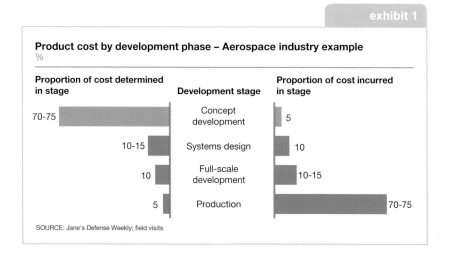

exhibit 1

Product cost by development phase – Aerospace industry example
%

Proportion of cost determined in stage	Development stage	Proportion of cost incurred in stage
70-75	Concept development	5
10-15	Systems design	10
10	Full-scale development	10-15
5	Production	70-75

SOURCE: Jane's Defense Weekly; field visits

Case for action

Many of today's Technical Development practices have been driven to some extent by the prevailing regulatory paradigm, which provides incentives to avoid process changes along the development timeline and even to avoid full characterization of the process.

As a result, products often make it to market with suboptimal manufacturing processes and quality levels of less than 2-sigma. In most companies, the manufacturing function is left to optimize the process over time. This results in higher costs and risks from delayed product launches, quality issues and inability to meet market demand.

The regulatory paradigm is changing, however, and those changes will make a new approach viable and optimal. Key elements driving this shift are the regulatory changes, ICH Q8/9/10, together with the broad push for the Quality by Design (QbD) approach to filing.

Excellence in Technical Development

We believe Technical Development excellence has five key components: (1) **technology platforming**; (2) **managing the interfaces** and organizing optimal structure for Technical Development between R&D and operations; (3) **product launch and manufacturing effectiveness** with process capability, standardization based on process platforms and quality effectiveness with statistical methodologies such as PAT and CTQ; (4) **investment optimization** for commercial process development and process technology innovations; and (5) **resource utilization**, in managing costs through lifecycle, clinical manufacturing, balancing efficiency with CMO partners.

1. Technology platforming

Almost all major biotechnology companies, and some major pharmacos, have introduced some manufacturing platform standardization. They design a portfolio of products to be manufactured on the same platform and use standard resources, such as manufacturing equipment, unit operations, materials, analytical instruments and engineering design knowledge. While the approaches vary by company, there is little argument about the magnitude of their effect on process capability improvements.

Some companies think this platform process is impossible or too restrictive. Yet once the platform is in place, developers spend their time focused on the truly tough challenges of a given process, rather than on the basics that are already built into the platform approach.

Platform strategy can greatly improve the efficiency of capital and human resources. It can reduce the need for additional manufacturing equipment and sites, avoid unneeded capital pre-investment, allow for diversification of demand on network sites, and guide make-versus-buy decisions. For example, some pharmacos utilize standard equipment types for formulation (e.g. granulators, tablet presses) and chemical synthesis across their development and manufacturing networks. A few bolster this approach with common launch sites used to produce clinical and commercial launch supplies. When process and market demand are stable, product can easily be transferred to a supply site or vendor. With such approach, these companies have been able to spare capital through diversification, and engineering, analytical, clinical and regulatory resources through reduction of process reengineering.

From the viewpoint of technical resources, platforming requires less diverse engineering talent, builds deep knowledge of platforms, and allows companies to repeat proven practices easily. It also requires less engineering and maintenance, raising capital utilization.

One leading biotech company has used technology platforming to develop a robust system that allows it to take an antibody from primary sequence to a clinically suitable production process in four months. The company's platform includes a practical set of options for media and growth conditions, etc., allowing it to select parameters that quickly lead to a stable process. Chromatography media and buffers are highly standardized, as is viral filtration and inactivation. This standardization allows scientists to scan a set of likely conditions quickly, leading to a faster custom "on-platform" process. The benefits don't end there, as clinical and commercial manufacturing facilities are configured to receive these processes without significant capital expense.

2. Managing the interfaces and organizing optimal structure for Technical Development

Technical Development requires close collaboration between R&D and operations. This inherently imposes challenges in organizational structure. While some aspects of the Technical Development function are much closer to the R&D function, late-stage process development can benefit significantly from close ties with Operations. One approach does not suit every situation, but the issues that arise from ineffective collaboration between R&D and Operations deserve attention.

Good practices in this area include a shared sense of ownership across the project team, equal status for clinical operations and CMC (both a notch down from clinical/regulatory strategy) and seamless transitions within CMC during hand-offs. Pharmacos have approached this issue in a variety of ways, ranging from implementing empowered, rigorous project management to aligning incentives across functional leaders to complete reorganization.

3. Product launch and manufacturing effectiveness

Process technology decisions affect development cost as well as technical skill and personnel requirements for commercial manufacturing. These technology decisions also affect maintenance and, ultimately, capital requirements and efficiency.

The key drivers for improved process capabilities include design of experiments (DOE) methodology to define the process design space and techniques to establish yield at launch. Companies that adopt these best practices enjoy a significant reduction in re-filing for small changes in processes. Fundamentally, changing product and process development practices using a handful of proven practices (from both within and outside pharmaceutical) can have huge benefits to the industry in profitability, reliability and quality.

In addition, statistical tools and methods such as PAT, CTQ, FMEA, and DOE can significantly reduce in-process quality related interceptions. Quality can represent up to 25% of manufacturing headcount in pharmaceutical industry.

Most pharmaceutical companies have made increasing use of Quality by Design (QbD) techniques in recent years, although the maturity of QbD implementation varies across companies. That maturity can be measured along two tiers: (1) Design tier: methodologies and tools to develop the QbD design space and define the manufacturing control strategy; and (2) Quality and operations tier: leveraging manufacturing capabilities, quality & operating systems, infrastructure, and mindset to enable full value of QbD.

Many companies are already aiming to develop and launch all new products based on QbD processes, which have proven to be effective levers in enabling efficient technology transfer, scale-up, and qualification for products transitioning from development to commercial launch.

While companies have traditionally focused on achieving excellence in their new products, they can make huge strides in in-line products as well. One generics company used a combination of QbD and lean techniques (primarily OEE & process flow improvement) to reduce the unit cost of their best-selling product by about 60%. The company had produced this solid dose for many years utilizing the initially filed process. They weren't attempting to improve the process, despite its apparent shortcomings or the product's importance. The operations and quality organizations had gathered data that supported process, cleaning and analytical changes that would improve manufacturability. Influential gatekeepers, however, considered it taboo to change a filed dossier.

To overcome these objections, managers built a comprehensive business case around the bottom-line benefits of changes on process cost, time and quality. Senior corporate leadership recognized the benefits, relaxed internal barriers and allowed the project to go forward. The filings were approved and the new process benefits actually exceeded expectations.

4. Investment optimization in technology development

Portfolio governance and investment decisions impact the overall productivity and effectiveness of the Technical Development organization and the development process overall. Investment decisions in commercial process development are a key area that many pharmaceutical companies continuously review due to the high costs and uncertainty of success during product launches.

While back-loading (delaying specific steps in process development) allows optimal use of resources on high-probability molecules, delaying such decisions can also bring process development onto the critical path of the launch. There is a constant tension at the cross-functional project team level between the benefits of delaying work (avoiding cost if the program is killed) and accelerating work (reducing the risk of delays, increasing efficiency due to fewer set-downs, and reducing comparability risk). Good practices in this area include clarifying trade-offs at project team and

project governance for investment level. Some companies find it useful to develop a menu of alternative approaches for the timing of investments with clearly understood trade-offs.

Best practice companies define about three "development pathways" as default options, with clear guidelines as to when to front-load, back-load, or a middle-of-the-road approach, based on criteria such as whether the molecule is a fast follower and the competitive landscape. This approach makes transparent what is actually critical path and what is not. For example, the bulk of "process challenge" activities are to support regulatory needs and commercial transfer, and can be conducted late in the clinical program. One large pharamco was able to reduce its overall technical development costs by 30% with no negative commercial impact by shifting from totally front-loaded to a menu approach, which emphasized backloading.

Innovative manufacturing process technologies, such as cell separation and continuous reactor technology, can also create competitive advantages. Semiconductor firms have aggressively made these kinds of process investments to manufacture next-generation products, but only a few pharmaceutical companies are seizing this opportunity. The challenging business case under high uncertainty doesn't allow technology investment topics to get adequate attention. Front-runner companies tend to take a long-term view, basing investment decisions on 5- to 7-year returns, and driving in parallel technology investment priorities based on clear business need such as cost reduction, growth in emerging markets, or longer term network optimization.

5. Resource utilization

Leading companies have always focused on managing both the capital and operating resources required over a product lifecycle. However, conservative estimates of time-to-market, market demand, and lack of insight into internal resources all contributed to poor outcomes. Today, leading companies plan realistically, employing flexible facilities whenever possible. Resource needs, particularly in technical development, are better understood, providing management knowledge about outliers.

As more companies have started relying on CMO partners, the management of capital efficiency based on Technical Development has become more complex. It is no longer about optimizing processes for internal platforms but also about developing processes that can be transferred to CMO partners effectively.

Another area that requires attention is developing strategy and processes for clinical manufacturing. Here companies must trade off the flexibility to launch out of any site versus optimizing utilization of a single plant. For example, one company supports all of its clinical needs at a single site, although its pipeline is five times larger than when that site was built, due to acquisitions that had their own dedicated facilities.

Good practices in effective management of capital include top-down transparency into resource utilization, for both process development and clinical trial material. Leading companies closely manage a backlog of work (e.g., near 100% asset utilization) but ensure negligible delays to the critical path of important programs. These companies use more than 70% of the clinical supplies manufactured for actual trials (less than 30% getting scrapped)—as opposed to the 5% being utilized in trials we see at many companies.

***

Diagnosing and implementing a holistic excellence program in pharma Technical Development requires a few essentials: (1) Adopting best practices from other industries such as aerospace and automotive; (2) establishing a transparent business case for implementation; (3) designing in tandem a strategy for plants, assets, and quality systems; (4) aligning with portfolio optimization efforts; (5) the assessment of both new and in-line product; and (6) establishing a longer-term roadmap for the achievement of excellence.

With increased focus on driving excellence based on operational and technological advances, pharmaceutical companies can create a significant competitive advantage. So don't let the flap of the butterfly's wings halfway around the world—or in the adjacent Technical Development lab—cause chaos in your Operations group. Instead use the power of Technical Development excellence to drive efficiency and effectiveness from the very start.

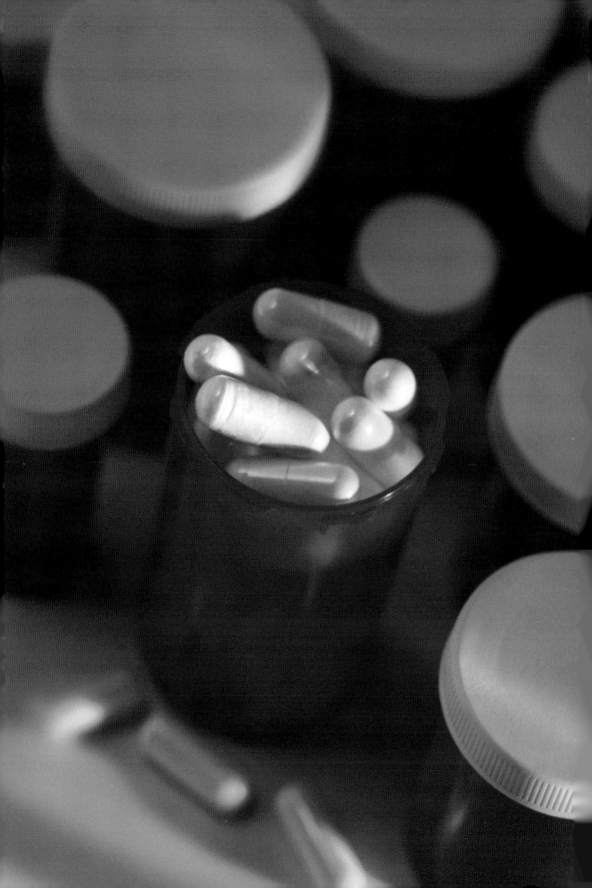

Delivering
sustainable future state

Improvements that endure: The secret ingredients

Peter De Boeck, Thibaut Dedeurwaerder, David Keeling

Have operational excellence programs gained ground in the pharmaceutical industry in the last 10 years? According to the 26 industry executives surveyed during a recent roundtable on "Leading Change through Operational Excellence," the answer seems to be yes. Survey results showed that some companies and plants have made substantial improvements—and others haven't. Results also suggested that sustaining improvements is difficult if they aren't built into the program from the start.

Taking stock : Has operational excellence begun, and what has it delivered?

When we conducted a similar survey some 10 years ago, lean operations were still considered a novelty in the pharmaceutical industry. Executives today say that 75% of pharmacos have embarked on wide-scale operational excellence programs that cover at least five sites in their networks. All programs use a toolbox—so they go beyond pure cost-cutting—and lean is the preferred methodology for 56% of the toolboxes (Exhibit 1).

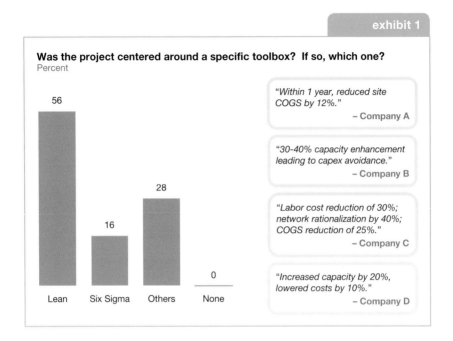

exhibit 1

Was the project centered around a specific toolbox? If so, which one?
Percent

56

28

16

0

Lean   Six Sigma   Others   None

"Within 1 year, reduced site COGS by 12%."
– Company A

"30-40% capacity enhancement leading to capex avoidance."
– Company B

"Labor cost reduction of 30%; network rationalization by 40%; COGS reduction of 25%."
– Company C

"Increased capacity by 20%, lowered costs by 10%."
– Company D

Survey participants testify to impressive results. In all of the efforts, productivity improvement was the core or among the core ambitions. Participants are enthusiastic about the impact, yet the spread remains high: best performers claim up to a 40% reduction in conversion costs, while the average ranges from 10% to 15%.

What are the challenges ?

Despite this step forward, executives recognize that the journey to operational excellence is long and requires effort and persistence. When asked about their biggest concerns, they mentioned setting aspirations, transforming people, and sustainability.

Defining the right aspirations for an operational excellence program does pave the way to success. "Not all solutions work," one participant testified, "especially given that productivity improvement is often just one part of an excellence program."

Setting the right aspirations often proves difficult indeed. When asked to name the three issues they struggled with most, participants provided some illuminating responses:

- 70% admitted to difficulties in setting quantitative targets. As one participant explained, "Agreeing on ambitious yet realistic targets was difficult, as we all had different agendas and opinions. And since we didn't dedicate enough time or energy to cascading these targets down in the organization, we had to deal with a lot of negative energy around the real objectives."

- 70% said they lacked a clear change story about their aspirations. "It's difficult to explain the need for improvements the day after you announce record-breaking results, and to make people understand that in the long term such a program will benefit all stakeholders, including shareholders and workers."

- 52% of the participants said aspirations were not shared among senior management. One said, "Operational excellence should start with a change in behavior at the top, and not everyone understood that in our company."

- Finally, 48% were unable to define a clear and tangible future state. "We did have quantitative targets," one reported, "but they didn't translate into clear shop-floor-based opportunities, so the program wasn't tangible or actionable enough to drive change."

Some companies have set clear aspirations using a holistic approach that includes strong senior commitment, benchmarks and shop-floor-based opportunity assessments. The main advantage is that targets are set according to concrete opportunity levers, which makes the target more tangible, provides clear direction and makes it easier for people to contribute and show leadership.

The second critical success factor is the program's setup from the workers' and managerial point of view. When asked which attributes their architecture lacked, respondents mentioned three elements (Exhibit 2):

- 60% said their programs were too technically oriented. "We focused too much on technical elements, like whether our OEE should be 67.5 or 68.5 %," one said. "We neglected actual management, including KPIs and organizational design, and the people who had to execute it, including capability-building and changing mindsets. So we faced a lot of resistance when we wanted to implement the technical changes."

- Companies struggled with mobilizing the right human resources around their program. Some 39% lacked any form of training academy, 51% could not exchange resources across sites to stimulate standardization and best-practice sharing, 42% lacked career paths for their high-performing

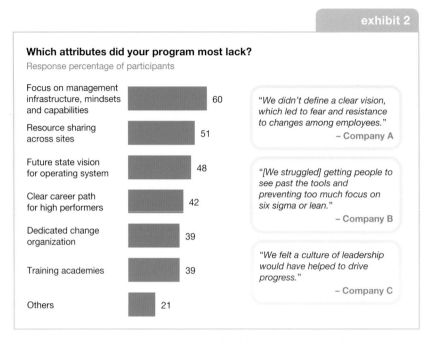

exhibit 2

Which attributes did your program most lack?
Response percentage of participants

Focus on management infrastructure, mindsets and capabilities	60
Resource sharing across sites	51
Future state vision for operating system	48
Clear career path for high performers	42
Dedicated change organization	39
Training academies	39
Others	21

"We didn't define a clear vision, which led to fear and resistance to changes among employees."
– Company A

"[We struggled] getting people to see past the tools and preventing too much focus on six sigma or lean."
– Company B

"We felt a culture of leadership would have helped to drive progress."
– Company C

operational excellence staff, and 39% said they lacked a dedicated change organization supporting the program. "We believed we could just give aspirations to the sites," one respondent said, "and then expected them to reinvent themselves without the quantity or quality of resources they needed."

Sustainability is the third and final major challenge. Almost half of the participants recognize a gradual decline in performance after the early successes. In analyzing survey results, we found that three out of four companies that did sustain improvements addressed employees' mindsets and behaviors, compared to only a third of the companies that didn't. And 78% reported that continuous improvement had become part of their daily business, versus 17% of those who did not address mindsets or behaviors.

"We realized too late that impact was not about being technically right. It required changing day-to-day behaviors and ways of thinking on the front line. Probably our own mindsets were not ready to accept that at the outset of the program." (Exhibit 3)

* * *

Pharmaceutical companies now recognize operational excellence as a means to improve productivity and create long-term value. But only a few have truly grasped and sustained improvements from operational excellence programs.

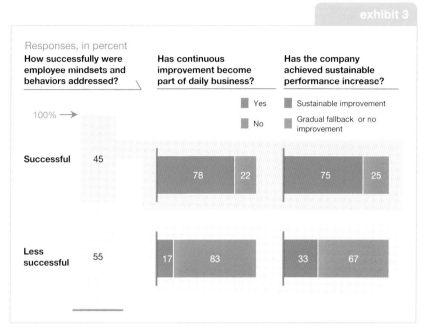

Responses, in percent

How successfully were employee mindsets and behaviors addressed?

Has continuous improvement become part of daily business?

Has the company achieved sustainable performance increase?

■ Yes   ■ Sustainable improvement

■ No   ■ Gradual fallback or no improvement

100% →

Successful	45		78	22	75	25
Less successful	55	17	83		33	67

We now expect a new wave of efforts, as we have seen in automotive and other industries, that will have more success and impact. This time around, more companies will succeed by choosing the right aspirations—and launching a holistic program that focuses on management and frontline workers, not just technical improvements.

Prescription for sustaining performance improvements

Elissa Ashwood, Maia Hansen, David Keeling, Janice Pai

Many pharmaco leaders trying to "lean out" operations have had limited success despite extensive investment. Those who have succeeded know that "hard change" requires "soft" skills. This article presents five insights and stories from the front line that operations leaders should take to heart when conducting large-scale operational changes.

The highly skilled pharmaceutical manufacturing workforce has taken on many operational challenges over the past decade, including new product launches and speed to market. So when pharma companies decided to "lean out" operations in response to declining margins and volume, people expected this workforce to impress the world with operational innovation. Instead, sustained organizational improvements have been elusive, leaving many leaders wondering what to do differently.

Pharmacos are not alone. Historically, across industries, 70% of transformation efforts fail (Exhibit 1), mostly because of "soft" factors: people's resistance to changing their behavior. Leaders considering or conducting large-scale change efforts should think carefully about how to create the needed change within senior leadership and the rest of the organization.

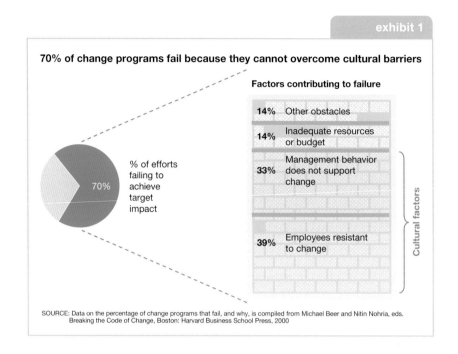

exhibit 1

70% of change programs fail because they cannot overcome cultural barriers

Factors contributing to failure

% of efforts failing to achieve target impact — 70%

14%   Other obstacles

14%   Inadequate resources or budget

33%   Management behavior does not support change

39%   Employees resistant to change

Cultural factors

SOURCE: Data on the percentage of change programs that fail, and why, is compiled from Michael Beer and Nitin Nohria, eds. Breaking the Code of Change, Boston: Harvard Business School Press, 2000

Why the soft side is important

To date, most of the process improvements in pharma have been driven by technical change—deployment of Six Sigma, automation, and an extensive lean toolkit—plus huge investments in top talent and physical plant networks. However, something is holding pharmacos back from delivering at their full potential and sustaining the value.

Building technical change skills has improved workforce capabilities, but not managers' abilities or willingness to lead people through transformational change. As one plant manager put it, "Give me the new process, we'll put it in and train people on it. All they need to know is what to do."

This manager was setting his plant up for one-time change—his people would comply, but they wouldn't think about the process differently, so no continuous improvement would follow. In fact, at the slightest obstacle—one person out sick, a delay on a machine, a new supervisor—this line would likely revert to the old process and improvements would evaporate.

In our experience, organizations overlook up to half of the potential savings when they implement or expand operational improvement programs inspired by lean, Six Sigma, or both, because they don't engage people effectively. Some companies set their sights too low to create breakthrough change; others falter by implementing lean and other performance-enhancing tools without recognizing how existing systems or mindsets might undermine them.

Still others underestimate the investments required in people, particularly at the plant leadership level.

The broader challenge is integrating the soft side with the "hard" operational tools and approaches, including the development of leaders who can help teams identify and make efficiency improvements continuously. Neglecting the soft side of lean—enabling leaders to drive continuous improvement and change the way employees think and work—can delay or even derail an operational transformation.

True transformational change shifts people's thinking so substantially that they never go back to the old way of thinking. For example, a line operator we'll call "Mary" had duties that included setting up and cleaning processing equipment. She was an efficient team member and always followed procedures. One day, the operational improvement team came to the shop floor to share an analysis that showed high variability in yield. Given the great cost of this process, the team explained that increasing yield would be incredibly valuable. When Mary learned that losing a single gram of active ingredient cost thousands of dollars and wasted hundreds of doses of lifesaving drugs, she identified three alternative hosing configurations that reduced loss by 15%, improving overall yield by 3%.

Contrary to management's belief that line operators wanted to do their jobs with as little effort as possible, Mary and her colleagues began to look for other improvements. With the right tools, encouragement from her supervisor and a supportive visit from a senior Operations leader, she and others kept finding ways to improve the process. Visiting six months later, the team found the entire flow of materials across the floor had been reorganized to minimize time lost in transfers. Changing the hose was a one-time event, but changing Mary's view of her job created an ongoing series of improvements.

To get the most from large operational improvement programs, top companies look beyond the technical aspects of lean and Six Sigma and embrace the softer side.

Why soft is hard in pharma

What created the workforce's current attitude toward performance improvements? The pharmaceutical industry has been interested in continuous improvement for years. Most of these efforts arose from the need for quality and compliance with the goal of creating "right first time" or variability reductions. Many programs focused on learning technical specifications and processes and adding checks where needed, rather than instilling a passion in people for creating better methods. When people did get excited about improvement, incentive systems and risk management practices often squelched new ideas. Changing a process was seen as risky and even a threat to quality standards. Regulatory sanctions, public humiliation and termination of those who made mistakes made it clear that the only safe path was to follow all procedures, no matter if a better way seemed possible.

"When we say 'no-fail environment,' we mean that if you fail, you won't be in this environment anymore," one pharma operations manager told us. Against this backdrop, it is not surprising that many people see process improvement as dangerous.

Structural barriers, like those between quality and operations, increase the difficulty of making changes. Even changes that improve quality and efficiency can meet structural resistance. At one plant with a particularly complex reporting structure, approval for change had to come from three separate leaders who had no shared goals and rarely interacted. Despite an opportunity to move from fourth- to first-quartile performance, this site could not make change until leadership was reorganized at the next level.

In our experience, leaders who have created sustained performance changes have done five things differently:

1. Set high aspirations grounded in reality

In an effort to create evolution instead of revolution, many organizations have aimed for incremental changes and about 5% year-over-year improvement. This approach fails in several ways. First, it encourages managers to sandbag their targets, reserving just enough budget slack to reach their goals without having to make any real changes. Second, we know from POBOS benchmarking data that average plant performance across operational measures is steadily improving at 5-7% a year. So a low incremental change target will never be enough to competitively improve performance—and it might not be enough to keep from falling behind.

More important, incremental goals lead to incremental change. To illustrate this, a group of managers were asked to observe and improve a simulated changeover process. Within a few minutes, the group identified changes, resulting in 10% improvement. Then, the managers were told that they needed to reduce their time by 80%. They objected until they were told that others had managed to achieve this goal. The managers got to work, and all were able to reach at least a 60% improvement. Instead of trying to run the existing system faster, they thought differently and modified the method—an approach they never would have taken in an environment that only asked for a 10% improvement. The managers learned through the exercise that much of the work of transformation is about redefining "what good looks like."

Transformational leaders apply the lesson of this game to ask themselves two questions: What goal is inspiring enough to merit all of the hard work of change, and how will we give people confidence that it can be done? One leader tells the story of a big goal—30% cost reduction within three years, expectations of improvements in quality, supply, and the skill sets of the organization. Upon learning of this audacious goal, the plant managers were in shock. The leader asked one question: "Just come back and tell me: Why can't you do it?"

This leader realized the importance of grounding the high aspiration in reality. Before a single commitment was made, plants conducted diagnostics to get a bottom-up view of how costs could be cut. Once managers understood what was possible and expected, they saw the plants with new eyes. Why were there six people on a line watching bottles go by? One manager watched for an hour as one of his best supervisors walked boxes back and forth and spoke with no one. These real-life experiences helped plant leadership see that despite a sense that everyone was extremely busy, they could reduce waste. Having a tangible aspiration created tremendous energy and friendly competition among plants. One manager remarked, "It is a lot more fun to work toward being the best than it is to just avoid making mistakes."

2. Align senior leadership

Deciding to go after transformational changes requires political wherewithal, and successful leaders have learned not to go it alone. They focus on aligning the senior team to both the hard and soft aspects of transformation. We take three main lessons from these teams:

- **Get beyond comparing success among the teams.** Each operations leader comes with his or her own business units strengths and challenges. Formulations and markets are so different that it is not always clear who is most effective. Focus instead on creating a fact-based burning platform that is meaningful to everyone.

- **Recognize that leaders step up at their own pace—and that some never get there.** An early skeptic can become and advocate and role model. But about 20% of leaders will not make it through the transformation, and it is important to acknowledge this up front. Some will opt out because they don't support the direction, and some will not be capable of the softer leadership skills required to lead through difficult times.

- **The strongest transformation leaders may do not have clear vision at the start.** Many leaders emerge from the process challenged with a new aspiration and building new skills through the process of leading change.

Transformational leaders use the aspiration process to create alignment and reduce skepticism. In addition to compelling data, they may need to "see for themselves" what is possible and hear from other leaders' concrete examples. Ultimately, when it is clear that a leader is not supporting the direction after ample opportunity to be convinced, that person should be removed from the team leading the change. Removing a senior leader is a highly visible signal to the organization of the commitment to the transformation, as is removing middle management blockers.

As the team aligns, they need to communicate a common message. This is more about making decisions together and coming away with the same definition of success than it is about polished speeches. While the "what" and the "why" of the change story should be the same, at the heart of the change story are the individual's thoughts, feelings and commitment, and the most relevant messages for each group.

3. Take a balanced approach

Operational improvements in the pharmaceutical industry have traditionally been managed as a series of projects. Engineers identify a specific issue or improvement area and design a project to suit a specific need. Oftentimes, they identify a tool that could be helpful across the organization and set up a project that involves plant-wide training and a list of initiatives, managed at an individual or department level. These efforts often fall short because they fail to change the way work is done.

Successful leaders realize that real change is complicated and must address not only the technical aspects but also the way people are managed and rewarded, and the mindsets they hold about "the rules" and "what it takes to be successful here." This can be a complex process in a plant with more than a thousand people and multiple product streams that don't intersect.

To reduce the complexity, leaders should focus on comprehensive change in a targeted area. This focus allows the team to experiment with all of the needed variables without disrupting the entire plant. Hese units of change, which we refer to as "mini-transformations" include a specific portion of the value stream and everyone on that operating area who needs to enact the change.

A balanced diagnostic identifies the areas of opportunity from the technical, management and organizational standpoints. Managers identify the current state and potential improvements: what will change physically about the operations, how the area will be managed differently, and the behavioral and capability shifts required to achieve the desired outcome. Exhibit 2 shows an example of how a fill-finish area defined the transition from current state to future state, and rooted all the changes in broad operational goals for the area.

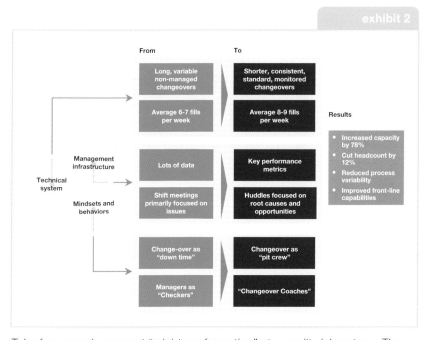

exhibit 2

Take for example a recent "mini-transformation" at a quality laboratory. The diagnostic identified levers to optimize labor and equipment utilization, and gaps in mindsets that could impede the change. The team put together a plan that addressed these gaps holistically, giving lab personnel the technical capabilities to improve labor scheduling, changing mindsets around siloed behaviors, and building the roles, responsibilities, and capabilities of all personnel in the laboratory to meet the objectives. The laboratory met its initial goal of reducing operating cost by 30% and increasing right first time performance, while building technical and leadership skills. They have since established new, more ambitious goals.

4. Lead through the line and build capabilities

One common pitfall of operational improvement programs is their reliance on dedicated staff resources to drive the program. These people—green belts, black belts, project managers, human resource and organizational development consultants and external experts—typically have the technical and analytical capabilities to diagnose and implement changes. But their ability to drive sustainable change is limited. Without shifting ownership of change to line leaders, the line organization may not build capabilities, and no new changes will follow the first investment.

Successful transformation leaders address this issue in two ways. First, they move the organization from expecting change to "come to them" tov taking responsibility to lead the change. This also involves a shift in mindset of the change-dedicated resources, who need to focus more on coaching and building capabilities of the line leaders. To reinforce this shift, one organization changed the evaluation measures for change-dedicated personnel. Instead of merely evaluating technical capabilities such as lean knowledge, they were judged on how well they built leadership capabilities, such as coaching and feedback, according to plant leadership's evaluations.

Second, transformation leaders develop the capabilities of the line leadership—both technical and interpersonal. Supervisors must learn to serve the line rather than "boss" it, to look for root causes of problems collaboratively without casting blame, to see beyond the shift to the importance of the work being done, and to understand how his or her personal strengths and vulnerabilities affect the way he or she leads the team. (See sidebar: "Boosting the impact of frontline managers.")

For example, line leaders supporting the mini-transformation in a quality control department were not initially ready to lead the transformation. Many in the group were promoted because of their technical process capabilities— they had neglected people leadership and avoided challenging performance discussions. As implementation began, supervisors were trained for a few hours on time management skills and coaching, and then had six weeks of daily practice and coaching from dedicated change support. They also spent time improving problem-solving, trust and accountability, and addressing cultural barriers. From the leader of the area to the technicians, the managers' new skills helped them drive the program themselves and sustain long-term gains.

As this story illustrates, change requires a short-term "over-investment" of resources. It includes not only support for the current area of change, but often addressed the next cadre of leaders who will implement changes in their areas or sites. Committing these resources gives the area the best chance of success and builds the capabilities of people to spread the change quickly.

These people should be the best of the organization, even though they may be needed elsewhere. If five leaders invest in an initial pilot area, and they later lead change in five additional areas with five more invested, in six months, every site will have experienced change leaders. In addition to building capabilities, this approach signals that the organization is committed to developing people. It also quickly builds a common language about what is changing, and creates cross-site relationships that will accelerate best-practice sharing. A little competitive spirit among sites can also create the tipping point for site leaders who are on the fence about whether they want to embrace the change.

Management should reinforce the same messages and skills as frontline supervisors. In many successful transformations, the top leadership team sets aside a couple of hours every month, or a half-day every quarter, for their own skill development. This kind of training refreshes managers' evergreen skills, and creates expectations that everyone will focus on the same agenda. This can help give middle management the confidence to do things differently and then sustain change when conflicts arise. Connecting middle and senior management with the mini-transformation can also break down barriers between the operator and management. Many managers are surprised to discover the depth of commitment and knowledge in the front line, break down hierarchies and improve their relationships and problem-solving abilities.

As one operator said, "The general manager will do anything for our plant. He's really busy but he gets out to see us, so I wasn't surprised to see him [involved in the transformation]. But managers we've never seen before have come out on the floor. At first we were worried, but then they started to fix some things we thought were unchangeable. That was pretty cool. And they listened to things we've been saying for years and let us make some of the changes. Why would you put the supplies you need every day all the way across the floor? But we did—until they asked what slows down the job. It makes you feel good that someone thinks your work is important. We have a job to support our families and make good products to help people. We want the company to do well."

5. Design for scale

Transforming operations can be challenging in the pharmaceutical industry, given its complex supply chains that balance tax advantages, local market access, talent availability and a host of other factors. Plant networks are dispersed and specialized and highly dependent on each other, as products often shift from one facility to another between processing steps or at the packaging line. Transforming a plant network is exponentially more valuable that improving a single plant, with value added as practices are standardized and improvements made among interdependent plants.

Of course, planning and sustaining a large transformation takes more choreography that changing a single plant. Transforming multiple plants across geographies could take years. What lessons can we learn from successful transformations of this kind? While sites are working "in" the transformation, central resources need to be a step ahead and work "on" the transformation architecture to make sure that impact is fast but sustainable. A good architecture can boost impact and build capabilities in the field and at headquarters.

Management must first know where to get the impact. If three plants will provide 80% of the financial benefit, and six will provide the remaining 20%, the initiative should focus first on the three. One company that recently embarked on transformation of its manufacturing network sequenced their sites into three distinct support models, shifting support according to the potential impact and the organization's readiness to change.

At the site level, develop a sequencing plan to address all major value drivers. One successful site transformation team built their plan from the end state—declaring that "the entire site will be transformed in a year." They divided the site into mini-transformation areas, grouping those that logically worked together to create impact in a value stream area. They started with two, where they scored some initial successes to get the plant excited, and trained a cadre of leaders to lead the subsequent areas. In the second set of areas, they reached a critical mass of the site (about 70%) which became their tipping point of the transformation They reached the entire plant within a year (Exhibit 3).

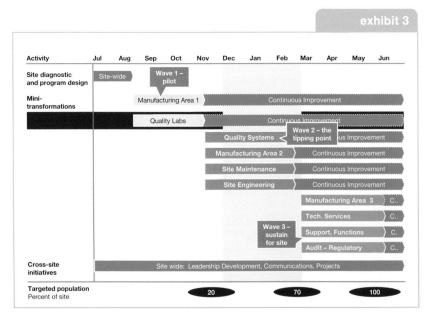

exhibit 3

At the center, before the diagnostic action begins, successful transformation leaders get capabilities in place for a transformation-enabling PMO to keep senior management, and themselves, aware and accountable, and to gather expert resources who can support sites to create the needed changes. It is tempting to wait to build the PMO until later in the transformation, but leaders who start a second transformation have learned that transformation infrastructure takes a while to build and is needed sooner rather than later. As one leader explained, "Have you ever grown tulips? You have to plant them in the fall, because they bloom in the spring. If you get to spring and you want tulips, you're too late."

Beyond the PMO, all support functions need to be brought in at the beginning of the transformation. This may feel unnecessary at the time because some operations personnel aren't even convinced there is anything to change. But as soon as the diagnostic makes the opportunity tangible, needs may emerge quickly.

One large global operations team considered all of the field implications but assumed the center would be ready when needed. It seemed to happen overnight, as sites started asking for help with training, terminations, new measurement systems, changes to financial reports, and requests to stop many processes that had been required. Instead of center pushing the front line, the front line was ahead and the center struggled to catch up.

Transformation situations are often a good catalyst to rally the sites and the center around some priorities, such as training or better approval processes.

Finally, while initial targets and changes should be as short-term as possible to help people shift into new ways of doing things, the medium term needs to be sustainable or people will give up. Managers must monitor the energy of the organization and be responsive. Sites use drop-in visits, pulse surveys, and coffee talks to judge where an extra boost of support or fewer demands may be warranted.

As transformations can take a while, it can also help to find milestones to celebrate. Create closure on each phase before moving onto the next. Then kick off the next phase by telling the change stories all over again and invigorating a new round of people who might not have heard it before.

The prescription

The most encouraging news from leaders who have created sustained transformation is that it can be done. The elements that make a transformation work are challenging but not impossible individually. The senior leader's challenge is to ensure that all of the elements of success are in place: 1) the aspiration is high enough and made tangible through bottom-up diagnostics; 2) senior leadership alignment is not assumed but considered its own project; 3) the approach is balanced among technical, management and "soft" mindset changes; 4) capabilities are built to change the way line leadership leads; 5) the overall transformation is designed with enough support from the center and at each site to help create sustainable local wins.

Like most prescriptions, knowing the answer is a great start, but being committed and rigorous about taking the medicine—and doing things differently—are the real challenges.

Boosting the impact of frontline managers

Aaron De Smet, Monica McGurk, Marc Vinson

In most of the companies we've encountered, the frontline manager's role is merely to oversee a limited number of direct reports, often in a "span-breaking" capacity, relaying information from executives to workers. He or she communicates decisions but does not make them; ensures compliance with policies but does not use judgment or discretion—and certainly does not develop policies; and oversees improvements without contributing ideas or even helping to implement improvements, since that's the workers' job. In our experience, this approach makes companies less productive, less agile, and less profitable.

In difficult economic times, employee productivity is more crucial than ever. For frontline managers to be more productive, they need the time—and the ability—to address the unique circumstances of their plants, foresee trouble and stem it before it begins, and encourage workers to improve themselves.

The shortcomings in the frontline manager's role are rooted in the early days of the industrial revolution, when manufacturing was broken down into highly specialized, repetitive, and easily observed tasks. No one worker created a whole shoe, for example; each hammered his nail in the same spot and the same way every time, maximizing effectiveness and efficiency. Employees didn't necessarily know anything about the overall job, so supervisors (usually people good at the work itself) enforced detailed standards and policies—essentially, bridging the gap between workers and policymakers. Many manufacturing companies still use this approach, and it can deliver high-quality results on the front line, at least in the short term.

Although attention to execution is important, focusing on it exclusively can have insidious long-term effects. It leaves no time for dealing with new demands, such as raising production volume or quality, let alone seeing the big picture. The result is a working environment with little flexibility, little encouragement to make improvements, and the risk of low morale among workers and their managers.

At a North American medical-products distributor, for example, one supervisor told us the company "is like California—forest fires breaking out everywhere and no plan to stop them. A lot of crisis-to-crisis situations with no plan. We've been in this mode for so long, we don't know how to stop and plan, although that's what we desperately need to do. I wish I knew how to intervene."

Frontline managers were so busy jumping in to solve problems that they had no time to step back and look at longer-term performance trends or to identify—and try to head off—emerging performance issues. It's no wonder that the company's performance had begun to decline: inventories and shipment errors were rising. Companies can also get into frontline trouble if they fail to manage operations well.

At best-practice companies, frontline managers allocate 60 to 70% of their time to the floor, much of it in high-quality individual coaching. Such companies also empower managers to make decisions and act on opportunities. The bottom-line benefit is significant, but to obtain it companies must fundamentally redefine what they expect from frontline managers and redesign the work that they and their subordinates do.

They must help frontline managers become true leaders, with the time, the skills, and desire to help workers understand the company's direction and its implications for themselves, and to coach them individually. Such managers should have enough time to think ahead, uncover and solve long-term problems, and plan for potential new demands.

A nursing supervisor at a European hospital that empowered its nurses offered perhaps the clearest description of the way frontline leaders ought to think—which couldn't be more different from the role of traditional frontline managers: "I am a valued member of this team, who has responsibility to make sure my ward nurses have the right coaching to improve patient service while contributing to the overall functioning of our ward. For the first time, I feel as important as a doctor or an administrator in the success of this institution."

That kind of frontline leader can consistently help employees enhance their impact on an organization's work.

Driving quality performance in pharma manufacturing

Eric McCafferty, Janice Pai, Ric Phillips

Leading manufacturers in many industries have improved quality by driving more efficient and effective quality systems and managing and measuring quality performance while instilling a culture where continuous improvement of quality is paramount. Pharmaceutical and medical product companies should do the same and adopt world-class manufacturing practices that create competitive advantages by reducing regulatory risk and production costs.

Drug and medical product manufacturers continue to face significant challenges in quality and compliance due to rising risk, regulatory requirements and cost pressure. Compared to other industries that have historically faced intense operations performance pressures, pharma manufacturers tend to trail in innovating their quality approach, resulting in less efficient processes and more regulatory risk.

Many pharmacos hesitate to change their approach to quality management, citing the constraints of strict regulations. But even in the tightest regulatory climates, some companies have managed to raise quality significantly and reduce regulatory risk.

The world's leading manufacturers—including producers of semiconductors and goods for the automotive, aerospace, and electronics industries—consistently use a set of practices to improve their quality and compliance. These include regularly re-optimizing processes for measuring and controlling product quality. The economics of quality are critical for these industries—in some cases, a few points of difference in yield can determine profitability or market leadership.

In contrast, quality control in pharmaceuticals and medical products has historically taken a back seat to innovative science and compelling marketing, the standard drivers of industry profitability. But in the last decade, executives have had no choice but to sit up and take notice as poor quality and related compliance issues have cost the industry hundreds of millions of dollars in fines and billions more in lost revenues. Addressing compliance eats up big chunks of management's time and attention and, in some cases, we have seen companies experience increases of up to 20% of overall cost of goods sold due to compliance-related network inefficiencies, cost of firefighting and consultants, wasted material, additional inventory, etc.

While some pharma companies are improving their manufacturing quality substantially, many more have been slow to study and adopt world-class practices. They may not feel the imperative for change until a major compliance issue occurs. And rather than building quality into and across manufacturing processes themselves, many companies have relied on risky and costly inspections late in the manufacturing process. This approach is not sustainable, especially as the FDA and other regulatory agencies have shifted their focus to monitor not only a company's outputs but also the consistency and effectiveness of its processes and systems.

In the face of a challenging regulatory environment, some leading pharmaceutical and medical product companies have found ways to improve quality and costs significantly. They use three basic approaches:

1. Focus on product and process attributes that are critical to quality, and drive effective and efficient controls around these attributes

2. Drive a robust performance system to manage and measure quality performance across the organization

3. Set clear aspirations around quality performance and embed a culture where continuous improvement of quality is paramount.

Companies that succeed in implementing this shift in quality approach can create a competitive advantage through superior performance on cost and quality: they dramatically reduce variability, the risk of noncompliance, and time to market while freeing up funds for investment.

What pharma companies should change

As the pharmaceutical sector has grown—revenues in the United States have tripled in the last decade, while those in Western Europe have doubled— regulators around the world have changed their approach in ensuring that drugs are safe and effective. As late as the 1980s, for instance, the primary focus of the FDA was to prevent fraudulent drugs from reaching consumers. By the late 1990s it focused more on the drug makers' processes. Today the FDA has taken a system-wide approach to evaluating the quality of pharmaceutical manufacturing plants and networks.

But some pharma companies haven't adapted well. Many continue to focus mainly on near-term regulatory inspections and have been spending increasing amounts of money to fix problems only after they arise, or adding layers of tests and resources that raise costs and slow processes. The common pitfalls of this approach include gaps in identifying important sources of variability, insufficient and ineffective testing during production, and failure to resolve quality issues in a timely manner. Such flaws can add up to big problems—and big fines.

New processes can help pharma companies keep up with best practices in manufacturing and significantly reduce compliance risk at low cost. Although managers and plant personnel must spend time to drive the change, transforming a company's quality culture and performance may not require large investments in people or equipment.

1. Focus on product and process attributes that are critical to quality, and drive effective and efficient controls around these attributes.

Top manufacturers consistently meet customer requirements and achieve regulatory compliance by relentlessly driving improvements in their quality activities. To do it efficiently, companies need to identify the handful of factors that truly affect quality—something many companies haven't done. We worked with one company that spent as much time perfecting a drug's color as it did ensuring its effectiveness and shelf life.

In our experience, identifying and ranking the key quality attributes of most products isn't complicated. Operations managers can tap internal sources, including sales, marketing, product development, and technical staff. External sources, such as physicians and customers, can contribute invaluable insights, particularly on ranking customer needs, which can vary from product to product. Taste isn't highly valued for painkillers, for example, but it might be important for children's cough syrup. Many companies don't spend enough time on this step. Instead, they devote inordinate amounts of time to complex internal processes and extensive, often redundant, processes to support noncritical activities.

Once pharma companies identify product attributes that most affect quality, they can work to align their efforts with those attributes (see Exhibit 1 for an example of a CTQ matrix). A good quality and compliance system should allocate resources to achieve consistency on the most critical attributes, but many pharmaceutical companies have overly complex systems. Since these companies have not identified the few factors for each production line that are critical to the quality of the end products, they often test and retest too late in the process. Many of these screenings have limited value and result in missed opportunities to identify and isolate variability upstream.

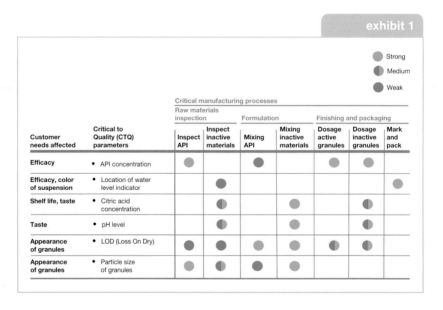

exhibit 1

Legend: ● Strong ◑ Medium ● Weak

Customer needs affected	Critical to Quality (CTQ) parameters	Raw materials inspection		Formulation		Finishing and packaging		
		Inspect API	Inspect inactive materials	Mixing API	Mixing inactive materials	Dosage active granules	Dosage inactive granules	Mark and pack
Efficacy	• API concentration	●		●		●	●	
Efficacy, color of suspension	• Location of water level indicator		●					●
Shelf life, taste	• Citric acid concentration		◑		●		◑	
Taste	• pH level		◑		●		◑	
Appearance of granules	• LOD (Loss On Dry)	●	●	●	●	◑	◑	
Appearance of granules	• Particle size of granules	●	◑	●	●			

A streamlined quality system not only improves efficiency by removing wasteful activities but also reduces the opportunity to make mistakes. One pharma company significantly raised efficiency by optimizing the layout of its manufacturing facility and encouraging workers not to leave unused tools and supplies lying about. Before the change, the lab staff spent 60% of their time walking around, moving supplies and tools from one workstation to another, talking, or waiting—and adding no value (see Exhibit 2). After the company engaged the front line in lean tools such as standard work and workplace organization (applying "5S"), the lab doubled value-added time, reduced

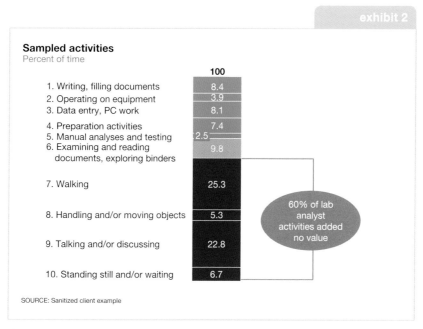

Sampled activities
Percent of time

100

1. Writing, filling documents — 8.4
2. Operating on equipment — 3.9
3. Data entry, PC work — 8.1
4. Preparation activities — 7.4
5. Manual analyses and testing — 2.5
6. Examining and reading documents, exploring binders — 9.8
7. Walking — 25.3
8. Handling and/or moving objects — 5.3
9. Talking and/or discussing — 22.8
10. Standing still and/or waiting — 6.7

60% of lab analyst activities added no value

exhibit 2

SOURCE: Sanitized client example

the number of deviations associated with the manufacturing processes, and reduced compliance risk by removing unnecessary equipment and subsequent validations.

Another way pharma companies can make their quality systems more efficient is to work harder at building quality measures into the manufacturing processes themselves. Rather than inspecting finished products and failing to generate insights into the causes of defects, world-class manufacturers monitor the performance of production lines and predict variability that may result in defective products. They consider the prevention and detection of errors paramount, and see errors an opportunity to improve, not as a source of remediation. This can translate into hands-on, practical improvements in day-to-day work.

At one medical product maker, line workers frequently identified defective products and immediately took them off the line without halting production. The workers fixed the defects and reintroduced the goods into the production line without trying to determine why a defect had occurred or working to prevent it from occurring again. After they discontinued this practice, the company uncovered and addressed important problems and improvement opportunities.

First, executives discovered what front-line employees had apparently known for a long time—that because defective products had been taken offline, repaired, and put back online, an artificially high number—90% or more—passed the first inspection, when in reality only 30 to 50% should have been approved. For one product line, managers learned that they should aspire to a true first-pass inspection acceptance rate (the products that meet specifications without any rework) of at least 95%.

Then the company conducted root-cause analysis of why many products would have failed the initial quality inspection, and developed systemic solutions to prevent the issues from recurring. With this knowledge, the company improved the manufacturing process, significantly lowered the risks related to poor quality, and focused on the attributes critical to quality.

It took more than 18 months to implement the design changes fully, but a few process fixes yielded almost immediate results. Within just six months, the manufacturer doubled the first-inspection acceptance rates of several product lines. As a result, quality is now embedded in the manufacturing process, and cycle times are 20% shorter.

2. Drive a robust performance system to manage and measure quality performance across the organization.

A system that drives the active management of daily quality performance is critical to ensure effectiveness and efficiency in quality practices. One key aspect of this management system is focusing performance discussions around the few metrics that truly matter. One common mistake that can inhibit strong performance discussions is using large numbers of metrics— sometimes more than 50, at the plant and corporate levels—often without consistent definitions. When choosing performance metrics, operations leaders should concentrate on tracking the few that help plant managers understand what drives better performance, such as first-pass yields, internal quality observations, or quality cycle times. Within the plant, a cascade of metrics derived from these key metrics should be developed to make the goals tangible enough for the front line.

Knowing the first-pass yields of a particular manufacturing line, for example, can be critical. Yet this same metric may be meaningless when aggregated at the corporate level across different products, lines and plants. Similarly, FDA penalties imposed on a company may give senior management an indication of overall regulatory performance, but may not reveal what needs to change at any one plant.

In our experience, many pharma companies can apply techniques from other industries to improve quality performance. Simple tools on the production line—such as whiteboards with important line-level metrics, as well as depictions of what defective devices, tablets, or other products actually look like—are vital to increasing transparency and promoting constant improvement.

3. Set clear aspirations around quality performance and embed a culture where continuous improvement of quality is paramount.

Top manufacturers have reinforced quality and management practices across the organization by persuading employees that quality is paramount in everyone's role, and that improving quality is vital to the success of the business. These organizations set their quality aspirations higher each year and excite and empower their employees to keep improving quality practices and management systems.

To understand the culture and mindsets around quality, leading pharma companies gather insights on their through interviews, surveys and focus groups. At one company, such an effort revealed that employees across the organization did not understand how their day-to-day actions impacted quality performance, and that senior leaders didn't stress the importance of quality through their own behavior. The front line and supervisors lacked the awareness and capabilities—from technical expertise to communication skills—to manufacture high-quality products. Armed with these insights, the company developed a plan to close the capability gaps.

The resulting changes to the organization and employees' behavior led to a rapid and measurable shift in the company's approach to improving quality. Within a year, people across all levels could articulate quality objectives and aspirations, and a new sense of empowerment emerged around the ability and responsibility of employees to raise and address potential risks. Three new behaviors emerged:

■ Senior leaders deliver cultural messages clearly tying quality performance to the business imperatives, and continually reinforce them through communications, meetings, and site visits. Whenever the CEO discusses operational objectives, for instance, he says that one of the ultimate goals is to achieve industry-leading performance on critical quality metrics. Other senior managers ask plant managers and staff about quality during every visit and support quality improvements.

■ Plant supervisors are trained to model and coach the desired behaviors to improve manufacturing quality. Initial analysis showed that supervisors spent most of their time in meetings and reviewing corrective actions. To be more proactive than reactive, they now walk the floor regularly and encourage on-the-spot discussions around potential quality issues (see Exhibit 3). They regularly discuss the progression of the quality targets, which are posted at each manufacturing line, rather than simply reviewing metrics in the comfort of their offices. Through regular dialogue and problem-solving and coaching sessions, supervisors ensure that issues are resolved in an efficient and effective manner, and they have made individuals and areas accountable for quality performance.

- Front-line workers are meaningfully and regularly engaged in improving the company's quality performance. After all, corporate leaders and even senior engineers don't necessarily know when a particular machine is the root of a serious quality problem. To get workers to contribute, the company first ensured that they had the right technical expertise. Operators received additional training on how to monitor variability in production processes, conduct structured root-cause problem-solving, and simplifying and standardizing processes. All manufacturing personnel have the authority—and the confidence—to stop production lines for recurring problems and put together the right teams to fix them. In addition, quality performance is part of individual and team performance reviews, and the company publicly rewards employees who receive top scores.

The tasks involved in such a cultural transformation, while often straightforward, are critically important, and most pharma companies simply aren't undertaking them. Creating a corporate culture where every employee understands the importance of quality and takes responsibility for it propels all the components of an improvement initiative. For pharma companies, this can't be limited to one executive responsible for quality; all leaders must work to create a culture where quality products are a top priority.

Transforming quality

A biologics plant began their quality transformation where it would typically be expected—in its Quality laboratories—but quickly shifted gears to affect the entire organization, particularly manufacturing. The personnel there tended to see yield improvements as part of the engineers' role and accepted their own quality performance.

The senior leadership team set a higher aspiration for overall plant quality performance—communicating the effects of poor quality through poignant stories. Each gram of product lost was worth hundreds of doses, for example. When a team of front line operators analyzed the issues, they found many opportunities to decrease process variability and increase output without capital investments or process changes. Their innovations grew from idea to idea: they standardized every bit of the process, embedded in-line testing, and worked with their supplier to ensure higher-quality input into the process. They measured and managed performance daily—by creating a new set of yield metrics clearly tied to the critical process steps—and had regular problem-solving dialogues around the variability of the individual

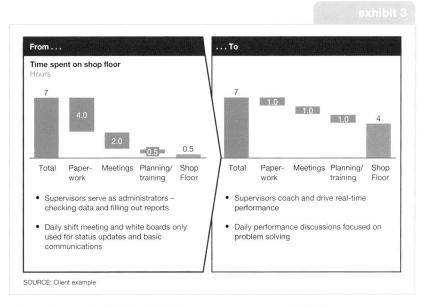

exhibit 3

From . . .

Time spent on shop floor
Hours

7

4.0

2.0

0.5   0.5

| Total | Paper-work | Meetings | Planning/training | Shop Floor |

- Supervisors serve as administrators – checking data and filling out reports

- Daily shift meeting and white boards only used for status updates and basic communications

. . . To

7

1.0

1.0

1.0

4

| Total | Paper-work | Meetings | Planning/training | Shop Floor |

- Supervisors coach and drive real-time performance

- Daily performance discussions focused on problem solving

SOURCE: Client example

steps. A consistent desire for better performance and yield became embedded in the manufacturing front line and management.

When the Head of Quality for the corporation came to visit one manufacturing site, he was greeted a manufacturing supervisor, who said, "Thank you for visiting our area. As you know, we are the most influential group affecting product quality, and we're happy you're here to see our improvements."

This manufacturing group had improved the efficiency and effectiveness of their quality processes, used the management and measurement of performance to drive improvement in performance, and embedded a culture across the organization that improving quality was paramount to their daily work.

* * *

Transforming quality requires a relentless focus on the most important drivers of quality, a determined effort to build quality into manufacturing processes, and a commitment from the leadership to align management processes with this goal. Pharma companies that move too slowly to address this challenge risk much higher costs and much more trouble from regulators.

Indeed, a significant benefit of a greater emphasis on quality is a better relationship with regulators. Although a spirit of collaboration cannot be achieved overnight, it can lead drug makers and regulators to share information and insights. Such a shift from a purely transactional, audit-based dialogue to a more productive, collaborative one can help companies shape manufacturing processes more efficiently and further improve quality.

Sales & Operations Planning: Making it stick and maximizing its value

Jochen Großpietsch, Sanjay Ramaswamy

While most companies have implemented S&OP processes, many struggle to extract real value from the activity, and even more fail to unlock the hidden potential in using this cross-functional process as a "pivot point" to drive change through the supply chain. But by tailoring the process design around the decision needs of each product segment, and having senior management model the right mindsets and behaviors, companies can balance supply and demand and transform performance through the supply chain.

Global manufacturers know that improving supply chain processes can cut costs, increase customer satisfaction and boost sales. They also know that synchronizing complex, far-flung operations is difficult. Few companies have mastered it.

A well-structured, cross-functional approach to Sales and Operations Planning (S&OP)-related activities, focused on on-time and in-full deliveries to customers, can bring transparency, synchronization and rigor to the whole organization—allowing previously hidden product delivery issues to become visible and be resolved before they become problems. S&OP allows fact-based decision-making that helps companies improve the balance of supply and demand—the key to success in any supply chain organization. The process also allows companies to mitigate risk, undertake fewer activities that don't add value, and make more educated decisions about supply and demand trade-offs.

Getting it right offers substantial benefits, and they can often be realized relatively quickly. We have seen companies improve customer service levels from below 90% to above 99% in a couple of S&OP cycles, boosting sales by improving transparency on market opportunities and available manufacturing capacities. At the same time, the introduction of well-run S&OP processes allowed one company to reduce inventory and related costs by over 30%.

Those who don't get it right continue to struggle with overproduction, stock-outs, added production cost, write-offs, and the frustration of constant misalignment between technical and commercial operations.

Many companies have experience with S&OP and acknowledge its merits, but few have fully harnessed the process or enjoy all of its benefits. So what are the companies that get it right doing differently?

Based on our work with some of these firms and interviews with clients and internal experts, we understand what it takes to set up and sustain an effective S&OP process—and the five pitfalls companies face.

First, sales and operations planning is not "one size fits all." Requirements differ from one company to the next, and even more important, from one product segment to the next. The process must be tailored to a company's unique needs and situation, taking into account product characteristics (including demand variability and supply stability), business variables, and organizational infrastructure and capabilities. A generic process cannot unleash the full potential of the multiple supply chains or supply chain segments that make up a typically portfolio.

Second, process effectiveness requires cross-functional cooperation and decision-making—a challenge for the typical siloed organization. An effective S&OP process cuts across sales, production, quality assurance, and other relevant support functions. It requires coordination, training, and the involvement of sales managers, production planners, logistic schedulers, quality managers and executives from all functions. Too often, the right decision-makers don't attend meetings, driving a cycle of lowered expectations and effectiveness.

Third, a lack of information integrity can undermine the process. Success relies on high-quality, timely sales forecasts and accurate accounts of production volumes, capacities and inventories. Deploying an S&OP process often reveals gaps in relevant data, while organizations prepare and rewrite reports and gather data that are only marginally helpful. Learning how to gather the right data for decision-making can take time.

Fourth, success relies on the right processes and mindsets—not just technology. The first focus is on the design of processes and rules along three phases of the S&OP cycle—demand planning, supply planning, alignment—and defining clear responsibilities for all stakeholders. The second focus needs to be on changing the way managers think and act—enabling them to recognize the end-to-end trade-offs and providing the right incentives for sound decision-making. ERP systems and software modules for planning can help with data integration and availability, but should be tailored to the needs of each supply chain segment. The S&OP process must drive software choices—not the other way around.

Finally, managers and senior executives must balance long-term and short-term perspectives and resist the temptation to spend every meeting on day-to-day firefighting. This is particularly true in supply-constrained organizations, where managerial attention is focused on the short-term production period and product delivery instead of a longer planning horizon. Many companies find it helpful to establish separate but interlinking S&OP processes to cover short- and long-term horizons, such as discussing operational short-term decisions monthly, while addressing more strategic long-term decisions once per quarter. This requires change management discipline and distinct approaches for different types of decision-making.

Too often, we see a combination of these pitfalls thwarting the S&OP process. Meetings revolve around immediate production details, participants do not have the power to make decisions, planners have no end-to-end view of product availability, and IT systems govern the pace and type of information exchanged across the supply chain.

In the following two sections, we discuss how to set up S&OP processes and manage the transformation in a sustainable way—while avoiding the pitfalls. Our recommendations draw heavily on best practices in the consumer packaged goods, high-tech and chemical industries.

How to design S&OP processes to maximize the benefits

The S&OP process design creates the framework for all execution. Successful companies pay attention to five design areas: defining the scope; clear roles and accountabilities; well-defined processes with a focus on exceptions; the right process parameters; and adapting the approach to the company's specific situation.

First, the scope of the S&OP process should be structured according to the globalization of the products and the interconnectedness of the supply network. If a product sells in only one region, for example, there is no need to address it in global meetings—unless trade-offs must be made due to shared, limited capacity with global products. In general, local products should be handled locally, regional products regionally and global products globally.

Second, it is crucial to define ownership and accountability clearly in the orchestration and execution of the cycle. One person should own and facilitate the S&OP process. He or she should be well-respected and have cross-functional impact, but not necessarily parallel reporting responsibilities like the global head of supply chain. Additional executive participation can help enforce decision-making and commitment from the right people. In the execution of the cycle, functional decision-makers should attend some meetings and own some of the outcomes. For example, the head of regional sales should own the regional demand meeting, and the COO or head of operations should own the global supply meeting.

Third, the S&OP process should be structured in demand, supply and decision phases:

- **Every S&OP cycle starts with a demand phase.** The objective is to accurately forecast demand, not taking supply constraints into account. Major points of discussion are changes in demand, new products or changes in the market environment.

- **The second phase is focused on supply.** At the end of this phase, planners aim to propose a production plan and corresponding plans for other supply chain areas that fulfill all demands with the best service level possible. Typical discussions in this phase may cover optimizing cost and inventory, and the initial resolution of capacity constraints.

- **Supply planners cannot resolve all capacity constraints immediately;** some conflicts require a broader discussion in the organization. This is the final step: the decision phase. The objective is to resolve the remaining issues and make decisions on trade-offs, such as prioritizing markets and products. In a well-run S&OP process, only a small portion of the products will be up for discussion at this stage, on an exception basis, ensuring a focus on the most important issues.

All SKUs should be incorporated into the process without exception, but the more SKUs are on auto-pilot, the more discussion can focus on major issues. There is no reason to discuss SKUs if demand for them does not fluctuate significantly, production capacity is sufficient and there are no supply risks. Naturally, checks should be in place to identify emerging supply risks and changes in demand.

Success story: Focusing managers' attention on the right topics

A pharma manufacturer segmented its planning approach to reduce inventory by 33% while maintaining target service levels of 99%. It began by dividing products into three segments:

Steady flow: Mainly high-volume products with flat sales

Responsive large: High volume and highly variable sales, often driven by the downstream supply chain (distributors, export, etc.)

Responsive small: Low volume and highly variable sales—such as tender products and irregular production for export.

The company treated products in each segment according to differentiated processes for each phase of the S&OP process.

For steady flow products in the demand phase, the company used automated demand forecasting based on historic patterns. For the responsive products, it forecast some sales using automated, history-based routines, and forecast peaks manually. But management directed its full attention to manual input for the responsive large items.

In the supply phase, the company implemented fixed production cycles to improve production stability and efficiency. The steady flow products were produced every 2 weeks, optimizing safety stock and production frequency for lowest total cost. The responsive products were also optimized for the sequence of production, but specific slots were allocated to large items. The supply planners then tried to match capacity needs for each period and with available capacity in slots blocked for flexibility across products. At the end of the planning process, they were identifying exceptional cases where they needed to make trade-off decisions.

In the decision phase, most discussions focused on exceptions in three priority areas. For new products, managers aligned ramp-up scenarios between markets and manufacturing. Next on the agenda were big demand peaks for large responsive items, as their volumes often exceeded capacity and required pre-production. Finally, the team discussed smaller items that caused capacity conflicts, together with any other upcoming issues. The recurring production for the steady flow products almost never made it to the agenda—helping the team focus on the most important decisions.

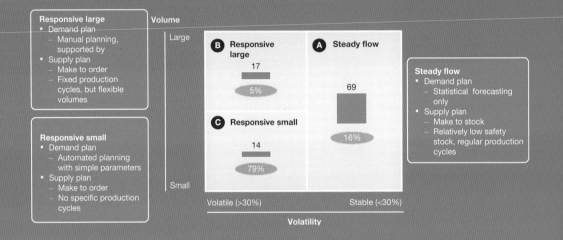

As fourth principle of successful S&OP, companies should base process parameters on product and business characteristics such as cycle frequency, planning horizon, planning granularity, and frozen window. The table below indicates how certain companies across industries have made different design choices in setting up their S&OP processes.

Finally, the emphasis on different phases in the S&OP process should reflect industry dynamics. A typical approach in the consumer packaged goods industry might emphasize the demand phase—forecasting and close integration of key accounts and customers into the S&OP cycle. The pharma industry, in contrast, typically pays more attention to the supply phase, since demand tends to be stable. When a product release process is long and variable, and production capacity is constrained, companies must focus more on scenario analysis and risk mitigation.

Tailoring the process, agenda, templates and tools, and attendance based on the above factors can make an immediate difference.

exhibit 1

Industry Sector					
	Pharma		High- tech	Consumer packaged goods	Chemical
Design Parameters	Drugs	Vaccines			
Cycle Frequency	Monthly	Weekly or Monthly	Weekly	Weekly or Monthly	Monthly
Planning horizon	12 months	18 months	4 months	12 months	6 months
Planning granularity	Week - Month	Week	Week	Week	Month
Frozen period length	3 months	3 months	1 month	1 week – 1 month	1.5 to 3 months

How to make it stick to sustain impact and value – S&OP transformation

Defining the right S&OP process design is not enough: the biggest challenge is actually transforming the organization to embrace a new way of working. Our research has shown five success factors that enable a transformation and allow the company to make the biggest improvements supply chain performance.

First, speed of design and execution are crucial. When implementing an improved process, companies should scale up the introduction quickly across the end-to-end product flows. It could start with one key product from supplier to customer, and then scale across the product portfolio, refining the design as needed during the process. Successful companies avoid lengthy preparatory phases and insert the necessary support tools and systems in phase with (or even slightly lagging) the process changes. Speed in implementation does not come at the expense of accuracy in the S&OP process cycle itself; on the contrary, the foundation of successful S&OP is fact-based decision-making. Momentum will build as participants see the benefits during the first few cycles of the process.

Second, executives should model the right decision-making behaviors. This usually starts at the top: by attending meetings and asking a couple of pointed questions, prepared beforehand, the CEO and other executives can spur

participants to prepare for meetings and improve performance. When the S&OP process starts to get traction, managers must help make the difficult decisions and trade-offs that might otherwise bog down the organization. Once management realizes that the S&OP process enables quicker, better decisions, they will be willing to incorporate it into their way of doing business, and it will drive greater and sustained cross-functional participation.

Third, the process owner and accountable managers (and by extension, everyone) should ensure that key decisions are made within the S&OP process, not outside it. All too often, S&OP meetings are limited to information-sharing, and no decisions are made. If decisions are made outside the formal S&OP-related processes, decision-makers will not show up to alignment meetings. Instead, they will send subordinates with no authority.

Fourth, the implementation of new S&OP processes needs to be supported by a targeted capability-building. The quality of the processes depends greatly on the preparedness of the planner, such as the use for statistical forecasting in demand planning, or the right calculation of optimal order sizes. At the same time, running an effective S&OP process requires strong communication and other soft skills. Training that addresses both technical and qualitative skill sets can therefore help make S&OP a success.

Fifth, making performance transparent keeps the focus on business needs. Key performance indicators should be an integral part of the cycle. The linkage of (functional) accountabilities to business performance will help the process take hold—and change the way people think.

Finally, more broadly, the S&OP process can and should be used as a focal point to drive business-wide transformation in supply chain processes. Once it is established as a truly cross-functional decision-making process, it becomes a natural starting point to cascade and propagate changes to the demand and supply sides of the business. Such an approach also helps reinforce the importance of the process and drive the attendance and behavior necessary to a virtuous cycle.

S&OP – What is it?

The generic S&OP process has three consecutive phases: demand, supply, and decision, that repeat on a rigorous cycle and become the pulse of the supply chain organization. The generic cycle relies on basic tools and templates to improve transparency and facilitate the exchange of information across the organization.

S&OP processes can be established on two distinct time horizons. In pharma companies, an operational S&OP process is usually conducted monthly, dealing with short- and mid-term topics, such as the allocation of capacity to meet demand. In addition, a strategic S&OP process focuses on more long-term decisions, such as investments in new capacity and portfolio questions.

Success story: Biologic pharmaceutical manufacturing

The biologic pharmaceutical business presents major supply chain challenges, including a manufacturing cycle of up to two years, highly variable yields in some production steps, and unpredictable demand for some products. Building new capacity, meanwhile, takes three to five years.

One pharmaceutical company aimed to triple revenue in five years but was saddled with a patchwork of acquisitions that it had not fully integrated. With no clear processes to guide them, and a lack of alignment on operational planning, managers spent their time firefighting. Everyone involved, from manufacturing, sales, quality, product release, logistics and regulatory, was continuously trying to solve next month's issue, while nobody worked to identify or mitigate potential supply disruptions six months down the road.

Not surprisingly, many customers were dissatisfied; fewer than 30% of the company's products arrived by the date promised. Some products were oversupplied in some markets, leading to write-offs of expired product, while others had backlogs of more than six months.

To fix these issues, the company initiated a supply chain transformation using the S&OP process as the critical first step and focal point to implement change. Cross-functional members of the organization worked together to make supply allocation and product trade-off decisions to manage supply constraints.

To take control of the demand phase, they set a three-month frozen window where no demand changes were allowed, and switched from point forecast to range forecast for 18 months. A new demand template captured probabilities and distinguished between tender and commercial forecasts and between constrained and unconstrained forecasts.

For the supply phase, they implemented a more robust and standardized planning process, agreeing on explicit assumptions to replace various homegrown spreadsheets and systems. Regulatory Affairs and Quality Assurance participated in supply meetings to cover registrations, validations and release processes. The company increased planning granularity from months to weeks and included shared asset and external manufacturing capacities more directly in planning.

Sales nominated a single person per region to represent their interests in S&OP meetings. Meeting preparation was streamlined to reduce rework and the need for other meetings and reports. The rigorous plans for supply and demand were shared openly within the team to reduce surprises on both sides of the table. Senior managers turned their attention to this process, adopting a rigorous decision-making focus with deliberate role modeling of the required behaviors.

The new approach dramatically increased managers' trust in forecasts and plans. In addition, more planning granularity brought issues to the surface sooner and helped the company make more synchronized, transparent decisions. After a few S&OP cycles, associated changes in tools, planning roles, and other planning and scheduling process changes were also implemented—always using the S&OP as a focal point to introduce and drive the necessary changes.

Customer service started to move in the right direction, and in a more intangible measure of success, people inside the firm began reaching out to become part of the process and to have products from their plants or regions included in subsequent cycles.

Eventually, S&OP became a true cross-functional business process. It is now the primary decision-making vehicle for operational planning across the whole business. The company also now has a platform in place for coordinating cross-functional actions and ensuring sustainability.

The value of flexibility:
Pharma supply chain 2020

**Thomas Ebel, Jochen Großpietsch, Ulf Schrader,
Marco Ziegler**

*Pharmaceutical companies have traditionally focused on quality
and security of supply at the expense of speed and flexibility,
where they trail other industries by a wide margin. As the
market becomes more volatile and pressure on working capital
increases, pharma companies need to rethink their approach to
flexibility.*

Over the last decade, supply chain managers in industry after industry
have not only helped cut costs but dramatically improved flexibility.
Computer manufacturers now deliver laptops to retail customers
a week after getting the order—out of contract factories in China.
Copying what they see on catwalks in New York and Paris, fashion
retailers can now deliver the latest trends around the world—three
weeks later.

Pharma companies rarely make headlines with their supply chain
flexibility. While other industries seem to live by the week or even
the hour, pharmacos count the months and years. Aiming to protect
high margins and ensure the availability of lifesaving drugs, they still

focus primarily on product quality and regulatory compliance at minimum unit cost, and spend less time and effort creating flexible and fast supply chains. In many cases, unit cost reductions have been achieved at the expense of flexibility, for example by optimizing chemical production with long campaigns, minimal changeovers and production partially ahead of demand. Throughput times of about 400 days from raw ingredients to finished goods testify to the

exhibit 1

ESTIMATE

Dimension	Indicator of flexibility	Pharma	Electronics	Consumer goods
Sourcing	Share of sourced volume with volume commit Percent	~50-70	~10-20	~20-30
Sourcing	Order lead time for packaging materials Days	~10-40	~20-30	~10-20
Production	Share temps of total blue collar staff Percent	~10	~20-40	~20-30
Production	Direct/indirect labor ratio	1 : 1	10 : 1	8 : 1
Time to customer	Total throughput time Days	~400	~80	~40

SOURCE: McKinsey

inflexibility in the pharma supply chain (see Exhibit 1)

Changing conditions, however, are forcing pharmacos to rethink their approach to flexibility:

■ **Commercial markets are becoming more volatile** as companies focus on emerging markets with less mature distribution channels and a higher share of tendering. As tenders mean often big orders on short notice, many companies are not able to deliver the tenders they are granted

■ **Regulators are increasing the pressure** and responding to compliance issues with import bans. The FDA recently banned imports of products from Apotex and Ranbaxy, for example, which led to significant market share shifts in the US

■ **Payors are pushing more aggressively for cost savings**, such as regular tenders and rebate contracts for generics in the German market

■ **As the generics business model becomes more important**, generics companies need to manage hundreds of launches each year, and uncertainties about timing require high flexibility

■ **Unexpected pandemics and epidemics** require fast ramp-ups of new supply chains and last-minute supply of millions of doses, such as H1N1 vaccines

■ **Complexity is increasing** in product ranges, with more markets served, line extensions, me-too products and OTC, and in supply chains, especially those that rely on global production strategies and many handover points

■ **Increasing focus on working capital driven** by liquidity shortages and the need to finance new pipelines and acquisitions.

How can pharmacos benefit from more supply chain flexibility, and how can they become more flexible? The right supply chain requires flexibility along five

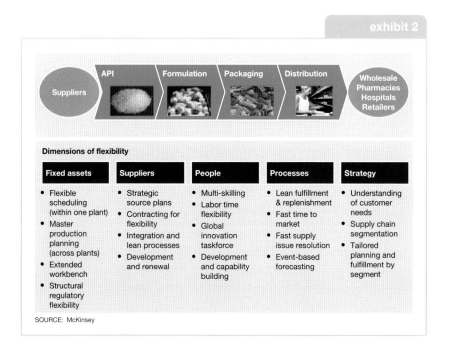

exhibit 2

Dimensions of flexibility

Fixed assets	Suppliers	People	Processes	Strategy
• Flexible scheduling (within one plant) • Master production planning (across plants) • Extended workbench • Structural regulatory flexibility	• Strategic source plans • Contracting for flexibility • Integration and lean processes • Development and renewal	• Multi-skilling • Labor time flexibility • Global innovation taskforce • Development and capability building	• Lean fulfillment & replenishment • Fast time to market • Fast supply issue resolution • Event-based forecasting	• Understanding of customer needs • Supply chain segmentation • Tailored planning and fulfillment by segment

SOURCE: McKinsey

dimensions: assets, suppliers, people, processes and strategy (Exhibit 2). Leaders across industries leverage all these dimensions to outpace their peers.

Asset flexibility—the breathing network

The normal fluctuation of demand and order patterns, plus seasonal and other special events, such as tenders, launches, loading of new channels and markets, require scaling volumes up and down quickly at a reasonable cost, avoiding idle costs in particular. Companies can calculate "upside asset flexibility" by measuring the unit cost increases (overtime, extra shifts, speeding in of materials and so on) required to produce an additional 50% of volume with three months of pre-advice. Downside asset flexibility is measured in the same way, taking into account all idle costs and production utilization variance per unit.

We find that companies with asset flexibility can target a higher asset utilization while meeting service and cost goals, and a higher ROIC than their peers. The companies in this group leverage the full range of options to create a flexible asset base:

- **Flexible scheduling within individual plants:** Pharmacos can pull many levers to expand capacity before resorting to expensive overtime, extra shifts or Sunday work. In one case, to help break a capacity bottleneck in packaging, we created a heat map at the packaging line level to identify capacity shortages against planned orders three to four months out, and leveraged flexible product line-allocation to achieve output targets for bottleneck SKUs. This included reserving full lines for bottleneck SKUs and shifting other SKUs to new lines, even at the cost of longer changeovers of different packaging formats. Producing ahead of time, postponing non-critical orders, and shifting small production batches away from automated packaging lines into manual packaging allowed the company to meet the increased demand with minimal additional unit cost.

- **Master production planning across plants:** Companies can use master production planning to optimize utilization across plants and avoid bottlenecks with a time horizon of three to nine months. This requires regulatory flexibility (see below), reactive and frequent demand planning (including a rigorous challenging of demands and planned orders) and a strict, cross-functional planning process that allows managers to make decisions on shifting volumes in the network in a regular rhythm. Some pharmacos need to take more radical steps to manage assets up and down. They may mothball plants, for example, to react to demand

disruptions or overoptimistic growth or launch forecasts. Petrochemical
and agricultural companies routinely use this technique to reduce running
costs to virtually zero, while reserving the asset and restarting production
when needed. More pharmacos are considering this option and finding
ways to address the regulatory challenges of mothballing.

- **Extended workbench (in-house-external):** Dynamic capacity
  management processes can leverage shifting volumes between in-house
  and external facilities. This can be done in a monthly S&OP process based
  on a forward-looking capacity heat map by line, technology or product. In
  one project, we used a mid-term capacity preview to level utilization in the
  target range of 70-80%. For lines below the target, the third-party sales

department aggressively filled all volumes with new orders or brought forward existing orders. For overutilization and bottlenecks, the company set up agreements with contract manufacturers that allowed producing about 60% of additional volume with three months of pre-advice at the current unit cost.

■ **Structural regulatory flexibility:** Fluid utilization of assets requires a regulatory strategy that allows more freedom to shift volumes between assets. Especially for high-volume, stable, easy-to-make products, second sources in the network need to be registered and ramped up to relieve launch sites or centers of excellence in Europe or the US and free capacity for difficult-to-make products, new technologies, and launches. By shifting to Eastern European, Indian, and Chinese plants as second sources, structural flexibility and cost improvements can go hand-in-hand.

There is certainly a benefit in shifting a share of the utilization risk to a third company, and many pharmacos are investigating selling parts of their plant base. Lilly, for example, recently sold an American API site to Evonik, which agreed to supply intermediates and APIs to Lilly out of this site for nine years.

Outsourcing does not necessarily make a company flexible, of course. Flexibility comes from relying upon the right approaches and processes to adapt up and down resources, be they in-house or external. Besides flexible contracting, it requires transparency of demand, capacity by line, and effective cross-functional S&OP processes to minimize idle cost and supply disruptions.

Suppliers—flexible partnerships

How flexible can suppliers be? Or rather, how flexible do you want them to be? In the automotive industry, cost control, reliability, quality and flexibility can go hand-in-hand. For example, a tier-1 supplier of automobile seats needs to meet high flexibility requirements to qualify as a preferred supplier to a big OEM company. The supplier needs to move capacity at five days (one shift) to meet base demand, dedicated lines with production in the same takt as the OEM to ensure synchronous flow, proof of parts availability, just-in-time delivery, and the ability to deliver emergency orders with 24 to 48 hours' notice. Together with real-time information about OEM production planning, gapless measurement of supplier performance, and an intense regimen of on-site controls and joint improvement projects, many suppliers coordinate their work as closely as possible with the OEM's final assembly.

Pharmacos often fail to obtain similar levels of flexibility: strict minimum-volume commitments, fixed annual delivery plans, long lead times for call-off orders, lack of emergency supply commitments of suppliers. They tend to focus instead on price savings or on protecting the status quo as long as suppliers meet quality requirements or provide access to critical technologies or markets.

Consequently, as our experience shows, it takes more than rewriting a few contract terms to create a flexible supply base:

- **Strategic sourcing plans:** Source plans need to be reviewed by product, and corrective actions need to be defined. Are backup or dual sources in place for critical products? Are supply contingency measures defined with preferred suppliers, such as strategic stocks and backup facilities?

- **Contracting for flexibility:** Standard KPIs and terms for supply flexibility need to be defined (e.g., call-off order lead time, emergency stock cover, supplier consignment stock/VMI, penalties and bonuses linked to delivery performance) and converted into contractual terms. Targets need to be defined by supplier segment and contracts up for renegotiation reviewed against them to gradually renew the contract base. Licensing agreements can often be enriched by flexible elements, such as introducing the right of parallel development and building a second source, which can cover a share of demand at more attractive prices or cover demand peaks that cannot be fulfilled by the contractor.

- **Integration and lean processes:** While contractual terms set expectations, it is crucial to improve operational processes with the supplier. What information will allow the supplier to improve production and source planning? How can joint planning and forecasting be improved and the call-off order process accelerated? We have seen supplier workshops use joint target-setting to improve processes with little cost and major boosts to flexibility.

- **Supplier development and renewal:** Successful companies have dedicated resources and processes for new supplier screening, auditing and development, thus ensuring a constant renewal of the supplier base with alternative sources and fresh ideas for continuous improvement.

Creating a flexible supplier base requires effort and enhanced capabilities in the sourcing organization, but it also takes a shift in procurement focus from price savings and order fulfillment to total cost of ownership, value-creation and continuous improvement. Suppliers in pharma have a long way to go. Global scale based on cost and innovation leadership in a focused set of technologies is instrumental for living up to the rising requirements of flexible partnerships.

People flexibility—the motor of innovation

People flexibility is essential in order to assign staff to tasks according to changes in demand and to ensure a fast and effective rollout of improvements. And since supply chains are global and span a wide range of suppliers, factories, logistics hubs and commercial sales organizations, pharmacos need highly skilled and internationally experienced talent who can drive supply chain innovation projects around the globe and sustain an edge on competitors. Leading companies ensure that their people are driving innovation, not impeding it, by using some of the following approaches:

- **Multi-skilling:** Flexible shop floor staffing is a key enabler for productivity improvements. By introducing multi-skilling for operators and flexible staffing across departments (e.g., between bottle and blister packaging), one team was able to keep machines running during breaks, fix small breakdowns faster, and speed changeovers. The operators performed small to medium maintenance tasks and equipment controls standalone during idle times, giving the specialized engineering staff more time to conduct root cause problem-solving around recurring errors and thus contribute to improving OEE and throughput time.

- **Labor time flexibility:** Many pharmacos are far from reaching the full potential of labor time flexibility. By introducing annual time accounts and flexible shift systems, companies can manage more ups and downs with existing employees and without raising costs. Companies should keep the right share of temporary staff across production and logistics departments to fluctuate with demand. Taking it further, many firms can benefit from cross-company sharing of resources. For example, a labor pooling contract with adjacent plants helped a flu vaccine producer contain production costs in peak seasons and speed time to market.

- **Global innovation task force:** Building or sustaining a competitive edge in geographically and functionally dispersed supply chains takes global leaders. Be it the managing improvement projects, the management of such as lead time reduction across the global plant network, establishing reactive, reliable and cost-effective supply chains in emerging markets, or setting up new distribution models to capture commercial value, pharmacos need a group of strong, internationally deployable global project managers. They establish best practices, ensure a fast rollout across local units and provide ongoing performance monitoring, coaching, and support. This is still a weak spot with most pharmacos, who can learn from the dynamic development culture in many high-tech companies, where leading change in war rooms and global supply chain projects is a #1 prerequisite for management talent of all tenures.

Needless to say that building a flexible workforce requires an integrated development and capability-building program across operations.

Processes—enablers for speed

How can a thousand new laptops, manufactured in China, arrive at a European retailer's ramp barely a week after he placed the order? Part of the answer is that computer manufacturers and their logistics providers have spent years streamlining their processes by stopwatch, driven by the fundamental need to minimize inventory risk exposure and fill retail shelf space before competitors take it. Why can't pharmacos challenge the speed of their fulfillment processes and carry lean beyond the shop floor across their end-to-end supply chain processes? Excellent processes are key to outpacing the competition, and leading companies focus their efforts along four dimensions:

- **Lean fulfillment and replenishment (Exhibit 3):** For one client, we conducted a detailed mapping of the finished product replenishment process from formulation and packaging plants to distribution warehouses. Following the "staple yourself to an order"-approach, the team mapped all process steps from generating a net demand/order in the sales country, over the order processing and scheduling in the plants, down to dispatching, transport, goods receipt and quality control in the distribution warehouse. The client reduced lead times by about 70%, from 75 to 25 days, with improvements such as speeding order processing from 15 to 5 days (through a change from monthly to weekly demand runs and accelerated order handling), introduction of a two-week scheduling window in the plants (every product needs to be packaged within two weeks of order entry in the plant, a period that allowed room for stable, cost-effective production), speeding the quality release of finished goods

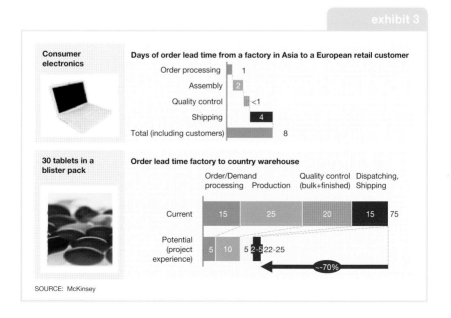

exhibit 3

Consumer electronics

Days of order lead time from a factory in Asia to a European retail customer

Order processing — 1
Assembly — 2
Quality control — <1
Shipping — 4
Total (including customers) — 8

30 tablets in a blister pack

Order lead time factory to country warehouse

	Order/Demand processing	Production	Quality control (bulk+finished)	Dispatching, Shipping	
Current	15	25	20	15	75
Potential (project experience)	5 10	5 2-5	22-25		

~-70%

SOURCE: McKinsey

from five days to one, and accelerating dispatching and goods issue from five days to one. These improvements required no investment, but a rigorous description, training, parameterization and enforcement of the new process

■ **Fast time to market:** While speed of replenishment is important for regular supply, it is crucial for launches, where each day of lead time after market approval equals a day of sales lost of overall lifetime value of the drug. For one client, we implemented a fast-track process for design, printing, packaging and distribution of launch products after FDA/EMEA approval, which has reduced the time-to-market after approval by up to 80%, from 100 to 20 days, depending on the market. Printing packaging materials takes three days now rather than the 30 in the regular process, with 24-hour production on a reserved printing line and release of materials by quality staff directly at the printing house within one hour, fast transport and accelerated distribution in the wholesale channel, closely tracked in interaction with logistics and wholesale partners. The additional cost for the fast-track process were far outweighed by the savings of an "early" market entry.

■ **Fast supply issue resolution:** Most companies have a bi-weekly or monthly S&OP process between plants, regional headquarters and sales countries. Just having a standard process in place is not enough, however. We see three criteria to take S&OP further towards fast and effective reaction to the market: A structured communication of changes across the chain (e.g., forecast uptake, unplanned breakdowns, supplier insolvency), fast escalation of real issues to top management, and fast cross-functional decision-making (e.g., by setting up a top management decision procedure requiring 24-hour resolution or daily follow-up).

■ **Event-based forecasting:** To ensure fast and effective reaction to major events (such as success of tenders for certain molecules, success of patent lawsuits, approval of drugs in new markets or molecules for new indications), pharmacos need to make a step change in forecasting. While limiting the effort required for transactional forecasting by automation and pull-based systems, they need to focus forecasting expertise and manpower on major events as stated above, and leverage more sophisticated approaches such as event-based forecasting. This includes developing scenarios for major events, assessing risks and probabilities for each scenario, the definition of actions along well-defined decision gates, and the assessment of alternative actions by means of risk-adjusted NPV. We have seen in many projects that shifting forecasting to focus on major events, instead of transactional forecasting for thousands of SKUs, in line with strong market intelligence and business judgment, allows supply chains to react faster with minimal additional resources.

Strategy—investing wisely

Highly flexible supply chains are clearly not the most effective setup for every product segment and demand pattern. The delivery of products with stable demand, such as high-volume blood-pressure drugs, or medium-volume oncology drugs, requires a stable, cost-optimal replenishment process. But SKUs with variable or seasonal demand, such as vaccines and hospital supplies, may need fast reaction times to minimize high inventory exposure and capture full sales potential.

Thus, leaders typically segment their portfolio in few supply chain segments, rather then running a "one size fits all" approach, which requires excessive planning efforts, often fails to meet customer requirements and may lead to costly emergency actions. They (*remark: the leaders*) tailor supply chain processes to meet the requirements of each segment, and develop a specific supply chain segment strategy:

- **Understanding customer needs:** Every strategy must start with a deep understanding of customer requirements: How are order patterns and variability in demand driven by patient consumption, channel structure, number of customers, ordering process and commercial incentives? What is the required delivery frequency and order lead time? Does a wholesaler with an average stock of two weeks require an order line fill rate of 99.8% from pharmacos? Only companies that have a thorough understanding of these factors can be more flexible and focus on the products, markets, and customers that pay off most.

- **Demand-driven segmentation:** One project illustrates a simple segmentation for flexibility requirements. Beginning with an understanding of demand patterns by SKU, a company defined a replenishment strategy and decoupling points for each segment. Roughly half of SKUs had stable sales with a standard deviation of weekly demand of less than 30%, and these were replenished in a simple pull system, with controlled stocks and a straightforward reorder-point replenishment method from finished goods to raw materials. In production scheduling, the big SKUs were planned as a stable, recurring element in a biweekly or monthly fixed cycle. This strategy allowed a 40% reduction in inventory and required less manual planning and forecasting effort. For SKUs with erratic, hard-to-forecast sales, such as medium-volume SKUs in markets with few wholesale players, or small SKUs ordered infrequently, the company established a fast pack-to-order process that decoupled bulk materials in a controlled stock to allow replenishment within two weeks (see Exhibit 4).

■ **Tailored planning and fulfillment processes:** In our experience, segmentation works only where segment-specific strategies are defined for all key processes , including forecasting and demand planning, service

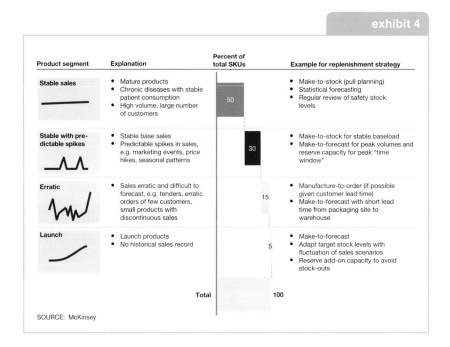

exhibit 4

Product segment	Explanation	Percent of total SKUs	Example for replenishment strategy
Stable sales	• Mature products • Chronic diseases with stable patient consumption • High volume, large number of customers	50	• Make-to-stock (pull planning) • Statistical forecasting • Regular review of safety stock levels
Stable with predictable spikes	• Stable base sales • Predictable spikes in sales, e.g. marketing events, price hikes, seasonal patterns	30	• Make-to-stock for stable baseload • Make-to-forecast for peak volumes and reserve capacity for peak "time window"
Erratic	• Sales erratic and difficult to forecast, e.g. tenders, erratic orders of few customers, small products with discontinuous sales	15	• Manufacture-to-order (if possible given customer lead time) • Make-to-forecast with short lead time from packaging site to warehouse
Launch	• Launch products • No historical sales record	5	• Make-to-forecast • Adapt target stock levels with fluctuation of sales scenarios • Reserve add-on capacity to avoid stock-outs
Total		100	

SOURCE: McKinsey

level and inventory management, production scheduling and capacity planning. This tailoring effort can be an opportunity to standardize processes and define improved targets, decision rules, and escalation procedures.

Overall, segmentation results in higher overall product availability with even lower inventories, with less firefighting and last-minute changes. It can also lead to lower costs overall, thanks to reducing scrap, preventing overstocking, and reducing the need for highly expensive emergency transportations

***

Flexibility can offer major benefits. Based on simulations and what we know from other industries, we estimate the potential at stake as 25% of EBIT— without major investments. For a $10-billion global pharmaco with EBIT of $2 billion, improvements would mean a 20% reduction in COGS, or about $400 million in savings. This is possible with optimized product/plant allocation, reduced idle time, stable production schedules with high adherence and total cost savings from flexible, performance-oriented contract structures. In addition, the example company would lower inventory by 40%, or about $500 million, with a faster replenishment processes, clear segmentation strategy, and reduced throughput times in manufacturing and packaging. The company could also raise revenues with better market penetration, fast delivery into new markets, fast ramp-up of launches, and fewer stock-outs.

Leading pharmacos have started thinking about how to take their supply chains to the next level of flexibility. While they may never be as flexible as the nimblest computer manufacturer, the old, rigid pharma supply chains will soon be a thing of the past.

Value-creating
purchasing

Lorenzo Formiconi, Martin Lösch, Jean-Philippe Talmon, Marco Ziegler

Pharma companies have not traditionally made purchasing a priority. But new pressure on profits, and structural changes in the industry, are driving many to reassess its importance. New research reveals what purchasing leaders can achieve, and how they do it.

A RENEWED INTEREST IN AN OLD BUSINESS

Stable growth, healthy margins, and virtually no control on important spend buckets like marketing, research, and development have relegated the role of purchasing in pharma to little more than a back-office transactional function. But a new focus on cost has sparked interest in the "art of buying," with several pharmacos embarking on purchasing initiatives to capture value from what many consider no more than low-hanging fruit.

Unfortunately, it's not easy to achieve purchasing excellence, and even companies with the highest aspirations need to overcome cultural and organizational hurdles.

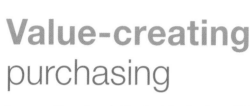

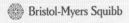

"Project Forward, [which includes] all divisions in procurement and IT, [will save] $1.6 billion over two years."
– Daniel Vasella, Chairman and CEO

"[We expect significant] savings from procurement and streamlining various operations as we become a biopharma business.   This initiative should be complete in 2012."
– Jean-Marc Huet, SVP & CFO

"[We] set an ambitious five-year savings target of more than $1.2 billion through changes in the way we procure goods and services. We achieved that goal 18 months early—and set a new target to deliver an additional $1 billion over the next three years."
– Richard Spoor, SVP Global Procurement

AstraZeneca

"In February we announced a major program to improve asset utilization in our supply chain. We are tackling procurement. And…we are doing everything we can to drive out complexity in different parts of the organization."
– David Brennan

Pharmacos typically face several barriers to better purchasing. Many have a highly fragmented organization and a silo mentality, both the result of geographical dispersion. Country, regional and global organizations may manage overlapping spend without a common understanding about how to collaborate.

Second, managers have low transparency on spend, costs per unit, prices for alternative materials and services at different suppliers within the same category, and so on, thanks to fragmented reporting systems.

Third, a corporate culture driven by risk awareness will pay high premiums to keep overall risk profiles low. This attitude—originating from the need to ensure supply and sustain growth, but also extended to sourcing of indirect cost categories—has in some cases prevented the adoption of more modern risk and volatility management approaches.

Fourth, purchasing staff may lack incentives in terms of remuneration, and more important, in terms of reputation and career opportunities. Purchasing positions can therefore look unappealing, and talent moves towards other functions.

In this context, how can pharmacos create value in purchasing? Can examples within or outside the industry help them navigate there? What are the mantras for the purchasing of the future in pharma?

In a McKinsey purchasing survey based on executive interviews and quantitative data from more than 400 corporations[1] including 20 pharmacos, we found that pharmacos lag top performers from industries such as high-tech, automotive, and consumer goods. We identified four areas where the gap is especially wide: a robust category management approach, the opportunity to challenge the business system, focused purchasing talent management, and effective knowledge creation and distribution (see Exhibit 1).

Does matching top-performing industries represent an unrealistic aspiration for pharma because of its unique industry requirements? Maybe not. In fact, a few pharmacos in the survey were able to achieve top scores in selected purchasing excellence dimensions, closing much of the gap with the top-performing industries: their example could represent a starting point for other pharmacos.

---

1   Based on McKinsey's Global Purchasing Excellence study—a large-scale, empirical study correlating procurement practices with corporate performance. Results are based on in-depth interviews with Chief Purchasing Officers and extensive written surveys of large corporations from all major industries and across all geographies. More than 400 survey responses have been analyzed so far, and results correlated and validated with confidence level of over 95%.

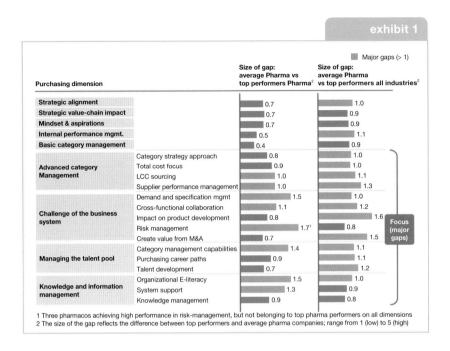

exhibit 1

■ Major gaps (> 1)

Purchasing dimension		Size of gap: average Pharma vs top performers Pharma[2]	Size of gap: average Pharma vs top performers all industries[2]
Strategic alignment		0.7	1.0
Strategic value-chain impact		0.7	0.9
Mindset & aspirations		0.7	0.9
Internal performance mgmt.		0.5	1.1
Basic category management		0.4	0.9
Advanced category Management	Category strategy approach	0.8	1.0
	Total cost focus	0.9	1.0
	LCC sourcing	1.0	1.1
	Supplier performance management	1.0	1.3
Challenge of the business system	Demand and specification mgmt	1.5	1.0
	Cross-functional collaboration	1.1	1.2
	Impact on product development	0.8	1.6
	Risk management	1.7[1]	0.8
	Create value from M&A	0.7	1.5
Managing the talent pool	Category management capabilities	1.4	1.1
	Purchasing career paths	0.9	1.1
	Talent development	0.7	1.2
Knowledge and information management	Organizational E-literacy	1.5	1.0
	System support	1.3	0.9
	Knowledge management	0.9	0.8

Focus (major gaps)

1 Three pharmacos achieving high performance in risk-management, but not belonging to top pharma performers on all dimensions
2 The size of the gap reflects the difference between top performers and average pharma companies; range from 1 (low) to 5 (high)

SOURCES OF VALUE IN PHARMA PURCHASING

1. Implement advanced category management

Sharpen your category strategy approach

Purchasing leaders have a culture of exploiting every opportunity to reduce their total cost of supply using a well-established category management process, where purchasing is recognized as a value-driver by all business functions. Top performers integrate basic instruments, such as better spend transparency, clear-cut category definitions and responsibilities, a deep understanding of the company's day-to-day business, and overall spend size and drivers. They also use more advanced approaches, such as a purchasing strategy tailored to take advantage of the specificities of the supplier market in each category; a total cost focus that helps them capture and compare costs and benefits of different purchasing options throughout the life cycle of the purchased good; active LCC sourcing; and a well-structured approach to supplier management based on objective performance measures.

Pharmacos can benefit from advancing beyond the basics in category management. One pharmaco that recently focused on improving its category management for packaging materials saved over 10% by more carefully screening the supplier market, expanding the scope of its RFPs to more candidates, and more aggressively negotiating conditions with the selected partner on the basis of insights gathered during the RFP process.

Create transparency on total cost with a benchmarking mindset
An important element of an advanced category management is full transparency on the total costs—direct and indirect—of a good or service before starting negotiations. Transparency allows the company to set realistic targets in advance to get the best possible price during negotiations.

Two approaches can improve cost transparency: benchmarking and clean sheets, sometimes used together. The former is easier—it requires only that companies broaden the scope of an RFP and compare quotations—but has its limitations in concentrated markets with few players that know each other's price ranges.

The second requires more effort to understand and model the relevant factor cost for a good or service, but allows companies to gauge the supplier's underlying cost base and gain leverage for negotiation. Pharmacos are focusing more on cost transparency, having noticed that most suppliers enjoy high margins. Supplier markups of up to 80%—as in a recent case with a contract manufacturer (see Exhibit 2)—are not uncommon and represent golden opportunities for additional savings[2]. Transparency can and should then extend to capacity and utilization, providing powerful arguments for cost reduction through in-sourcing or outsourcing, or even for negotiating rebates from suppliers with the threat of in-sourcing.

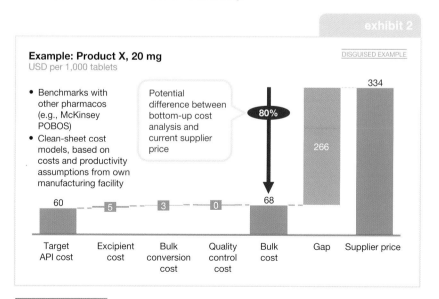

exhibit 2

Example: Product X, 20 mg
USD per 1,000 tablets

DISGUISED EXAMPLE

- Benchmarks with other pharmacos (e.g., McKinsey POBOS)
- Clean-sheet cost models, based on costs and productivity assumptions from own manufacturing facility

Potential difference between bottom-up cost analysis and current supplier price

80%

Target API cost	Excipient cost	Bulk conversion cost	Quality control cost	Bulk cost	Gap	Supplier price
60	5	3	0	68	266	334

---

2 McKinsey's proprietary operations benchmarking (POBOS) compares unit costs and plant performance on a normalized basis.

Push low-cost country (LCC) sourcing beyond the obvious

Most pharmacos already source part of their chemicals and API needs from LCCs like India and China. Leaders have managed to get to the next level by developing comprehensive LCC sourcing strategies across their entire spend portfolio; for the leaders, LCC sourcing is a key part of global category management, with a growing focus on indirect materials and services.

For example, one pharmaco reduces costs for stability testing by 40% after a new product introduction by outsourcing the service to a provider in Eastern Europe. Another pharmaco requires managers of most spend categories to screen and assess LCC sourcing opportunities regularly, and to evaluate suitable LCC alternatives before every negotiation round.

More generally, we have seen pharmacos including more non-traditional spend categories, such as contract manufacturing, packaging equipment, and tooling for machinery, in their LCC sourcing portfolio, often realizing double-digit percentage savings.

Sourcing leaders who consider total cost of supply in every decision sometimes reach with counterintuitive conclusions. One compared LCC sourcing alternatives for bulk manufacturing, for example, and found that total cost of supply from some remote low-cost countries was higher than their current supply in Western Europe (see Exhibit 3), and limited its sourcing to regions with clear cost advantages.

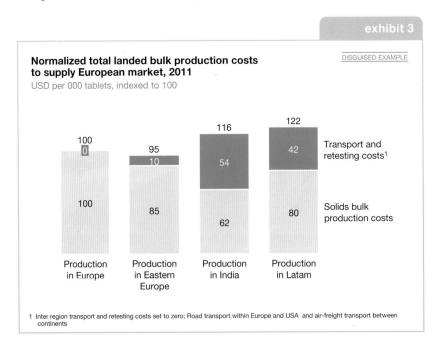

exhibit 3

Normalized total landed bulk production costs to supply European market, 2011
USD per 000 tablets, indexed to 100

DISGUISED EXAMPLE

100	95	116	122

Transport and retesting costs[1]

Solids bulk production costs

Production in Europe | Production in Eastern Europe | Production in India | Production in Latam

1 Inter region transport and retesting costs set to zero; Road transport within Europe and USA and air-freight transport between continents

Implement "automotive-like" supplier performance management
McKinsey research shows that automotive companies are top performers in supplier performance management. They actively manage their supplier base, include deliverables and performance metrics in contracts, and standardize supplier scorecards to track and remunerate performance.

Toyota, Honda and others have established regular quantitative assessments to drive continuous improvements in supplier performance and ensure productivity increases balance cost increases in the face of technological progress and rising commodity prices.

To implement "automotive-like" supplier management, however, pharmacos have to rationalize their supplier base first. In fact, our survey indicates that a purchasing associate in pharma is responsible for nearly twice as many suppliers as other sectors, on average, and only half of the spend (see Exhibit 4). Without reducing the number of suppliers and concentrating on the few that matter, any aspirations towards effective performance management are doomed.[3]

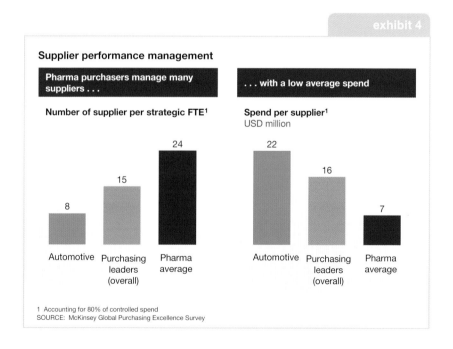

exhibit 4

Supplier performance management

Pharma purchasers manage many suppliers . . .

Number of supplier per strategic FTE[1]

- Automotive: 8
- Purchasing leaders (overall): 15
- Pharma average: 24

. . . with a low average spend

Spend per supplier[1]
USD million

- Automotive: 22
- Purchasing leaders (overall): 16
- Pharma average: 7

1 Accounting for 80% of controlled spend
SOURCE: McKinsey Global Purchasing Excellence Survey

---

3   For a detailed analysis of the opportunities, pitfalls and organizational implications of supplier management in contract manufacturing, see "Mastering the supply management challenge" on page 232.

2. Challenge your business system

Dare to challenge demand, not just price

A robust category management process pushes purchasing organizations to go beyond classical annual price rebates in direct spend and start addressing demand-related levers. Top sourcing organizations excel in extending their activities into demand areas, and tend to start by addressing spend categories that have gone unnoticed in the past.

Consider the case of a pharmaco where purchasing helped to reduce occupancy costs by over 10% by switching headquarters locations to newer buildings with more efficient layouts. The change was sparked by realizing that existing locations had poor utilization rates due to an old layout and furniture: the company's sourcing group assessed relocation alternatives and selected the best fit together with the local business leadership.

In another situation, purchasing managed to reduce facilities and site service costs—a varied category including cleaning, security, building and equipment maintenance, gardening—by around 15%. It did this by realigning service-level requirements in non-critical dimensions and aggressively renegotiating agreements with service providers.

Connect purchasers to the business

In most industries, commercial negotiation tactics account for as little as 20 to 30% of the potential impact of purchasing improvements. The rest comes from managing product specifications and demand—practices that purchasers can learn from close cooperation with the business functions.

In addition to classical price negotiations, top sourcing leaders therefore challenge the business system itself. By stimulating the dialogue between purchasing and the business functions, these leaders take a more entrepreneurial view of purchasing, which helps them overcome organizational fragmentation. Especially in direct spend categories, the opportunities can be huge: one pharmaco reduced its API spend by as much as 37% by challenging product specifications and current processes (see Exhibit 5).

Deep cross-functional relationships from collaboration also help purchasers address sacred cows—spend categories that have historically been beyond the influence of purchasing. Pharmaco fragmentation offers ideal habitats for sacred cows, including marketing, research and development, and critical outsourced business. But cross-functional links can help overcome these hurdles.

At one pharmaco, sourcing and marketing collaborated to reduce the number of speaker training events for congresses and other marketing events, saving

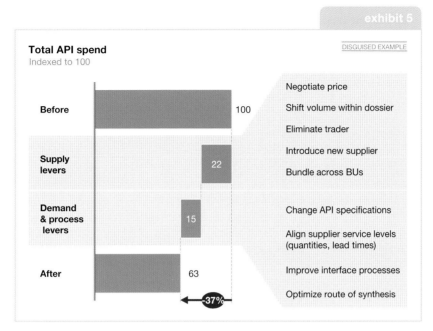

exhibit 5

Total API spend
Indexed to 100

DISGUISED EXAMPLE

Before — 100

Supply levers — 22

Demand & process levers — 15

After — 63

-37%

Negotiate price

Shift volume within dossier

Eliminate trader

Introduce new supplier

Bundle across BUs

Change API specifications

Align supplier service levels (quantities, lead times)

Improve interface processes

Optimize route of synthesis

more than 20%. In another case, the sourcing group and the businesses reduced over 15% of IT helpdesk costs by replacing the support in the local language with standard English support, thereby increasing the possibility of cross-country back-ups, and by fully offshoring the service to India.

Collaboration does not need to stop to at the company's gates, as there are plenty of opportunities for cooperating and bundling spend with external organizations. Some pharmacos are recognizing the value of collaborating with competitors on categories distant from the sources of competitive advantage, such as distribution, where sharing of logistics assets— warehouses, fleet, suppliers—significantly contribute to cost reduction.

And opportunities can multiply when searching for collaboration beyond the pool of competitors. In operations, for example, it is a common practice in several industries to share processes and assets for power generation, security or cleaning services to raise scale and lower costs.

Leverage purchasing as a source of innovation
Top performers realize that purchasing can catalyze innovation once it relies on professional category management and has established its role within the organization. In fact, purchasing associates will see a number of innovations while screening supplier markets in search of less-expensive items, from new packaging solutions up to best-of-breed dosage devices or test kits.

The main challenge in leveraging suppliers as a source of innovation is setting the right incentives and context for purchasing associates. They need deep knowledge about marketed drugs and their effects—and how to push an innovation through all approval stages.

Don't just avoid risk—manage it

Purchasing leaders manage supply and supplier risks and dedicate resources and expertise to this task. In its best expression, purchasing integrates risk modeling and scenario planning with the corporate risk management. In pharma, some players are also timidly taking steps toward managing risk and volatility in a more active way. One pharmaco has reduced its electricity costs in Europe by 7% by replacing yearly fixed-price contracts with a brokerage approach that included risk-based purchasing on the forward electricity market (see Exhibit 6).

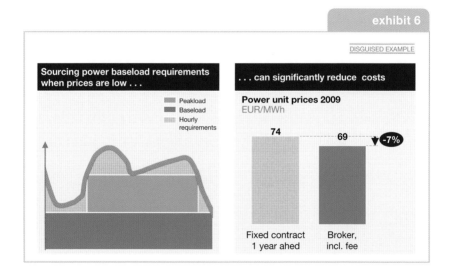

Another company increased self-insurance on its company vehicle fleet and accepted the risks of being exposed to the volatility of cash outflows for reimbursements, convinced by a 10% forecast savings on insurance fees, net of expected cash outflows for reimbursements.

Create value from mergers & acquisitions

M&A in pharma is typically driven by top-line growth. This often obscures the operational synergies and the value purchasing could realize, with the result that purchasing representatives are only marginally involved in the due diligence process, with low or no saving targets during post-merger integration. Purchasing leaders, on the contrary, are involved early in the process and have high pre-merger targets. Based on our experience, purchasing savings from a pharma merger can easily exceed 5% of total spend.

3. Strategically manage the talent pool

Pharma purchasers have above-average educational qualifications. Still, education alone does not pay off in terms of the overall purchasing performance of the industry, which is lags significantly behind top performers. Sourcing organizations at most pharmacos seem to have difficulties attracting and retaining talented associates with the same pace they achieve in, say, sales or research. The problem is typically related to limited career opportunities beyond purchasing.

Sourcing leaders have a strategic priority in filling in their key purchasing positions with talent and rewarding them with good career opportunities in their "life after purchasing": by hiring strong people, these companies improve procurement's credibility, set the stage for successful purchasing initiatives, and create a base for attracting new talent.

Talent-development programs that help purchasers beef up their commercial acumen and establish relationships with internal customers are a common tool at top sourcing performers: for promising university recruits, this training might take the form of a rotation program offering a variety of experiences; for long-term staff some companies create tailored programs. Some pharmacos, for example, establish "procurement academies" providing training and workshops in selected product categories, individualized development plans, and advanced negotiation skills.

4. Foster knowledge and knowledge creation

Knowledge has always been intertwined with talent, and, like talent, it must be carefully managed. The purchasing survey shows that top performers achieved far higher scores in managing knowledge than low performers. But, interestingly enough, we found no correlation between superior knowledge management and IT spend and use (see Exhibit 7). The results hint at the fact that information is important, but people are the key.

For this reason, line management and knowledge managers should pay particular attention to the degree of formalization they aim at while codifying knowledge, and carefully evaluate benefits and costs in terms of effort and motivation.

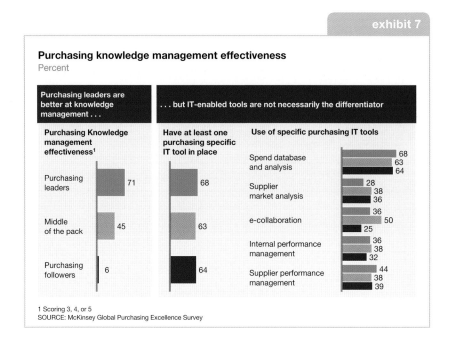

exhibit 7

Purchasing knowledge management effectiveness
Percent

| Purchasing leaders are better at knowledge management . . . | . . . but IT-enabled tools are not necessarily the differentiator |

Purchasing Knowledge management effectiveness[1]

Purchasing leaders — 71
Middle of the pack — 45
Purchasing followers — 6

Have at least one purchasing specific IT tool in place

Purchasing leaders — 68
Middle of the pack — 63
Purchasing followers — 64

Use of specific purchasing IT tools

Spend database and analysis — 68 / 63 / 64
Supplier market analysis — 28 / 38 / 36
e-collaboration — 36 / 50 / 25
Internal performance management — 36 / 38 / 32
Supplier performance management — 44 / 38 / 39

1 Scoring 3, 4, or 5
SOURCE: McKinsey Global Purchasing Excellence Survey

Getting there: Shoot for the stars but start at the ground

Below the top performers in our survey, many companies started on their path to excellence by challenging their transparency of spending. The fragmentation of reporting systems is the major hurdle to transparency. Nonetheless, in the absence of an integrated reporting system, entrepreneurial purchasing organizations temporarily run spend allocation and basic analyses manually, reallocating bookings into financial accounts into a spend category structure. Leaders often adopt this procedure in the aftermath of a merger, when reporting systems are not integrated yet.

Second, top performers set high aspirations and challenging but achievable goals. The clearer the goals—typically a quantified objective or set of metrics—the higher the probability that the company will achieve them. While this may seem obvious, we have seen many companies among the low and average performers that don't set any targets or make them vague in terms of quantification and timing. Conversely, among the top performers, purchasing associates have a clear-cut understanding of target cost reductions and timeline.

Third, leaders ensure that the boardroom backs their aspirations, regularly reviews their attainment of goals, and coordinates activities across businesses and functions. Typically, the transition begins when purchasing becomes a more frequent C-level discussion and the CPO and the CEO commit—together with other senior executives—to aggressive organization-wide savings targets.

Finally, leaders bet on talent, coupled with the right incentives, and quick results rather than on changes to the formal organization structure, to achieve the change. The basic philosophy is simple: talent is able to deliver impact, which in turn motivates behavioral change in the people around it. The alignment of the formal organization is a mere consequence, a recognition of what has already happened.

Pharma's typical geographical fragmentation is a barrier to this virtuous circle, since it reduces the transparency of performance across country organizations. For this reason, leaders ensure that the whole organization—not only the boardroom or few selected functions or countries—is aligned towards common targets and well aware of the results of purchasing's successes by improving transparency and communicating results. This pushes centralization of roles at regional or global levels, especially for purchasing categories presenting similar requirements on the demand side and overlaps on the supply side.

Leaders generally recognize the importance of being "close to the business" and rarely go too far in centralizing purchasing responsibilities. In fact, a common feature in successful purchasing initiatives is the early involvement of "local champions," who are made accountable for target-setting together with central purchasing as well as for the realization of results. While selecting, training, and coaching local champions absorbs resources from central purchasing, the multiplier effect they yield cannot be overemphasized. And they may demonstrate the acumen and motivation to take over more senior leadership roles in purchasing.

* * *

Purchasing is becoming an increasingly hot topic for pharmacos aiming to increase their profitability. Successful purchasing for pharma is characterized by robust category management, a strategic focus on talent management, and a willingness to challenge the business system. Pharmacos embarking on the path to excellence should focus on creating the necessary transparency, setting bold aspirations, getting backing from the boardroom, and communicating results throughout the organization.

Integrated productivity management

Sirish Chandrasekaran, Sue Ringus, Nick Santhanam

Many companies are unable to measure productivity in the face of shifts in production volume and mix, and few can connect operational metrics directly to financial performance. But by using an integrated approach, companies can measure productivity—and manage it. Beginning with a granular view of true production costs, and then normalizing for production volume and mix, managers can quantify changes in productivity, prioritize and track initiatives to drive improvements, and use a common language throughout the company.

Consider a common scenario: In a bio-pharma company, a shop floor supervisor keeps a close eye on scrap and labor utilization. She and her plant manager hold weekly meetings to discuss operations, and both believe their team is significantly improving productivity. But at the end of the month, they are surprised to see that financial results indicate a big increase in COGS. The plant manager and his manufacturing finance partner can't explain why the information tells conflicting stories, and they can't tease out the results of changes in production levels.

During the quarterly review, the CEO asks if the plant has gotten more productive. The plant manager answers, "It could be mix, it could be volume... but we think we're doing better." His predictions about next quarter's results are even less definitive. Both leave the conversation dissatisfied.

What's causing the confusion and painful conversations? One frequent reason is that financial and operational measures are not linked.

Connecting them—and getting a true measure of productivity—is critical for allocating resources based on needs and opportunities, identifying initiatives worthy of investment and rollout, and disinvesting in projects that do not meet ROI hurdles. In addition, anticipating and accounting for changes on the shop floor can help managers make better financial predictions.

Our research shows that integrating financial and operational productivity management can help drive company performance. It can improve quantitative measures, such as fixed and labor costs and material consumption and yield, and it can inform forward-looking conversations about leading indicators of success and how to drive improvement. In our experience, implementing such a system can produce dramatic results:

- 15% boost in material consumption/yield

- 25% lower labor costs per normalized unit

- 10% lower fixed costs, such as indirect labor, utilities and IT spend.

Many managers struggle with productivity measures based on the cost of goods sold that do not correspond to their perceptions and, more important, do not equip them to assess or act quickly to boost productivity. For many organizations, especially those with diverse product lines and global reach, the complexity of manufacturing processes has outpaced accounting metrics. As a result, quarterly financial performance is often widely divergent from what the operations managers believe they're seeing on the shop floor. Executives and managers at all levels operate in a perpetual state of surprise and firefighting.

WHAT DRIVES THE DISCONNECT?

Measuring productivity is challenging for three major reasons: the complexity of manufacturing environments, a lack of integration between financial and operational measurements, and organizational barriers.

Problem #1: Manufacturing is increasingly complex

Manufacturing complexity is the main impediment to measuring productivity. Varying product lines and product mix make comparisons across accounting and financial periods difficult.

Suppose, for example, that a bio-pharma company's total cost of producing two tablets, one coated and one uncoated, is $1. Using a standard cost method, managers estimate that the cost of producing two of each is $2. But they may not be able to reliably estimate the cost of producing one coated tablet and two uncoated tablets, or some other change in mix. In a real plant manufacturing 10,000 or more SKUs, the complexity of the problem is enormous.

It can also be difficult to assign material and labor costs to specific products in complex manufacturing processes, especially if production flows are not continuous and employees work on overlapping products. Interdependencies among products, such as shared production lines or production teams, add to the difficulties, especially with assigning fixed and variable costs.

Consider this example: A specialty chemicals company produces many different products with common raw materials and intertwining sub-processes. The company's recent roll-out of lean seems to be paying off—standard lean metrics are pointing towards improvements across the board. But the standard variance (e.g., "earned" or entitled total costs minus actual total costs) is negative. The shop floor supervisor is stunned, but the explanation is simple: The company's costing system artificially inflates the unit cost by assigning a set amount of fixed costs per unit produced, not based on the actual cost of production.

Long production times, high inventory and obsolescence also hinder attempts to match inputs to outputs and measure productivity.

For example, suppose a semiconductor component manufacturer's products have short times to obsolescence—about two months. Shop-floor productivity measures suggested improvements for the last three quarters, but the senior management questioned the manufacturing group's credibility because COGS had skyrocketed during the same period—primarily due to scrap.

The explanation? The company produced the "wrong" products a quarter before and must now scrap obsolete components. In the meantime, the site manager was not able to reconcile the operations scrap reports with the inventory scrap figures. Manufacturing productivity gains were lost in the noise of decreased product demand.

Problem #2: A disconnect between shop floor measurement systems and financial measurement conventions

In many organizations, standard measures of productivity on the shop floor do not tie directly to financial performance. For example, a shop floor supervisor may measure the team's labor utilization based on hours spent in a variety of activities including training and process improvement, while the financial metric of labor utilization may be based on hours spent only in direct production activities. Similarly, the team may track production scrap but not the cost of additional raw material inputs above the standard amount.

Another factor seems to be the lack of an IT infrastructure for gathering, integrating or analyzing factory data with financial data and posting results in a dashboard. Current operations and financial reports (e.g., manufacturing variance, site P&L, company P&L) can be hard to compare, and they are used in different forums by different decision-makers.

As a result, we have seen gaps as high as 200% between quarter-over-quarter change in financial metrics, such as gross margin, and change in shop-floor direct material and labor productivity!

Problem #3: Cultural and organizational barriers to joint efforts

In many organizations, the operations group has limited cross-functional interaction, hindering efforts to build common language and metrics. Functional groups, such as Operations and Manufacturing Finance, rarely come together to define metrics that serve multiple purposes, the critical link in performance measurement regardless of whether numbers are viewed through an operational or financial lens.

One common challenge is measuring labor productivity. Finance may track productivity in terms of regular and overtime pay relative to total hours worked to get a perspective on total cost per FTE, whereas Operations may measure productivity based on total labor, training and maintenance hours for an understanding of available time. Without common definitions, calculations and targets, the company is unlikely to improve overall labor productivity in ways that are measureable or meaningful enough to further the broader organizational goals.

A BETTER WAY

Overcoming these difficulties demands a new approach: integrated productivity management. We recommend six steps to create an integrated productivity management system:

1. **Disaggregate total costs.** Understanding of the factors that contribute to total costs is a powerful tool—and surprisingly absent in many plants. Using readily available data from purchasing and production management systems, companies can see how their overall cost base is split between direct and indirect materials, labor and support functions. Simply building such a picture can identify obvious targets for productivity improvement.

2. **Map processes into pathways.** Pathways are essentially "factories within a factory," the critical first step in disaggregating costs into meaningful groups. Pathways can often be identified by looking for common people, processes or products. Pathway breakdown should be intuitive and easily articulated across the organization, especially to the front line.

   While most pathways are end-to-end, some are cross-cutting. Even in the most complex manufacturing environments, certain aspects of production will share common features. A detergent manufacturer might produce liquid and powdered product in different lines, for example, but send both to a single packaging line. Building a picture of such production pathways establishes a framework for the next, more granular level of performance analysis (see Exhibit 1).

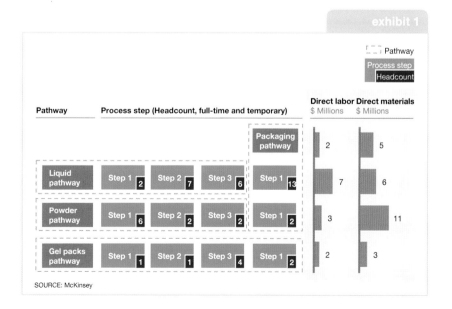

exhibit 1

SOURCE: McKinsey

At a fine chemicals company, we deconstructed all the operations at one site into ten pathways corresponding to different work areas in that site. We subdivided each pathway into five to seven sub-pathways based on the actual processes and raw materials involved and a common unit of output. This allowed the team to compare cost structures and level of granularity.

3. **Identify the key cost drivers for each pathway.** For each product in each pathway, companies can use historical cost data to understand how processes consume materials and labor. In this way, cost drivers estimate input costs based on output produced. Using regressions based on historical cost and output data, it is possible to establish statistically significant expected costs per unit produced. Material cost drivers are based on the physical units of output and vary by pathway or sub-pathway. At one bio-tech company, cost drivers were units, grams and milliliters produced. Regressions then capture the non-linear relationship between cost and volume. For example, a 15% increase in production volume for a certain bio-pharma product might require only a 10% rise in labor cost, since measuring and mixing did not take more time as volume rose.

    Operations input and ownership, especially from work area managers, is critical to ensure that the mathematical modeling is grounded in business and operational reality and the results interpreted correctly. For example, is an outlier a scrap event, an extraordinary yield event, or a data error? The combination of historical and statistical analysis can lead to breakthroughs in the accuracy of cost estimates.

4. **Create a synthetic "manufacturing unit" to account for mix and volume.** With the cost data created in step 3, a company can model expected production costs for any mix of product types and volumes. While it is impossible to add "apples and oranges," it makes sense to add the predicted costs of producing each and comparing them to actual incurred costs. Manufacturing units are not based on true physical output units but rather are synthetic units that normalize for mix and volume changes across time horizons and sites. The costs (dollars or hours) at the most granular level can be rolled up to the pathway and eventually site level to estimate costs and changes in cost productivity independent of SKU volume and mix (see Exhibit 2).

5. **Integrate cascading KPIs from executive to shop floor levels.** The new cost model provides a direct link between top level financial targets and shop floor actions. Because cost drivers at the sub-pathway level add up to pathway level, and then aggregate to the plant level, determining what pathways are responsible for changes in productivity across the plant is a straightforward process. Further, because pathway and sub-pathway definitions include existing teams and supervisors, each process

exhibit 2

SIMPLIFIED EXAMPLE

Pathway	Unit of measure	Period 0			Period 1		Period 2	
		Cost per unit	Units produced	Total cost	Units produced	Total cost[1]	Units produced	Total cost[1]
Pathway 1	Tube	$4	4	$16	10	$40	10	$40
Pathway 2	Liter	$6	8	$48	4	$24	10	$60
Pathway 3	Box	$3	12	$36	12	$36	20	$60
Total "scalable" cost[2]				$100		$100		$160
Normalized production volume			Mfg units: 100		Mfg units: 100		Mfg units: 160	
Notes		Baseline of historical plant performance (1 unit = $1)			Change in mix		Change in mix and volume	

1 Total cost based on 0% productivity change
2 Does not include indirect costs (e.g. indirect labor, overhead, corporate allocations, etc.)
SOURCE: McKinsey

has natural owners built in. Management can therefore cascade financial targets down through the organization and translate them into shop floor actions, or track the impact of an initiative. For example, if a manager believes his team can reduce scrap by introducing a new process, an integrated productivity management system allows direct material tracking at the sub-pathway or even product level to verify material cost reductions relative to baseline costs. The resulting impact on the overall site performance can also be determined when rolling up from product to pathway to plant levels. In addition, reviewing the pathway's direct labor spend relative to expected spend can highlight unintended impacts on labor costs (see Exhibit 3).

6. **Link to existing reporting mechanisms.** Finally, the system can serve existing primary reporting mechanisms, improving accuracy while presenting information in forms that will be familiar to executives. By establishing such links, companies gain immediate insight into the root causes of many manufacturing cost issues. In one case, a plant had made strenuous efforts to reduce scrap in key production pathways, but managers still had to explain increases in COGS. By reviewing pathway level detail, it was clear that the increasing costs could be attributed to higher volumes of a product line with higher material input costs. The managers were able to show that the scrap reduction program had in fact substantially improved direct material productivity.

exhibit 3

$ Thousands, unless otherwise noted

Change in productivity
▨ >3% gain
▨ ±3%
▨ >3% loss

2008
548 Manufacturing units[1]

Direct costs		Target	Actual	Productivity
	Direct material	4,000	3,850	3.8%
	Direct labor	1,000	1,050	-5%
	Total scalable cost	5,000	4,900	2%

Other costs		Target	Actual	Change[2]
	Indirect labor	2,000	2,150	-7.5%
	Overhead	1,450	1,380	4.8%
	Allocations	2,200	2,200	0%

Total costs		Target	Actual	
	Total	11,650	10,630	8.8%

Inventory		Target	Actual	Change[2]
	Raw and WIP	6,000	6,500	-8.3%

Scrap				
	Scrap	815	642	21.2%

1 Mix and volume adjusted normalized units across plant
2 Favorable change relative to target (i.e., 10% favorable change is 10% lower than target)
SOURCE: McKinsey

PUTTING AN INTEGRATED PRODUCTIVITY MANAGEMENT SYSTEM INTO PRACTICE

Locking in improvements requires a broad-based approach to incorporate new systems, practices and behaviors. Building a meaningful tool is the first step, but implementation requires changes in reporting, training and accountability. It does not require a complex new IT infrastructure. Five approaches can help ensure success:

Supplement monthly financial reporting with daily operating metrics.
Productivity metrics—calculated at the end of each month—act as trailing indicators. Including daily operational metrics as part of the integrated productivity management system provides shop-floor supervisors with leading indicators and reveals which levers will improve performance. For example, tracking in-process material scrap and labor utilization on a daily basis helps managers anticipate and adjust behaviors prior to publishing month-end productivity results.

Encourage a new dialogue. Integrated productivity management often demands new mindsets in organizations used to standard cost accounting and variances, and nearly always requires changing the vocabulary at all levels. Implementing an integrated productivity management system requires effort on the part of plant level personnel, but truly institutionalizing it demands a CEO-level commitment. Moreover, analyses from the integrated productivity management system must replace existing reporting methods. It cannot survive if viewed as merely "one more report" among a host of other separate and unrelated metrics.

Build the right ownership and reporting structure. The new approach typically requires a dedicated SWAT team led by manufacturing finance with representatives from Operations and IT to drive design, implementation and roll-out. Building an integrated productivity management system requires partnership among operations (Operations VP, work center managers) and manufacturing finance personnel (Manufacturing Finance VP, financial analysts), and requires IT support to access and manipulate data.

Create a granular view of the company. Leadership from Operations and Finance will distill the goals and remove roadblocks, freeing managers to define pathways and review cost drivers. In most instances, building and rolling out to a pilot site requires about three months of work. Among the most significant challenges is ensuring that all parties understand the goals and the benefits: the ability to isolate successes and challenges in productivity at multiple levels and to declare financial and operational victory with successful initiatives.

Invest in the IT infrastructure to automate reporting. This does not mean spending millions of dollars to build a complex ERP module. Rather, simple IT tools can automate data compilation. Any implementation requiring "high-touch" from Finance or Operations will tend to be more fragile, suffer from lower adoption, and worst of all, take time away from value-added tasks—reducing productivity. A robust implementation should therefore link to ERP systems and minimize the manual effort required to produce reports. At one company, the implementation team put together a simple set of Excel tools for automating the reporting in about two weeks.

* * *

Companies in almost any industry can implement an integrated productivity management system. It requires a commitment to understanding true drivers of costs and careful monitoring at all levels to ensure that productivity gains are real and as visible when walking around a shop floor as when reviewing quarterly financial performance. The ultimate result: a true partnership between Operations and Finance in which all parties speak the same language and see the same results.

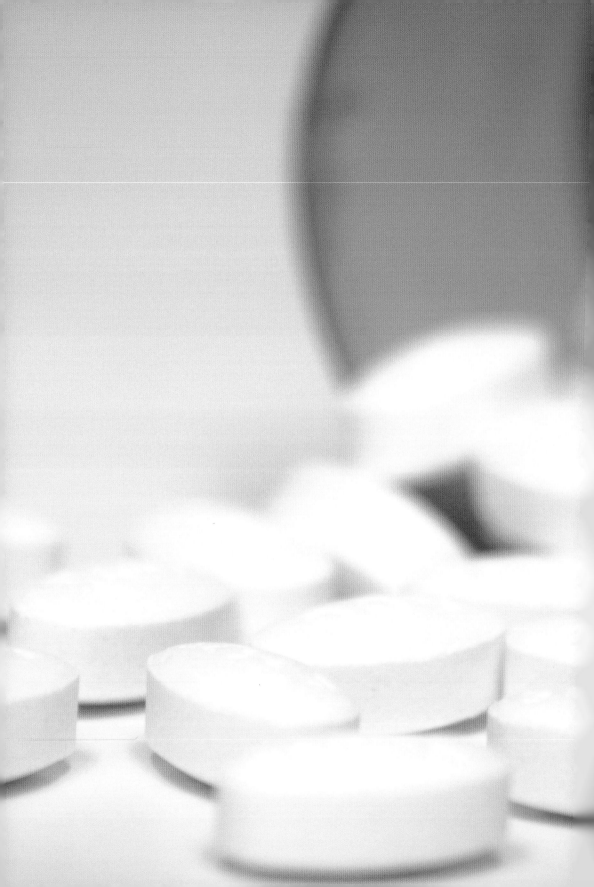

Developing new strategies for new times

Why quality-by-design
should be on the executive
team's agenda

Ted Fuhr, Michele Holcomb, Paul Rutten

Better practices in product and process development could raise the profits of pharmaceutical companies by up to 20%. Now is the time to implement Quality by Design.

New product development in the pharmaceutical industry is costly and time-consuming, and it often results in products that are expensive and difficult to make. It's getting harder to find safe and effective new products, but much of the expense, delay and rework in drug development occurs outside the clinical development process. Product and process development (PPD)[1]—the activities that include active ingredient manufacturing, formulation and analytical method development, regulatory review and approval, validation and preparation for commercial manufacture—account for 15 to 30% of overall R&D expenditures. Even more important, PPD directly determines production costs before and after commercial launch.

Of course, pharmaco executives are generally aware that their non-clinical development processes are less than ideal, but many

---

1   Product and process development (PPD) refers to a set of processes in pharma also known as chemical and pharmaceutical development (CMC), pharm sci, process development and tech development.

don't make a concerted effort to improve PPD. They may be focused on the demands of clinical trials, which largely determine whether a product gains approval for commercial marketing. Some don't believe better PPD can deliver the benefits in pharma that it has in other industries. Others think they have implemented the right tools and processes, but few companies use those tools systematically enough to reap their full benefit.

New approaches to manufacturing have clear benefits for patient safety and quality, but in this article, we focus on PPD improvements, which offer significant opportunity for value creation. Our models suggest that ineffective PPD is costing companies up to 20% of their potential net profits. Organizations across the industry that embrace the challenge can significantly reduce costs, improve products, shorten time to launch, reduce risk, and improve patient benefits. We estimate that for the industry as a whole, this opportunity could represent an incremental $20 billion to $30 billion in profits.

Building effectiveness in

Product development in nearly every industry is a major, complex undertaking, and pharma is no exception: development takes an average of four to eight years and about $1 billion (Exhibit 1). In most industries, most of the final cost of a product is determined early in the development cycle, when product parameters are defined. Thus, product development processes have a high impact on eventual manufacturing efficiency.

exhibit 1

Industry	Time Years	R&D capacity MY	Budget $ millions
Civil aircraft	4-7	5,000-10,000	2,500-5,000
Automobile	2.5-5	1,000-2,000	500-2,000
Pharmaceutical	4-8	500-1,000	500-1,500
Stationary gas turbines	3-5	500-1,000	300-500
Railroad rolling stock	2-3	50-400	20-160
Consumer electronics	0.5-1	10-100	5-50
Consumer durables	0.5-1	2-20	1-10

SOURCE: McKinsey

In pharma, PPD represents about 15 to 30% of overall R&D cost and time, can influence up to 50% of total R&D cost, and is a key determinant for all costs of goods sold from active pharmaceutical ingredient to final packaged product. And PPD is a critical contributor to the quality of the final product.

The efficiency of commercial pharma manufacturing operations established during product development lags other industries, despite similar expenditures. For instance, overall equipment effectiveness (OEE)—a standard operational performance measure—is 35-40% in pharma[2]. In consumer packaged goods, an industry with comparable processes, OEE ranges from 70 to 90%. Even comparably regulated industries, such as aerospace, regularly achieve average OEE rates above 50%. Pharma has a compelling case for increasing development cycle performance to reduce cost and bring the industry in line with others.

The QbD potential

To tap the PPD improvement potential, companies must adopt a new paradigm commonly known as Quality by Design (QbD).

One reason QbD has so much impact is that it enables companies to quickly amass and apply knowledge that is critical to the commercialization strategy. The more efficiently companies build this knowledge—including technical requirements, product profile, and regulatory compliance needs—the better they can use it to develop commercial manufacturing processes that minimize cost and risk, and maximize profits over a product's lifetime. Companies can accumulate this knowledge through more intelligent PPD investment and standardization of product development and technology platforms.

In addition to higher quality end-products, PPD offers many benefits: lower costs, shorter time to launch, improved patient benefits, and increased sales. We used a bottom-up approach to size the potential for pharmacos by quantifying each of these sources of value and estimating the impact of implementing QbD on an individual compound, a company, and the innovator pharma industry as a whole. We quantified the value PPD improvement brings, using conservative assumptions backed by industry experience and concrete examples.

We believe that improving PPD can increase an individual compound's lifetime value by 30 to 50%. Across a portfolio of compounds, this translates to a

---

2   McKinsey's proprietary operations benchmarking (POBOS) measures OEE at plant and line level for multiple technologies

reduction of 10 to 20% in annual COGS and 20 to 30% in PPD spending. Theoretically, across the entire innovator pharma industry, it represents an incremental $20 billion to $30 billion in annual profits (Exhibit 2).

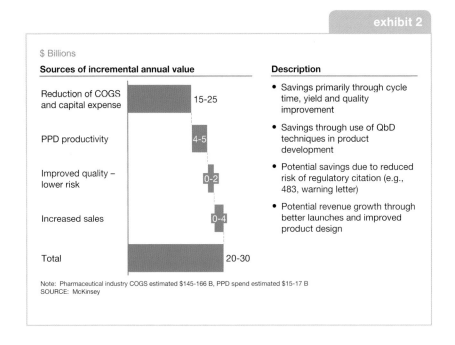

exhibit 2

$ Billions

Sources of incremental annual value

Reduction of COGS and capital expense	15-25
PPD productivity	4-5
Improved quality – lower risk	0-2
Increased sales	0-4
Total	20-30

Description

- Savings primarily through cycle time, yield and quality improvement
- Savings through use of QbD techniques in product development
- Potential savings due to reduced risk of regulatory citation (e.g., 483, warning letter)
- Potential revenue growth through better launches and improved product design

Note: Pharmaceutical industry COGS estimated $145-166 B, PPD spend estimated $15-17 B
SOURCE: McKinsey

We estimate that optimizing PPD practices would reduce COGS by 10 to 20%, which could produce $15 billion to $25 billion of annual savings on the industry's $145 billion to $166 billion COGS. In calculating this value, we included a reduction in manufacturing defects, cycle time, compliance cost, and commercialization cost, together with an increase in yield. For example, savings derived from cycle time reduction alone result in a 5% reduction in COGS.

Most important, companies can realize savings through QbD techniques without increasing PPD costs. Implementing QbD on the $15 billion to $17 billion industry PPD baseline can reduce PPD costs by $4 billion to $5 billion. In addition to value gained through operational efficiency, companies can find value in reducing compliance remediation costs and improving product-development-enabled sales, such as novel dosage forms or line extensions. We think some quality issues attributed to PPD could be avoided, which have imposed $1 billion to $2 billion in direct remediation costs on the industry from 1997 to 2006. The associated indirect costs—lost sales, manufacturing inefficiency, consulting fees, etc.—are easily in the billions of dollars. Improving PPD would prevent some of this waste.

Finally, PPD can increase revenue by ensuring smooth scale-up and product launch, and make it easier for companies to create differentiated products. The industry now derives at least $3 billion to $4 billion of value by through PPD-enabled sales. We estimate that PPD can further increase sales by up to $4 billion.

A large pharmaco, for example, failed to meet sales forecasts and overshot target COGS for an in-market pediatric product. Marketing and manufacturing executives were interested in reformulating the product, modifying the pricing structure, and making contracting changes. They engaged the PPD group within the company for assistance. Marketing surveys showed that patients would pay more for a pediatric liquid formulation than a solid formulation. The company implemented a QbD program to execute the new formulation. As a direct result of the program, the company developed the liquid formulation on time and within budget, and sales for the drug increased 48%.

Taking down the barriers

So what are the obstacles to widespread PPD improvement in pharma? The biggest one is the practice of transferring clinical trial production methods to commercial manufacturing. The driving force in PPD is speeding development in the clinical trial phase and producing drugs quickly so that the next clinical trial can launch without delay. Unfortunately, processes that are appropriate in trials may not be efficient for mass production. These sub-optimal processes often become the production processes for the commercially manufactured drug because management does plan for the optimization of these processes as part of the ongoing development and life-cycle management process.

The result is a variety of underdeveloped and inefficient product development practices: sub-optimal concepts, a lack of understanding of physiochemical process interactions, missed product parameter targets, high failure rates, long timelines, and inadequate prioritization. These problems are apparent in the high variance across the pharma industry of key aspects of product development, including the degree of development at different phases, investment strategy and governance models. This unevenness points to opportunities to identify and implement best practices.

A second obstacle to PPD improvement is an industry-wide tendency to point toward regulation and the governing bodies that enforce them as a primary source of development and manufacturing woes. Other regulated industries such as the aerospace and nuclear industries have very stringent rules, but continue to manufacture a much higher percentage of defect-free products.

The widespread use of QbD techniques in these industries enables them to achieve efficiency and extremely high quality despite regulatory restrictions which are similarly, if not more, stringent.

Seven years have passed since the FDA began to push the pharmaceutical industry to revolutionize how it develops and manufactures products and processes. Five years have passed since the adoption of regulations (ICH Q8 and Q9, Q10) meant to facilitate the implementation of QbD. But little has changed in most pharmacos. Today, as investors and the public push for increased ROI and quality from pharmacos, companies and regulators have an exceptional opportunity to join forces to push for better processes and lower costs through improved PPD.

Some industry proponents argue that pharmacos cannot adapt the QbD tools and technology from other industries to PPD without significant investment. Fundamentally, we believe that the tools are available and applicable in pharma and that skeptics underestimate QbD's potential.

Implementing QBD

Implementing QbD is complex and challenging; many of the concepts, frameworks, and tools are new to pharma PPD practitioners. As in any operational transformation, adopting QbD requires a cohesive set of technical tools, management infrastructure (such steering mechanisms and key performance indicators), and new mindsets and capabilities, including a training infrastructure, a knowledge base, and a high-performance operating culture within the PPD group.

But unlike lean programs, which pay off fairly quickly, the benefits of QbD may take three to five years to appear because it takes so long for pharma products to reach the market.

Many concepts have been associated with QbD, as evident in numerous publications and conference presentations. Generally, implementing QbD in pharma involves the combined application of design space, process analytical technology, statistical design of experiments, technology standardization, designing both production and quality methods according to the principles of "Poka Yoke" and even the introduction of new technology.

In our opinion, QbD also should include time-tested methods based on best practices in other industries and tailored to pharmaceutical development, like value stream mapping, design-to-cost and process risk analysis. The implementation of these tools does not require new regulations or guidance, as a handful of pharmacos have demonstrated, just dedication and know-how.

In practice, a QbD program is an integrated set of innovative techniques for designing high-quality products based on the most critical customer needs and compliance requirements at low cost (design to quality), along with methods for optimizing these new product designs for commercial manufacture (design for manufacturability. This combination creates a regimented yet smooth development process that yields superior quality, cost efficiency, and risk reduction (Exhibit 3).

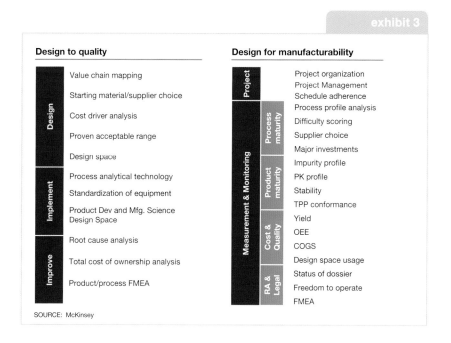

exhibit 3

Design to quality	Design for manufacturability

Design
- Value chain mapping
- Starting material/supplier choice
- Cost driver analysis
- Proven acceptable range
- Design space

Implement
- Process analytical technology
- Standardization of equipment
- Product Dev and Mfg. Science Design Space

Improve
- Root cause analysis
- Total cost of ownership analysis
- Product/process FMEA

Project
- Project organization
- Project Management
- Schedule adherence

Process maturity
- Process profile analysis
- Difficulty scoring
- Supplier choice
- Major investments
- Impurity profile

Product maturity
- PK profile
- Stability
- TPP conformance
- Yield
- OEE

Cost & Quality
- COGS
- Design space usage

RA & Legal
- Status of dossier
- Freedom to operate
- FMEA

Measurement & Monitoring

SOURCE: McKinsey

To govern the application of the new process, the PPD team should pass through a series of quality gates where predetermined product parameters must be achieved.[3] Managers control investment in drug candidates as they mature and move through the development process, and apply tools to ensure quality in the manufacturing process.

One international pharmaco, for instance, suffered from high costs in newly developed products and a lack of governance in the quality department in PPD. Individual products were up to 100% more costly than company executives estimated would be financially healthy. To reduce costs and improve quality, the company introduced a QbD program. Executives trained

---

employees in QbD tools and implemented a standardized project governance process that checks the application of those tools.

This approach guaranteed that PPD focused not just on R&D timelines, as before, but also on overall production process quality and cost. Executives understand that the application of QbD tools is not just mechanical, so they invested in creating a culture focused on the whole approach—for example, by introducing a shared language to communicate quality standards, exchanging people and knowledge across projects, and, perhaps most important, ensuring that QbD appeared on the top management's agenda.

CEO support

Implementing QbD requires investments in change management to ensure that the new methods stick. This requires a strong commitment from the executive team, including the CEO and his or her team, an overarching governance structure, and rigorous project management.

As a vital component of profitability, PPD requires that cross-functional performance objectives are in alignment. To ensure this, the CEO must create a compelling business case that lays out the company's overall objectives and each department's role in achieving them. Efficient PPD often entails multiple departments working in concert, including manufacturing, quality, regulatory, and R&D. Making the right tradeoffs between short- and long-term objectives, and among sometimes conflicting departmental needs, requires clear direction and strong arbitration.

Next, the CEO should build a strong and committed top team to provide direction and support to individual departments. Together they should craft a story to communicate the upcoming changes that excites people but limits the changes to those the company can realistically bear. It is important that all employees are clear on the high-level objectives and understand how they can contribute.

The top management team has an essential role to play in cascading the CEO leadership and direction to the senior management of the individual departments, so the changes may be integrated appropriately with other organizational processes. Improving PPD through QbD is primarily about execution, not approving higher levels of R&D investment. Delegating the task exclusively to the front line will not work. Naturally, scientists, engineers, experts, and smart regulatory negotiators are essential to a QbD program. Senior management must be educated enough to ask their scientific staff the right questions: not just "Is the project on time?" but also "What are the key risks?" and "Have we considered alternative designs?"

Implementing QbD takes a long time and requires active executive management throughout the process. To be successful, the program needs the support, governance, and cultural experience of the top team, who must be willing to make QbD a priority and act as role models through their own behavior. The top team should be visibly involved in a selected number of initiatives to send the message that solid progress is expected and will be rewarded.

* * *

We believe that the pharmacos, regulators, and the public at large can gain much from the broad-based adoption of QbD in the pharma industry. Not only are the benefits great: the opportunities are apparent. Perceived barriers to implementation are just that; supposed but not actual barriers. Companies that have successfully implemented QbD have shown that the rewards are worth the effort. We believe that pharma CEOs, COOs, R&D heads, heads of PPD and regulators alike should seize this opportunity.

Quality gates: Raising the standard of technical development

Michele Holcomb, Martin Møller, Paul Rutten

Good technical development can improve quality, lower costs, and get products to market more quickly, yet few pharmaceutical companies manage it well. Quality gates can transform the process.

New drugs have to be clinically effective. But to be commercially successful, they also have to be mass produced safely and reliably in a form that ensures a consistent therapeutic effect. This technical development process[1] absorbs between 15 and 30% of the development costs of a typical small-molecule drug, and even more in biologicals. Indirectly, it affects 50% of those costs if one includes, say, delivery of the supplies needed to run clinical and non-clinical trials. [2]

---

1   The process has other names, including chemistry, manufacturing, and controls (CMC); CMC development; process research; pharm sci; and chemical pharmaceutical development.

2   See "Why quality-by-design should be on the executive team's agenda" on page 194.

Good technical development can improve the quality of products and manufacturing processes[3], lower costs, and get products to market more quickly. Innovations in technical development can also open up new therapeutic uses, extend the life of a patent, and help products win a distinctive market position. Yet many companies still struggle to manage their technical development processes. Indeed, we believe that the pharmaceutical industry could raise its profits by up to 20% if companies systematically pursued opportunities to reduce the costs and increase the revenue of technical development. A management tool known as the quality gate is key to reaping such rewards.

Identifying risk early

Technical development is a complex and cross-functional activity that must overcome manufacturing challenges, take account of quality assurance, intellectual property protection, and regulatory compliance, and address scientific and medical issues. The traditional management approach is reactive: when problems occur, cross-functional groups come together to find solutions. But the end result is often higher costs or launch delays.

Part of the problem has been that R&D managers give scant attention to technical development, often regarding it as an enabler rather than a driver of value creation and focusing solely on development speed. Even when managers do try to assess technical development, the highly specialized and science-based nature of the work makes evaluation difficult. The first indication of trouble often comes only when the technical development team misses a critical project milestone.

Some companies are starting to do things differently. Quality by Design is a proactive, risk-based approach to technical development that helps identify potential problems before they occur, and puts mitigation strategies in place to ensure that the interests of all relevant functions are served quickly, smoothly, and cost-effectively. At the heart of this new approach are quality gates, used extensively in industries such as the automotive sector to manage the complex, costly, and time-consuming development process, and applied with great success in clinical development in the pharmaceutical industry. Many pharmaceutical companies claim to be using quality gates to manage technical development, too, but few do so rigorously enough to reap the potential rewards. Used well, quality gates can transform the technical development process.

Quality gates provide a mechanism to enforce regular, cross-functional evaluation of development risks. They measure the progress of the technical

---

3   See "Driving quality performance in pharma manufacturing" on page 132.

development project against a clear target state with attention not only to development speed but also future cost (or process robustness) and potential quality or regulatory issues. Any deviations are identified quickly and appropriate remedial action approved. Pressed managers are pleased to find that assessing a project at a quality gate is not a lengthy process—it typically takes less than half a day, and some companies use as few as four gates during the clinical development cycle of a new drug to assess whether it is ready for clinical trials, starting Phase II, scale-up, and commercial production (Exhibit 1).

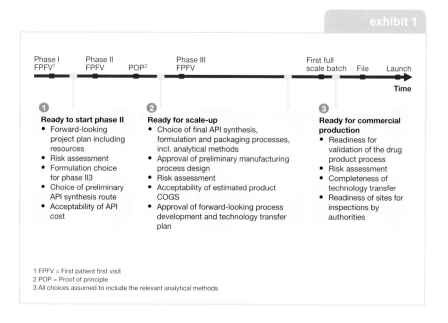

exhibit 1

Phase I FPFV[1] Phase II FPFV POP[2] Phase III FPFV First full scale batch File Launch

Time

1 Ready to start phase II
- Forward-looking project plan including resources
- Risk assessment
- Formulation choice for phase II[3]
- Choice of preliminary API synthesis route
- Acceptability of API cost

2 Ready for scale-up
- Choice of final API synthesis, formulation and packaging processes, incl. analytical methods
- Approval of preliminary manufacturing process design
- Risk assessment
- Acceptability of estimated product COGS
- Approval of forward-looking process development and technology transfer plan

3 Ready for commercial production
- Readiness for validation of the drug product process
- Risk assessment
- Completeness of technology transfer
- Readiness of sites for inspections by authorities

1 FPFV = First patient first visit
2 POP = Proof of principle
3 All choices assumed to include the relevant analytical methods

How quality gates work

Quality gate meetings are attended by key members of the project team and a management committee, often consisting of functional heads of chemicals, manufacturing, and controls (CMC), production, quality assurance, and regulatory affairs, and preferably a senior business leader such as head of R&D. All functions need to be represented to ensure the meeting focuses on time, quality and costs. The gates should be designed using three basic principles:

1. **They should be purposeful and proactive.** This means they should add value for all participants: they are not a reporting exercise. The objective is to smooth progress towards project goals, both in the near and longer term.

2. **They should be simple.** Each gate should require the minimum necessary preparation. The process should be easy to follow and communicate. Evaluation and target criteria should be clear and readily understood.

3. **They should be consistent and predictable.** Gates should use the same evaluation criteria for all projects, and progress should be tracked throughout the project using consistent metrics. In this way, information is easily accessible, comparisons can be made between projects, and those who perform the quality gate reviews gradually develop a valuable sense of pattern recognition.

Quality gates call for a collaborative working style, and participants must commit themselves to raising any problem as soon as possible. Discussions should be open and constructive, concentrate on finding solutions quickly, and culminate in defining next steps, individual responsibilities, and deadlines.

Measuring progress

At the heart of the quality gate process is a set of metrics that evaluate every aspect of technical development—the process, product, costs, legal and regulatory status, and chemistry, manufacturing, and control status (Exhibit 2). We call these "maturity metrics," their purpose being to measure progress towards developing and manufacturing a low-cost, high-quality product and delivering it on time. Each function is responsible for evaluating progress in its own area of expertise. But given the cross-functional nature of the work, other functions in the quality gate team need to endorse each evaluation.

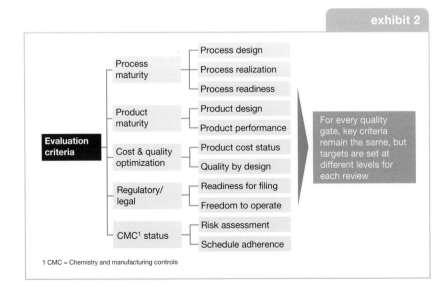

exhibit 2

1 CMC = Chemistry and manufacturing controls

A smart mix of qualitative and quantitative metrics can evaluate progress against defined targets without greatly increasing the workload of the teams involved. So, for example, a quantitative measure of process design maturity, itself a sub-category of process maturity, would be the number of impurities in the formulation. Qualitative metrics are needed for areas that are less easy to define, such as "freedom to operate," that is, whether a product infringes any patents.

The metrics are the same at each quality gate, though the targets are adjusted to reflect the different phases of development. A traffic light color-coding system then indicates the extent to which the project is on target, again using standardized definitions (Exhibit 3).

exhibit 3

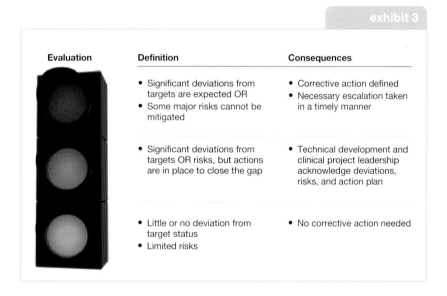

Evaluation	Definition	Consequences
	• Significant deviations from targets are expected OR • Some major risks cannot be mitigated	• Corrective action defined • Necessary escalation taken in a timely manner
	• Significant deviations from targets OR risks, but actions are in place to close the gap	• Technical development and clinical project leadership acknowledge deviations, risks, and action plan
	• Little or no deviation from target status • Limited risks	• No corrective action needed

This coding system is applied to every sub-category of the evaluation criteria. Exhibit 4 illustrates this for process design, showing the status of the active pharmaceutical ingredient, formulation, and packaging against certain targets. The warning signs here are that there is no map of the API value chain and solvent usage has not been analyzed.

The metrics not only record project progress to date—they also evaluate the risks involved in taking the project forward to the next stage, and offer a perspective on how the manufacturing process will evolve toward commercial production standards. Thus, the quality gate encourages agreement about what needs to be done to fix existing problems and reduce the likelihood of future problems.

exhibit 4

Evaluation criteria			Quality gate 2 – ready for scale-up		
			API	Formulation	Packaging
1. Process properties					
1.1	Process design	1.1.1	Process options	Final API synthesis route has been defined	Final formulation has been defined. Equipment train for production has been chosen	Final packaging process has been defined. Equipment train for production has been chosen
		1.1.2	Value chain map	Full value chain map includes yield rates, process times and all secondaries (e.g., solvents)	Fill value chain map includes yield rates, process times and all secondaries (e.g., solvents)	Fill value chain map includes yield rates, process times and all secondaries
		1.1.3	Difficulty assessment	Difficulties are listed, plan to handle is spelled out (QA, HSE, supplier capabilities, etc)	Difficulties are listed, plan to handle is spelled out	Difficulties are listed, plan to handle is spelled out
		1.1.4	Starting material choice	Starting materials including GMP/non-GMP status have been confirmed	Starting materials including GMP/non-GMP status have been confirmed	

The evaluations from all the various project areas are finally combined in a single chart, giving a clear overview of all aspects of the technical development process, and showing at a glance where risks and problems lie and decisions need to be made. The chart effectively dictates the agenda for the quality gate meeting (Exhibit 5).

Part of the value of the quality gate is the opportunity it gives participants to learn from the experiences of others on different projects. Much of the value of the process may be realized before the meeting, however. In the course of collecting the data needed for the quality gate, individual teams often start addressing problems they uncover straightaway. Individual, preparatory team meetings ahead of a quality gate are therefore important.

Some companies find it helpful to form a dedicated technical development project office to provide logistical support for the quality gate process. Ultimately, however, the success of quality gates depends upon those involved adopting a forward-looking, risk-based way of thinking about their work. Participants need to be comfortable collecting and sharing data that gives a realistic overview of project progress. And companies must raise the profile of technical development so that its value-adding role is recognized.

Pilot schemes can help. By using quality gates on one or two key projects with extensive management and administrative support, companies can fine-tune the process and demonstrate the value of the new way of working.

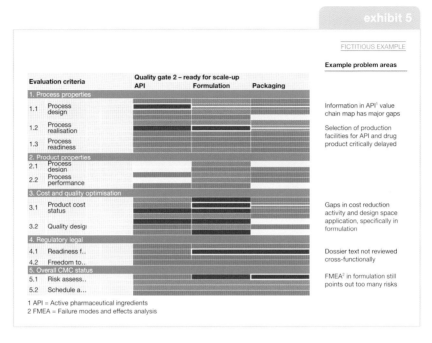

FICTITIOUS EXAMPLE

Example problem areas

Evaluation criteria	Quality gate 2 – ready for scale-up		
	API	Formulation	Packaging
1. Process properties			
1.1 Process design			
1.2 Process realisation			
1.3 Process readiness			
2. Product properties			
2.1 Process design			
2.2 Process performance			
3. Cost and quality optimisation			
3.1 Product cost status			
3.2 Quality design			
4. Regulatory legal			
4.1 Readiness f..			
4.2 Freedom to..			
5. Overall CMC status			
5.1 Risk assess..			
5.2 Schedule a…			

Example problem areas:

Information in API[1] value chain map has major gaps

Selection of production facilities for API and drug product critically delayed

Gaps in cost reduction activity and design space application, specifically in formulation

Dossier text not reviewed cross-functionally

FMEA[2] in formulation still points out too many risks

1 API = Active pharmaceutical ingredients
2 FMEA = Failure modes and effects analysis

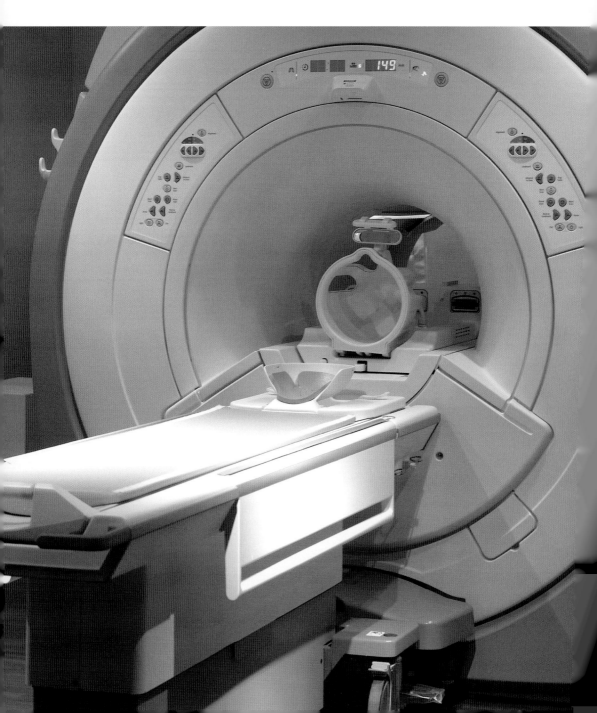

Design to value
in medical devices

Sastry Chilukuri, Michael Gordon, Chris Musso, Sanjay Ramaswamy

As price pressures increase, medical device makers need to rethink product development processes. Design to Value can help get costs under control—and deliver exactly what customers value.

"If medical device companies want to continue to make money as prices face continued pressure, their only option is to take cost out." This comment from the head of procurement at a major US healthcare provider neatly sums up today's situation in the medical device industry. The sector has always been challenging, with increasingly complex technologies and tough quality and regulatory hurdles. Until recently, however, device makers who overcame those barriers could sell their products at prices that made the effort worthwhile.

Today, medical device companies operate in a different world. In developed countries, healthcare systems are under acute financial pressure. Healthcare providers are responding by exploring every opportunity to increase efficiencies and reduce costs.

Developing economies are transforming the environment, too. As growth slows in established markets, opportunities are arising elsewhere. A rapidly growing middle class is demanding more medical devices of all types, but price sensitivity in these markets is acute. A sophisticated regional industry is growing to serve this demand, and ambitious new players from China and India are now keen to take their low-cost designs to enthusiastic hospital buyers in Europe and North America.

Now device makers have to find new ways to maintain their competitiveness. Like other industries before them—the automotive sector, consumer electronics and telecommunications, for example—they are paying new attention to the detailed design of their product ranges, looking for opportunities to eliminate excess cost wherever possible, to gain the flexibility to sell profitably in cash-strapped traditional markets and price-conscious new ones. History has shown that the winners will be those who can deliver exactly what the customer wants—nothing less, nothing more—at the best possible price.

Cheaper, but for whom?

This new game is challenging in developed and emerging markets alike. Success in emerging markets requires a deep understanding of stakeholders' needs—which is hard to get from a design office halfway around the world. One maker of electronic pacemakers, for example, developed a low-cost device aimed at the potentially huge tier-II market of lower-income customers in developing countries. By replacing the conventional programmable control with a simpler electro-mechanical version, the company dramatically reduced the cost of the device. The device was a market failure, however. Few customers in target regions could afford the combined cost of the pacemaker and the surgery to fit it. Few local hospitals had the capabilities to implant the devices, and those that did were suspicious of the mechanical controllers, worrying that they would need to carry out expensive secondary operations if devices failed. The company has since launched a programmable device, aimed squarely at the richer tier-I market. Surgeons, the gatekeepers in pacemaker selection, were more comfortable with the programmable devices, which they knew from their training in western hospitals. The programmable pacemaker has performed much better, capturing three quarters of its target market.

Even companies that are close to customers can misunderstand their needs. A US maker of electrotherapy devices, for example, embarked on a clever modularization program that allowed one device to be configured in many different ways at the time of purchase, or upgraded later as user needs changed. When it launched the product, however, more than nine out of ten customers chose the same basic configuration, and then rarely came back for more modules later. In the end, the modular architecture simply added cost to the product, and it lost out in the market to competitors with simpler designs.

Companies that do attempt to match product features and capabilities more closely to their customers' perceptions of value must answer a difficult question: Who are their customers? Fragmented decision-making in many healthcare markets makes it extremely difficult for companies to understand the requirements of all key stakeholders. To be selected for use, a device might have to be approved by a national or regional authority, selected by a healthcare provider, specified by a particular clinical team, and then chosen by doctors, often in consultation with patients. Finally, it may be the patient's own reactions to the device that define its success in use.

Each of these stakeholders will have an incomplete picture of product attributes: payors might not understand the importance of usability in patient compliance, while a physician may be unaware of the ongoing cost of supporting a product in the field. As a result, the incentives to purchase in many medical device markets may be fundamentally different from the benefits ultimately enjoyed by end users.

Where does the value lie?

To overcome these problems, medical device companies need new tools and a new way of thinking about product design. In particular, they need to be able to do two things effectively. First, they must find ways to understand exactly which product features their customers need and, critically, how much they are willing to pay for them.

Second, they must identify the most cost-effective ways of delivering those features to maximize available product margin. For many design and engineering teams in the medical device sector, this second requirement is particularly challenging. Years of focus on extending the technical capabilities of their products, with relatively little attention to design for manufacture or other cost-reducing strategies, have left them ill-equipped to find the powerful insights that drive cost out of their designs. These teams must find new ways of looking at the whole product design process, adopting best practices from their own industry and beyond.

Today, some smart medical device companies are recognizing that, by making this link between the true cost of features and their customers' perception of value, they can reliably deliver products that cost less and offer customers more. We call this approach Design to Value (DTV). Medical device makers have used it to deliver gross margin improvements of 20-25% over a typical 18- to 24-month period. Along the way, they have exploited quick savings that made the improvement projects self-funding. At the end of the process, they also have stronger product development functions, with departments working more effectively together and momentum in the organization for broader product and portfolio improvements.

What customers want

For all but the simplest products, purchasing decisions involve complex and subtle tradeoffs among features. Customers can rarely articulate the value they attribute to a particular feature in isolation. Fortunately, modern market research techniques can give a good indication of how the customer's perception of value is built.

Medical device companies have developed approaches to tackle the complex, multi-stakeholder environment. They first identify critical stakeholder segments for each stage of the product lifecycle, and define the influence of each on purchasing decisions. Stakeholders can be divided into two basic groups: gatekeepers, for whom a product has to meet a basic set of feature and cost criteria, and decision-makers who will actually make the final selection based on the differentiating features of the product.

For example, one maker of patient-operated blood-testing equipment identified four key segments across its product lifecycle. During the reseller adoption stage, pharmacies were a key gatekeeper, important in choosing the product, as were payors, who would fund it in their insurance schemes. Decision-makers included the patients themselves, who made final selection but were heavily influenced by their personal physicians.

Interviews and conjoint studies with representatives from each key stakeholder group then help companies to understand their differing priorities. In the blood-testing example, pharmacies valued the opportunity to maximize revenues, through ongoing sales of consumables for the meter. Payors tended to assume that all devices were equally effective, and focused their attention on the price of the device and its consumables. Health care providers were interested primarily in features that would ensure compliance with the prescribed testing regime. Patients, meanwhile, varied greatly in their requirements according to the nature of their disease. To understand what really drove their decision-making, the company needed to dig a little deeper.

Conjoint analysis is one technique that can provide a rich understanding of consumer needs. Customers consider various hypothetical product configurations and price points and choose between them. Regression techniques applied to their responses isolate the effects of individual features on the customers' perceptions of value. The results can be compellingly simple: an incremental "profit" value for each of a product's features.

Some medical device companies are now using conjoint techniques to navigate their complex stakeholder environments. The blood-testing company, for example, used the conjoint technique to test various product configurations in four different customers, segmented according to the nature and severity of their disease.

The conjoint analyses with each stakeholder group allow companies to construct a multi-attribute utility cost curve for each stakeholder. After including a basic set of product features to satisfy gatekeepers, this curve ranks each feature by the utility it provides to stakeholders and the cost of each feature. The curve can guide decisions about which features to include to maximize utility and minimize cost (see Exhibit 1).

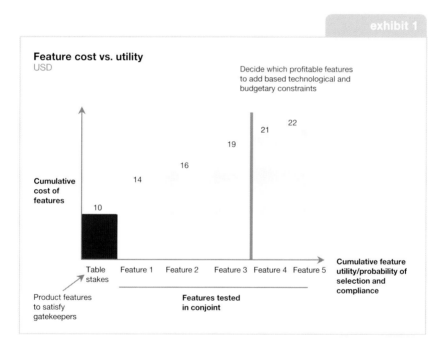

exhibit 1

Feature cost vs. utility
USD

Decide which profitable features to add based technological and budgetary constraints

Cumulative cost of features

10 14 16 19 21 22

Table stakes Feature 1 Feature 2 Feature 3 Feature 4 Feature 5

Cumulative feature utility/probability of selection and compliance

Product features to satisfy gatekeepers

Features tested in conjoint

A manufacturer of medical imaging equipment used conjoint studies in key customer segments to identify the factors most likely to build market share. The company found that price, brand name and image quality were the three most important decision attributes in the segment. Even though the company's products already ranked among the best in its segment in terms of image quality, the conjoint demonstrated that a moderate increase in quality had the potential to lift market share by 11%. Likewise, reducing downtime from four to two hours per month could increase market share by 7%, as could a 25% reduction in radiation dose, which would offer health benefits for patients.

What it really costs

The second critical element in the design-to-value equation is cost. Leading companies strive to deliver the features their customers most value at the lowest possible cost, overcoming the limitations of conventional cost engineering by adopting a clean-sheet approach.

While many companies invest heavily in product cost reduction, they usually do so by examining existing designs and identifying opportunities for incremental savings. Using Design to Value, companies first work to understand the likely limits of product cost reduction. Starting with a blank sheet and using knowledge of industry best practices for materials, processing and labor costs, they can build an estimate of the most efficient way to deliver the desired feature set (see Exhibit 2).

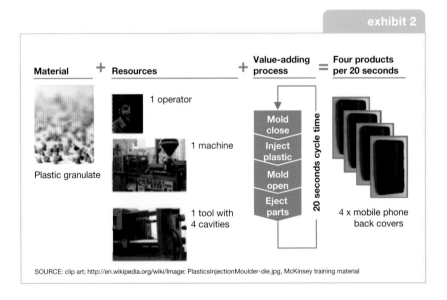

exhibit 2

SOURCE: clip art; http://en.wikipedia.org/wiki/Image: PlasticsInjectionMoulder-die.jpg, McKinsey training material

By comparing current or projected manufacturing costs with those in the clean-sheet model, companies can quickly gain insight into the areas of design most likely to yield the largest cost reductions. Opportunities identified in this way are often larger than those found in conventional cost engineering, since the technique encourages companies to consider changes to underlying product architecture and technology as well as individual components.

Clean-sheet analysis of its printed circuit board designs showed one device maker that it could reduce the eight separate boards in its existing design to just five, reducing the costs of the boards themselves, cutting assembly complexity and allowing the product's casing to be streamlined and simplified.

Tearing it down

Competitive teardowns are an important activity in many industry sectors. Pulling a competitor's product apart piece by piece and comparing it with one's own is nothing new, but it continues to deliver insights into opportunities for improvement or a new competitive edge. Some, such as the automotive industry, have spent millions raising the teardown process to an art. As competition increases and cost constraints tighten, companies in the medical devices sector are beginning to use this approach more widely.

In the design to value process, teardowns take on a new and central role as a context for cross-functional discussion and decision-making by engineering and marketing functions. Through teardowns of their own and competitor products, involving everyone associated with the product, including engineering, marketing, sales, manufacturing, quality assurance, and supply chain, companies can leverage all available expertise to optimize product design. Suppliers may even have roles to play in these workshops, as they may provide new perspectives on cost and functionality trade-offs (see sidebar: Medical device teardown case example).

The teardown process can be as useful with existing product lines as with new ones. In practice, comparisons of existing products often provide a range of ides that can be implemented quickly into the current design, while helping to generate a "wish list" of changes for forthcoming models.

In a competitive teardown of blood pressure monitors, one company compared its product with two competitors from the same segment. In a daylong session, the company identified 22 separate improvement ideas that could reduce manufactured cost by 18% without impacting customer value. Some of the ideas were simple and easy to implement: reducing complexity in the packaging and printed materials, switching to unbranded batteries, or replacing sewn labels with screen printing, for example. Others required more fundamental changes to the product: eliminating PCBs, reducing the size and thickness of the housing, or introducing surface mount components to reduce manufacturing costs. Finally, the company identified areas where it could eliminate features that were less valuable to users, such as an external power supply connector that was rarely used on what was essentially a portable device.

The teardown can also be a powerful source of other product improvement ideas. It helped one company realize that it would be cheaper to replace the custom-made black-and-white LCD screen on its product with an off-the-shelf color one that was more flexible and easier to use.

Discussions among functions during the teardown can also drive improvements. Conversations between the sales and design in the same company revealed the users found the elegant design of the product's accessories particularly appealing.   Eliminating the drawers where these accessories were stored and mounting them on external hooks, the company cut costs and emphasized one of the product's most compelling features.

* * *

The design to value approach is already helping medical device companies gain a much richer understanding of customer needs—and meet those needs more cost-effectively. While the approach has been proven in individual projects, some companies are now going further by building design to value skills and processes into their product development organizations (see sidebar: Making DTV happen). In a demanding but increasingly price-sensitive market, the ability to focus keenly on customer value can offer critical competitive advantages.

Making DTV happen

Companies are using Design to Value tools selectively to cut costs, raise margins and build market share. A small group of companies are going further, increasing margins by 20-25% across their entire product ranges. These companies do several things differently from their more cautious competitors:

- They set transformational goals for their products, using clean-sheet models to identify the minimum possible product costs and challenging design teams to achieve these levels, rather than being satisfied with incremental improvements.

- They emphasize impact and execution, with robust targets to check the progress of improvement ideas, and regular management reviews to highlight progress and remove roadblocks. This approach helps to deliver impact rapidly; ideas are often executed within a month of their identification, but it can also ensure ongoing improvement, with continual idea generation and feature modification throughout a product's lifecycle.

- They maintain an external perspective, understanding all decision-makers and stakeholders early in the product development cycle and revisiting the stakeholders regularly. They also repeatedly conduct teardowns on competitor products to understand design approaches, feature packages and cost positions. If customer insight or teardown skills are lacking, they train or hire external talent.

- They work to foster internal alignment, too. For example, one company encountered resistance to lower-cost products. Salespeople feared that the new products would cannibalize higher-cost alternatives. Once the sales team understood that the new product was aimed at a different customer tier, and that it gave them access to a new market and a competitive weapon to defend against new market entrants, they became fully supportive of the approach.

- They change their management systems and culture, with regular reviews of progress and incentives that encourage different functions to work closely together and ensure that quality, manufacturability and customer acceptance criteria are considered alongside cost.

- They implement a deliberate program to build Design to Value into their organizational DNA. Some companies establish a center of DTV excellence that provides specific skills and support to design teams. Others use specific projects as "gold standard examples," helping to educate the wider organization on the power of the approach.

Medical device teardown example

A medical-products company planned a series of tear downs to improve the design of its therapeutic medical device. To generate new ideas, executives invited colleagues from purchasing, marketing, engineering, and sales to see how their product stacked up against four rivals.

Seeing the products together was an "Aha!" moment for the purchasers, who quickly identified a series of straightforward design changes that, while invisible to customers, would significantly lower the cost of manufacturing the device. Meanwhile, seeing the configurations of

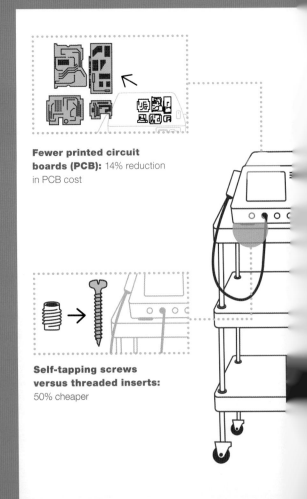

Fewer printed circuit boards (PCB): 14% reduction in PCB cost

Self-tapping screws versus threaded inserts: 50% cheaper competitors' circuit boards spurred the team's salespeople, marketers, and engineers to discuss the manufacturing implications of the company's modular approach to design. The engineers had long assumed that being able to mix and match various features after final assembly was advantageous and had emphasized this capability in the product's design. Yet the salespeople reported that most customers hardly ever ordered more than a handful of modules at purchase and rarely ordered more after assembly.

The conversations ultimately led to simplifications in the product's circuitry that lowered purchasing costs by 23% and helped marketers identify a new customer segment where the product might command a higher price.

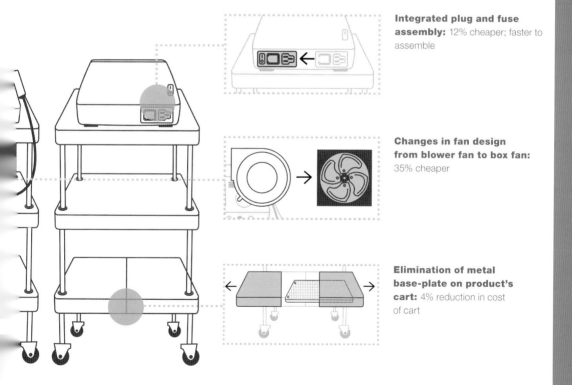

Integrated plug and fuse assembly: 12% cheaper; faster to assemble

Changes in fan design from blower fan to box fan: 35% cheaper

Elimination of metal base-plate on product's cart: 4% reduction in cost of cart

Smaller, leaner, nimbler: How some high-cost sites will survive

Andrew Gonce, Ulf Schrader, Ketan Shah

How can incumbent manufacturers facing high costs, falling volumes or threats from manufacturers in low-cost countries save their plants? The answer lies in transforming large traditional sites into smaller, leaner, nimbler plants to close the gap.

Pharmaceutical plant managers are facing multiple threats these days. Volumes are falling with looming patent expiries, competition is getting stiffer, especially from low-cost countries, and companies are looking to trim costs and streamline networks. Merger activity has only enhanced the threat of extinction for many plants. Some manufacturers have become more competitive by pulling multiple levers to close the gap and achieve first-quartile performance.

Multiple threats to high-cost plants

About $200 billion in revenue is at risk in the next four years from patent expiry, as volumes decline and generics penetrate the market. Few plants have been able to cut costs fast enough to keep pace.

Low-cost countries are gaining share quickly. Over the past five years, Indian manufacturers of sterile injectables have seen their US sales growth exceed 80% CAGR. Similar growth is taking place in other markets, particularly oral solids and APIs.   India has caught up in terms of technology and quality: it has more FDA-certified plants than any other country outside the US.

A recent analysis of a US company's competitiveness revealed that even as a first-quartile generics manufacturer, they face up to a 20% landed cost disadvantage relative to Indian manufacturers across their portfolio. A similar analysis in Europe revealed that only the top solid dose manufacturing sites could be competitive with new low-cost competition from India—even after the additional quality burden on the imported product (see Exhibit 1). Mean or below-average performers face even greater per-unit disadvantages—their landed costs can be triple those of Indian and other low-cost manufacturers.[1]

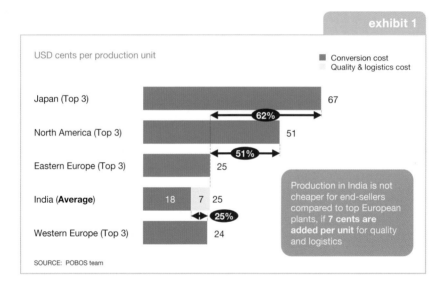

exhibit 1

USD cents per production unit

■ Conversion cost
░ Quality & logistics cost

Japan (Top 3)		67
	62%	
North America (Top 3)		51
	51%	
Eastern Europe (Top 3)	25	
India (**Average**)	18 7 25	
	25%	
Western Europe (Top 3)	24	

Production in India is not cheaper for end-sellers compared to top European plants, if **7 cents are added per unit** for quality and logistics

SOURCE: POBOS team

But moving production to India or other low-cost counties does not guarantee lower costs. Operations in India or China are not competitively advantaged with equipment purchased globally, and can have higher top management costs. Production wages are clearly lower, but so is average productivity. In fact, some companies that have set up operations in India for the labor advantage have had to invest millions more than expected to bring in the required skills.

Others have seen their final cost structures fall short of local competitors because they failed to change the way they operated in the new environment. So, while a high-performing Indian plant may outperform a European peer,

---

1   Both analyses based on McKinsey's proprietary operations benchmarking (POBOS), which compares unit costs and plant performance on a normalized basis.

there is no certainty that a new investment in India by a western manufacturer will outperform an existing high-performing site in the US or Europe. Companies therefore need to make a case-by-case analysis of off-shoring for Western markets to see if it really pays off.

Finally, merger activity and cost pressures continue to weigh on corporate leaders. Network rationalization can cut unit costs that are getting out of hand, and companies have announced aggressive plans to outsource. Following the Warner-Lambert and Pharmacia acquisitions, Pfizer rationalized half of its sites and shifted its footprint towards lower-cost sites. Similarly, Bristol-Myers Squibb targeted over half of its sites for closure and reduced headcount 10% as part of a significant restructuring effort.

Companies will continue to rationalize low-utilization, high-cost assets. How can sites survive?

Shutdowns are expensive

Plant shutdowns are not trivial—they typically take three to seven years. Tech transfer processes are long and expensive, too, with each product transfer costing more than $100,000—more if the product is truly global and requires filing with multiple boards of health. If the plant's portfolio is complex and some technologies unique, it will make the shutdown even more difficult and potentially risk the loss of some product families in the transition. In addition, severance costs are typically huge, companies may risk local, regional or national backlash, and the write-offs can be unpalatable.

Meanwhile, opening a new plant, even in a low-cost country, can costs tens of millions of dollars. Moving to a low-cost country is also not a slam dunk, as big pharmacos still worry about inherent country and quality risks, especially for some of their bigger products. They also face the challenge of finding the right talent to support and run a new site.

Some companies are finding alternatives to complete shutdown, however. They may sell the plant to a third party who operates it under contract and brings in additional products. To find a buyer, the plant still has to be cost-competitive for a contract manufacturer.

Fighting back

The secret to survival is not always targeting the lowest cost. A plant can survive if it is simply the best available alternative, especially when including landed costs and factoring in transfer risks. Plant managers can do themselves and employees a favor by cutting costs significantly when faced with this situation. Keeping costs in line can actually help bring in newer products and make the plant even more competitive, destroying the business case for moving production. This will not prevent the inevitable if offshore companies are far more competitive, but it may help delay the negative outcome, or make the plant a better candidate for sale and survival.

Managers should begin by assessing the gap between the plant and its competition, lay out a strategy, and then execute, execute, execute!

Assessing the gap

Not knowing where you stand among your peers inside and outside the company can leave you vulnerable to nasty surprises. One way to get an idea of where you stand is to use industry benchmarking, such as POBOS. It can also give you a directional idea of how far you need to go, and levers that might help. You can make comparisons to a "perfect plant" built upon top-decile performance indicators for a site of equal production demands.

Some sites also evaluate greenfield or zero-base options built upon an ideal footprint, product flow and talent base to get a sense of the gap (see Exhibit 2). Two sites, one in Puerto Rico and one in the US, took these paths to determine how to make 50% and 60% reductions in their workforces. The Puerto Rican site was able to redesign the manufacturing footprint, lab layouts, management structure, and product flow in response to a significant reduction in volume.

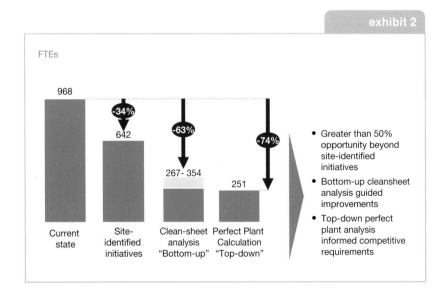

exhibit 2

FTEs

968

-34%
642

-63%

267- 354

-74%

251

Current state

Site-identified initiatives

Clean-sheet analysis "Bottom-up"

Perfect Plant Calculation "Top-down"

- Greater than 50% opportunity beyond site-identified initiatives
- Bottom-up cleansheet analysis guided improvements
- Top-down perfect plant analysis informed competitive requirements

Defining a strategy

Plant managers can find many ways to reduce unit costs beyond a simple headcount reduction and lean effort:

- **Reduce headcount—"right size":** Start by recognizing excess headcount and identify what you need to sustain the plant at lower volume. Employees will need to learn more jobs and be cross-functional. A study of standard work and value-add analysis showed that the packaging area at one site could be reduced by 39% immediately from right-sizing, and by an additional 22% from changeover and improved operations. The same approach in the quality labs showed that headcount could be reduced by up to 25% immediately without a loss in throughput.

- **Deploy lean—"clean sheet":** Do a lean diagnostic to find ways to reduce waste. Look at different ways to schedule production, labor, and shifts—fewer shifts and working days can cut costs dramatically, as can 4x10 shifts. Look for ways to make the workforce flexible or to minimize overhead and complexity. A large site in the US found that it could consolidate seven maintenance organizations into three or fewer by pooling work orders, sharing some responsibilities between crafts, and managing shift coverage. Eliminating these overlapping roles saved 10-15% on the maintenance cost base. Further analysis showed that if all seven organizations were consolidated into one, total savings would approach 25%.

- **Outsource:** Look at outsourcing to eliminate positions with low utilization. One company completely outsourced its HVAC maintenance, for example. Another evaluated outsourcing basic lab procedures by certifying suppliers and outsourcing reagent preparation, reducing lab technician time by 25%.

- **Manage complexity:** Look for ways to reduce complexity, such as trimming the "tail SKUs" that are a drag to production costs. Keep in mind that complexity can be a friend: producing low-volume SKUs efficiently can be a survival mechanism. It is important in such cases to understand cost per SKU and make it visible.

- **Optimize the footprint within the site:** Finally, look at ways to reduce the footprint within the site. Shut down or mothball modules that are not needed. This can significantly reduce utility needs, such as HVAC and boiler units. It may even make sense to invest in smaller, more efficient equipment and recoup investments from unused larger equipment, lowering maintenance and capex costs. Finally, a compact site is easier to manage with less supervision.

- **Other**: Look for any other incremental cost reduction opportunities, such as cost of supplies.

Execute, execute, execute

Of course, survival is not a walk in the park. Site leadership and employees have to accept that the platform is burning—and be willing to change. Honest communication about the situation is essential. Employees typically understand that sacrifices will be necessary to save at least some of their jobs. But this requires a new mindset, where all emplyees, from leaders to workers on the floor, thinks themselves as stakeholders in a small business.

The site will need a realistic but aggressive timeline and a clear plan to make it possible. Headcount cuts are not easy; making them as painless as possible for employees will help keep the process smooth.

Finally, the plant will need the right talent, such as lean experts, to define and reach the chosen goals. A strong and efficient PMO will help guide and keep the transformation on track. Employees will need capability-building and coaching to work across functions. They will need to make some quick wins to sustain the effort, which typically takes two years.

Case studies:

Many companies are facing the same situation in high-cost plants. Some have reacted by aggressively rationalizing, while others have allowed their sites to be less competitive as they evaluate their long-term options. Below are two case studies based on actual prior work by McKinsey teams within the past two years. The studies leveraged both lean and footprint consolidation levers to arrive at a best possible outcome.

A site faces dramatic downsizing or rationalization

A site in Puerto Rico producing branded pharmaceutical solids faced a significant risk of internal rationalization. Production volumes had fallen more than 70% from their peak in 2001 without any substantial changes in footprint or cost structure. POBOS benchmarking showed that productivity was in the fourth quartile compared to peers on a normalized unit basis. The site took action in two waves to quadruple productivity and regain competitiveness.

The first wave "right-sized" the organization to match volumes. The total site footprint was reduced 10-20% through closure and decommissioning of certain production areas and removal of rented trailer space. Consolidating packaging lines in particular yielded footprint and maintenance savings. The company also cut staffing by 35%, predominantly in packaging and quality related to the drop in volumes, the consolidation of some production, and quality automation.

The second wave began six months after the first, using lean levers and an additional 30-40% reduction in footprint, made possible by closing two major manufacturing areas. The plant also cut staffing by an additional 50% (60-70% in total), mostly by targeting operations and overhead layers.

In parallel, the site directly addressed the management culture. Site leaders recognized the challenge of adjusting to managing a significantly smaller and leaner organization. They redefined roles and departments to align the needs of the new site to the more competitive cost structure. In the end, the site radically altered its cost structure and will move from fourth- to first-quartile cost and productivity.

An incumbent faces low-cost country attackers

Threatened by low-cost manufacturers, an incumbent predicted a 20-30% landed cost disadvantage in its major market. Benchmarking revealed that the two largest production sites were within the top half of manufacturers but were disadvantaged relative to low-cost competitors. These plants, two to three times larger than the average in the benchmark set, had high exit barriers due to stranded costs and high transfer costs to a potential low-cost country site.

The company adopted a two-pronged strategy. First, it identified multiple cost improvement initiatives to close the cost gap with attackers. A lean initiative made variable and semi-fixed cost reductions. A procurement initiative reduced total direct and indirect spending. Together, these efforts targeted a total cost reduction of more than 20% savings within two to three years.

This program will make the manufacturer competitive in its major (local) market, but will not improve global competitiveness, essential for continued growth. So in addition to cost reduction, the company may have to look at other options to protect and grow share in global markets.

It remains to be seen if the now more-efficient sites will make any future move to a lower cost country harder. Other factors, such as tax and growth in emerging markets, will have to support any such move, as cost differentials alone will not make for an attractive business proposition.

Mastering the supply management challenge

Thibaut Dedeurwaerder, Chris Paulson, Ric Phillips

To manage increasingly complex supplier networks, pharmaceutical companies must develop new capabilities, organizational structures and management tools. They could learn much from the industries where mastering extensive external manufacturing has been a way of life for decades.

The days of large-scale vertical integration in the pharmaceutical industry may be over. Whether it was the acquisition of new technologies from external start-ups or the wholesale transfer of manufacturing responsibilities to external specialists, pharmacos have taken opportunities to cut costs, improve flexibility and reduce risk by expanding their third-party manufacturing capacity.

As the external supply base has grown, however, managers are increasingly recognizing the true complexities of the process. The opportunity may be large, but it brings new and significant risks. As they expand external manufacturing, companies need to learn how to reach a new level of supply management to capture the value.

Fortunately, others have travelled this road before. There is much that the pharmaceutical industry can learn from leading companies in other sectors – companies like Toyota, Dell, and Cisco – that have built successful mixed models of internal and external manufacturing. In this article, we will outline our view of these best practices, and discuss how they might be adopted and extended in the pharma sector.

Big pharma spreads out

Between 2001 and 2008 the pharmaceutical contract manufacturing industry doubled in size. It is forecast to continue growing at a rate of 11% per year and will likely be worth more than $26 billion by 2012[1]. Major pharmaceutical companies have announced plans for aggressive expansion of their external manufacturing programs. Pfizer says it wants to double the proportion of external manufacturing activities to 30%. Merck plans to outsource up to 35% of its manufacturing to India and China. By 2010, Bristol-Myers Squibb expects to have stopped production at half of its existing manufacturing sites. AstraZeneca says it expects to completely exit the manufacture of active pharmaceutical ingredients in the next 5 to 10 years.

At the same time, the contract manufacturing industry has become more sophisticated. Pharmacos now find it much easier to identify suppliers who can meet demanding quality and compliance specifications at lower cost than they can reach internally. Working successfully with contract manufacturers can also build capabilities or capacity to respond to technical and market changes. Technical evolution and the difficulty of forecasting demand frequently leaves pharmacos with overcapacity in older manufacturing technologies and a shortage of new ones. Contract manufacturers have been able to step in quickly to fill these gaps.

Perils and pitfalls

As outsourcing has grown, it has brought its own share of problems, however. Companies have found themselves struggling with late or incomplete shipments that have left them unable to meet demand, while a lack of transparency makes such problems difficult to predict and manage until it is too late. Poorly designed contracts mean costs creep up and companies find their suppliers difficult to control, while the sheer number of suppliers involved in some programs leaves pharmacos with the feeling that they are not building effective relationships with any. Perhaps most concerning of all are the major quality and compliance risks companies face through their third-party networks, from quality delays and cost increases, to potentially severe patient and regulatory failures.

---

1   Frost & Sullivan, 2Q 2008

Pharma executives frequently tell us they are frustrated with their suppliers. "We'd love to outsource more volume, but are concerned with aspects such as control of activities, supply chain transparency and how to maintain a proactive partnership," one told us. "We feel that only some of our current suppliers are able to offer us the strategic fit and perspectives we need." These problems have led some early adopters to slow or even reverse their outsourcing efforts. We believe this is a short-sighted response.

Hard, but not impossible

Such challenges are inevitable in any large external manufacturing effort, but they are not insurmountable. Many industries have faced the same issues and have learned to manage them, and pharmacos have yet consistently to adopt some core approaches. When we surveyed the purchasing performance of large companies across a range of industries, we found that the pharmaceutical sector, while far from the poorest performer, lagged significantly behind three other industries—automotive, electronics and packaged goods—in the sophistication of its management of external suppliers.

For this report, we examined the supplier management practices of several leading companies, including Apple, Dell, Cessna, Toyota, TSMC, P&G, and Cisco. All have made consistent cost, lead time, and quality improvements with comprehensive supplier management programs. From our review of publicly available information and in our conversations with experts from industry, we have identified three focus areas that appear to differentiate those who are mastering the supplier management challenge:

- *They create a supplier portfolio that suits their strategic needs.* For example, segmenting suppliers in a sophisticated way and then managing them accordingly is a practice we see applied relentlessly by leaders in other industries—they use clear criteria across areas such as technology, capabilities, product importance, and risk to segment. Then they tailor their entire management approach around this segmentation in terms of tracking, management reviews, plant visits, quality audits, and more. When they use the term "strategic partners," they mean three or four companies, not 50. By contrast, many pharma companies apply only simple criteria such as product sales volume to establish supplier segments, and then use a "one size fits all" management approach.

- *They design an organization specifically to manage that supplier network.* Leading companies treat external supply as an equal of internal supply. This means external supply managers report at the same level, have access to top talent in the organization, and are viewed as "up and coming" leaders. By comparison, despite regularly controlling 20-30% of manufacturing volume and managing a much more complicated network, many external manufacturing organizations report to lower levels, with fewer resources, and less management visibility than internal manufacturing. The perception that the external manufacturing organizations at many pharmacos are less important than internal manufacturing consistently frustrates supplier management leaders.

- *They work hard to drive improved performance at their suppliers.* For example, leaders hold suppliers to a level of risk management equal to their internal production facilities. They address quality or delivery issues with joint root-cause problem-solving. For example, an auto manufacturer placed five production engineers in one of their tier-2 suppliers to solve recurring cost and quality issues—for more than a year. By contrast, many pharmacos are much more reactive in supplier risk management, relying on reviews of batch records and infrequent formal audits instead of developing a proactive, on-site risk assessment and problem-solving approach.

Industry leaders have seen real results from focusing on these priorities. For example, Cessna was able to reduce costs by 15-20% and lead times by more than 75% by sending a team into supplier plants and focusing on joint process improvements. (Exhibit 1 shows a few practices of leaders. Later chapters will describe these in more detail). By improving its own practices in these areas to more closely align with leaders from other industries, the pharmaceutical industry could finally begin to enjoy the full value of more extensive external manufacturing.

Designing the optimum supplier portfolio

Third-party supply is already a significant and growing portion of pharma capacity. Many pharma companies have invested significantly in external manufacturing—some have outsourced more than a quarter of their overall production—but they are not yet capturing the full opportunity. Overly complex legacy networks that place more importance on historical performance than on long-term potential, and that have a tendency to treat all suppliers the same, have led to underperformance compared to other industries. Taking the following steps will help pharma companies design the optimal portfolio of external suppliers:

- Align the supplier selection process to overall business strategy
- Identify the full set of potential suppliers

exhibit 1

Best practices in other industries

Invest in a deep understanding of the economics of their key suppliers and create an expectation of transparency

Segment suppliers relentlessly with robust criteria that go well beyond "size," then use that segmentation to guide their management approach

Elevate supply management to operate as a peer to internal manufacturing, and develop or acquire the best talent

Demand and support operations excellence and continuous improvement at their key supplier's plants

Execute a quality and compliance risk management approach that takes a proactive approach to identify issues early

- Segment external suppliers using sophisticated criteria

- Use a rigorous process to select and negotiate with suppliers

- Create realistic competition between suppliers.

Most pharmacos have allowed their external supply base to grow organically, selecting and qualifying suppliers on an ad-hoc basis for particular projects, products, or markets. This evolution can produce a complex, expensive network that is difficult to manage. Large, unplanned supplier networks also fail to exploit either the cost advantages of allocating higher volumes to individual suppliers or the improved access offered by suppliers positioned close to rapidly growing markets. The best firms in other sectors, by contrast, take a much more rigorous approach. It starts *by aligning the supplier selection process to overall business strategy.*

Pharmacos may adopt any of several different competitive strategies, and each has implications for their optimum suppler portfolio. A company seeking cost leadership might aggressively seek low-cost country suppliers, for example, while another looking for technology leadership will want to forge collaborative relationships that give it access to critical skills and technologies.

Whatever their strategy, however, pharmacos must ensure they identify the appropriate supply base for their needs. They can do this by systematically collating knowledge from a wide variety of sources, including in-house expertise, trade fairs and industry publications. Depth of knowledge about the supply base is as important as breadth. Leading high-tech firms look hard at potential suppliers, tracking patent applications to identify technological leaders, for example.

We often see pharmacos fail to segment the supply base, relying primarily on volume or spend with a certain supplier, and many have far too many "critical" suppliers, ultimately reducing the focus of supply management activities. Leaders use *sophisticated segmentation criteria*, including criticality of the product, supplier capabilities, the supply landscape, and others (see Exhibit 2). Firms apply these criteria rigorously to the full supply base and use them to stratify the supply base for selection and, later, improve prioritization for active supplier management.

exhibit 2

Segmentation criteria	Example elements
1 Product value	• Revenue and margin generated by the product • Location on product lifecycle
2 Product criticality	• Impact of a disruption on supply assurance and profits
3 Product sophistication	• Technology or process complexity
4 Supplier capability	• Management performance (e.g., collaborative, proactive) • Productivity performance and quality/compliance record
5 Industry supply landscape	• Industry capacity constraints
6 Supplier strategic fit	• Presence in future growth areas
7 Supplier financial situation	• Financial stability, including historical performance and the product's importance to supplier
8 Product compliance risk	• Product compliance risk, including quality, safety, and regulatory compliance

Leading companies then use a rigorous supplier selection and negotiation process. One automotive company, for example, balances total cost of ownership (TCO), suppliers' overall track records, and their experience with specific technologies before drawing up a short list. Each supplier is assessed on potential TCO impact, strategic fit, compliance record, and history of serving the company. These categories are then weighted and used to rank all suppliers on the short list. This ranking can be used to drive negotiation priorities.

The best companies use smart negotiating techniques to get the best deal from their chosen suppliers. High-tech companies commonly rely on "clean-sheet cost modelling," which uses their own knowledge of material, production and supply chain costs to predict a supplier's true cost base. They use this information to push for the best possible price and identify opportunities for the supplier to execute performance improvements that can be passed on as cost savings.

Driven by technology, capability, or capacity, many pharma suppliers hold significant advantages over their customers. In order to create *competition between suppliers*, improvement potential needs to be clearly identified and defined during negotiations.   The potential may not materialize unless it is written into tough, enforceable performance criteria in contracts. The automotive industry has learned this painful lesson; the best firms now write comprehensive contracts that include multiple categories of terms and conditions, including ongoing price improvements, supplier service levels and logistics costs. They also prevent unexpected surcharges or cost increases by including agreements to cover variations in volume, raw material prices and transportation costs over the life of the contact.

Selecting the right suppliers is only the first step in a long journey. Leading companies pay even more attention to managing their supplier relationships. Relationship management is costly, and its value varies according to the category of supply, so the best companies segment their supply bases and allocate a different management approach to each. Strategically critical suppliers might be invited to contribute to product development, for example, or to participate in process improvement programs.

However strong their relationships with key suppliers, the best companies maintain leverage over them. Wherever possible, they keep dual sourcing opportunities available, for example, to minimize supply risk and maintain competition for supply to keep prices down and service levels up.

Designing the organization to effectively support external supply networks

Industries with a mature supplier management model have learned that, however broad their external manufacturing ambitions, it is changes at home that determine success. Historically, pharmacos have faced challenges in directing the appropriate talent and management to external suppliers. We believe that taking these actions will help:

- Elevate external manufacturing management within the organization

- Staff the organization with dedicated supply management professionals

- Develop a strong internal capability-building program

- Establish a rigorous ownership and decision-making process for cross-functional activities.

The first change that smart companies make is to elevate the role of external supplier management within their organization. To deliver this, the best companies *place supplier management at the same organizational level as manufacturing management*, and staff it accordingly. Toyota, for example, not only positions purchasing and supplier management at the same top organizational level as manufacturing in each of its regional divisions, it has also recently established a separate "supplier breakthrough" team, with the same seniority, responsible for ramping up and strengthening supplier capabilities.

Supplier management is different from manufacturing management and requires a unique combination of skills. Supply managers need a manufacturing specialist's understanding of a wide range of technologies, products and processes, together with a purchasing professional's negotiating skills. For pharmacos, these capabilities may be in short supply. The top performers recruit supply management professionals from other industries and identify talent internally.

The best companies will also take deliberate steps to continually *develop their talent in-house*. One high-tech company that we worked with has built a training program for external supply management that combines classroom learning with daily reinforcement on the job. That reinforcement included a green-belt project requirement, rotation into different categories of manufacturing, and regular feedback and coaching. The program has created deep "bench strength" that has helped support a rigorous recruiting program.

Finally, the supplier management function must consistently interface with other functions, from product development to supply chain. The best companies don't leave these interactions to chance. Instead, they *establish rigorous decision-making criteria* together with formal groups and processes to ensure that responsibilities are clear and execution is effective. For example, one of our pharma clients recently redesigned their supply management organization from the group up using the RACI tool (Responsible, Approve, Consult, Inform) to ensure process discipline, eliminate redundancies, and streamline the decision making process. They also developed a rigorous resource model that the leaders of the procurement, internal manufacturing, and external manufacturing agreed to.

Driving external suppliers' performance excellence

Pharma companies often find it difficult to replicate the success of other industries in working with suppliers. In pharma, event-critical supplier relationships tend to be more "hands-off" than in other industries, reducing transparency in day-to-day performance, collaboration and best practice exchanges, and limiting companies' ability to identify risks early. True operational excellence is especially difficult given the complexity of supplier networks and inherent product specialization, but we believe that improving these four areas will deliver improvements quickly:

- Develop KPIs that adequately reflect the priorities of the relationship

- Instill strong performance management discipline

- Develop advanced risk-management approaches

- Expect and support continuous cost and performance improvement from external suppliers.

With the right supplier base and supplier management infrastructure, pharmaceutical companies can drive the performance of their suppliers. Generally, supplier performance management evolves in three distinct phases: from simple monitoring through true supplier performance management to supplier development, in which the customer helps suppliers continually improve their performance.

As with supplier selection, companies need a smart approach to supplier performance management, segmenting their supplier base according to value and strategic importance and investing additional time and attention only where it is likely to be rewarded.

Supplier management starts with the *right performance indicators*, chosen to reflect the priorities in the supplier relationship. Quality, cost improvement and service KPIs are common, but smart companies also measure dimensions such as issue resolution or innovation performance where appropriate. Naturally, managers must rigorously collect and review KPI information and take action whenever performance falls short of expectations.

The best companies treat scorecards only as a starting point, however. Important suppliers are also subjected to a *rigorous performance management structure* highlighted by regular performance reviews. This improves their ability to identify potential issues and areas that would benefit from deeper involvement. In addition, regular reviews with suppliers allow the company to compare suppliers' performance against the competitive market and use "clean sheets" to compare changes to the suppliers' cost base with the best case.

As pharmacos rely more on external suppliers, supply and quality risks increase. Since the failure of a strategically critical supplier could be disastrous, leading companies take a proactive approach to risk management.

Some companies are now *developing more advanced methods for risk mitigation*, including formal methods for evaluating and mitigating supplier risk. They track a range of measures like those described above, triggering an alarm if a key supplier appears to be experiencing difficulties. At that point, leaders will conduct proactive, on-site risk assessments to get ahead of the problems. They will identify those issues and jointly solve the root causes of the problem.

Others are already adopting an approach pioneered in the automotive sector to map the principal sources of quality risk in key suppliers. Risk "heat maps" use a company's own knowledge of process risks to predict the parts of a supplier's operation that have the largest potential to create problems. These heat maps can be used to indentify critical criteria during supplier selection, and companies can engage directly with their existing suppliers to agree on appropriate risk management and mitigation techniques. For critical suppliers, top companies map the full operational taxonomy of past, current, and future risk in detail and carefully manage to those risks (Exhibit 3). One of our pharmaceutical clients developed a detailed risk management heat map and mitigation approach that they first installed at their own plants. They are now rolling out that approach to their most important suppliers.

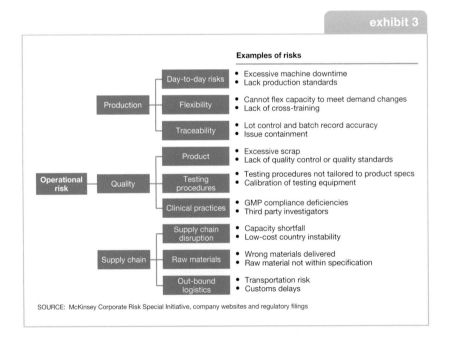

exhibit 3

Examples of risks

- Production
  - Day-to-day risks
    - Excessive machine downtime
    - Lack production standards
  - Flexibility
    - Cannot flex capacity to meet demand changes
    - Lack of cross-training
  - Traceability
    - Lot control and batch record accuracy
    - Issue containment

- Operational risk
  - Quality
    - Product
      - Excessive scrap
      - Lack of quality control or quality standards
    - Testing procedures
      - Testing procedures not tailored to product specs
      - Calibration of testing equipment
    - Clinical practices
      - GMP compliance deficiencies
      - Third party investigators

- Supply chain
  - Supply chain disruption
    - Capacity shortfall
    - Low-cost country instability
  - Raw materials
    - Wrong materials delivered
    - Raw material not within specification
  - Out-bound logistics
    - Transportation risk
    - Customs delays

SOURCE: McKinsey Corporate Risk Special Initiative, company websites and regulatory filings

One example of how pharma companies are adapting to mounting risks in the supply market is consortia-based risk pooling. In 2009, the Rx-360 consortium was founded to help pharma companies protect themselves against industry-wide quality threats like the adulterated heparin that led to

81 deaths in the U.S. and Europe. Participating companies plan to reduce risks with better audit standards, auditor training, and auditor certification, developing the infrastructure for audit sharing between companies, and rigorous tier-2 and -3 supply monitoring.

Finally, the best companies enforce their expectation that their suppliers will *continually improve cost and performance.* They write improvement expectations into contracts, but they also take a partnership approach, making joint investments with key suppliers where appropriate. The best companies are also using their own manufacturing skills to help suppliers improve, by teaching them new lean manufacturing techniques and helping to direct their application at supplier sites. In the spirit of treating partner plants as their own, leading manufacturers invest heavily in the success of critical suppliers.

***

It is time for the pharmaceutical industry to take the next step in supplier management. As other industries have proved, the value of well-executed third-party manufacturing is simply too great to ignore. As a first step, pharmaco leaders should take a hard look at their current supplier management practices and compare them with best practices from the automotive and high-tech sectors. If they can begin to close that gap, we believe they can dramatically increase the value delivered by their outsourcing programs, while simultaneously cutting risks and enhancing flexibility.

One size does not fit all: Emerging market distribution needs a custom fitting

Vikas Bhadoria, Raymond De Vré, Ulf Schrader, Ketan Shah

Pharma companies are increasingly looking to emerging markets to fill revenue gaps as patents expire. A single distribution strategy may not suffice for every emerging market, however, because each one features tiers with unique access challenges. Reaching these diverse and fast-growing markets requires a tailored strategy.

Growing importance of emerging markets

Emerging markets are fast becoming economic powers. Over the next ten years, they are expected to grow at 9% annually, compared to only 4% for developed markets, and represent about 43% of the world's GDP by 2018. Much of this growth will occur in cities considered tier-2 or below.

Likewise, pharma growth in emerging markets will far outpace growth in developed markets (see Exhibit 1), fueled by an expanding middle class and the increasing prevalence of lifestyle diseases stemming from growing incomes.

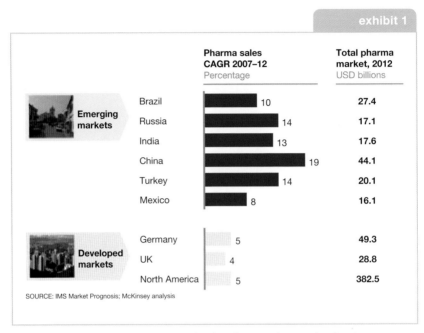

		Pharma sales CAGR 2007–12 Percentage	Total pharma market, 2012 USD billions
Emerging markets	Brazil	10	27.4
	Russia	14	17.1
	India	13	17.6
	China	19	44.1
	Turkey	14	20.1
	Mexico	8	16.1
Developed markets	Germany	5	49.3
	UK	4	28.8
	North America	5	382.5

SOURCE: IMS Market Prognosis; McKinsey analysis

While per capita consumption remains low for now, increasing buying power can grow the market exponentially. For example, if China's per capita pharma consumption were to approach a quarter of what it is in the US, China's market would be as big as America's. Although this is unlikely in the near term, opportunities in emerging markets can no longer be ignored.

Emerging markets distribution

Emerging markets differ in many ways:

- Patients, pharmacies and physicians are typically the key decision-makers, and payors have a smaller role
- Brand provides informal protection, while IP protection is relatively weak
- Branded generic penetration is much higher.

Emerging markets also differ from each other. For example:

- A significant portion of healthcare in Russia is funded from public sources; India and Brazil are predominantly "out-of-pocket"
- The hospital channel has a major influence in pharma distribution in China, while retail chains have a strong profile in Mexico, and more than half a million independent pharmacies dominate in India
- Government plays a limited role in Brazil and a strong one in Turkey.

Given the differences in markets and available infrastructure in each region, companies must customize their approaches. Large MNCs have focused mostly on tier-1 markets within emerging economies, such as Moscow, Shanghai and Mumbai. While major treatment centers and much of the population reside there, an even bigger population lives in tier-2 and -3 markets, and routine healthcare is becoming ever more accessible in these areas.

It is thus becoming more important to penetrate tier-2 and -3 markets, which are poised for continued economic growth (see Exhibit 2). While global pharma companies have made inroads into larger cities in some tier-2 markets, such as Nagpur in India and Kazan in Russia, many tier-2 and -3 towns remain hard to reach; distribution in emerging markets can be difficult. Each market, and some submarkets, are different and need a distinct and potentially hybrid approach.

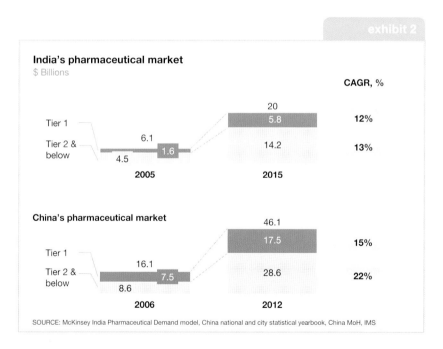

exhibit 2

India's pharmaceutical market
$ Billions

CAGR, %

Tier 1

Tier 2 & below

	2005	2015	
Tier 1		20 / 5.8	12%
Tier 2 & below	6.1 / 1.6 / 4.5	14.2	13%

China's pharmaceutical market

	2006	2012	
Tier 1		46.1 / 17.5	15%
Tier 2 & below	16.1 / 7.5 / 8.6	28.6	22%

SOURCE: McKinsey India Pharmaceutical Demand model, China national and city statistical yearbook, China MoH, IMS

Key challenges in distribution in emerging markets

Distribution infrastructure is not well organized in most emerging markets and even less so within tier 2 & 3 markets. Typical challenges to distribution include:

- **Poor access and infrastructure:** Poor infrastructure makes it difficult to reach and service tier-2 and -3 markets. Most lack established, cost-effective third-party logistics providers (3PLs) who can consolidate supply from multiple sources.

- **Market fragmentation:** Tier-2 and -3 markets tend to be fragmented, so reaching them can be cost-prohibitive. A sales force that reaches the interior can not only tap these markets but can also form the last leg of the supply chain.

- **Strong local dealers/stockists:** It can be difficult or even impossible to circumvent local dealers and stockists who have strong relationships with pharmacies and hospitals. So given the pharmacy channel's influence in decision-making, these local relationships are a factor in any successful distribution setup.

- **Tax laws and import processes:** Complex tax laws across state and provincial borders often require more local warehouses than needed for cost-effective distribution. Complicated customs clearance and import processes pose a challenge to timely deliveries—especially for products requiring cold storage.

- **Product security:** Repeated, manual handing of product raises the risk of damage and counterfeiting, and theft remains a key concern in most emerging markets. In 2005, 20,650 robberies accounted for $240 million in losses in Brazil alone[1].

- **Lack of talent:** Good supply chain talent with local expertise is hard to come by—this function has not yet matured in many regions. Top talent also tends to migrate toward tier-1 cities, although this situation is slowly changing.

- **Changing landscape:** The distribution landscape is changing rapidly, given that many companies and industries are focusing on emerging markets. Local players, such as Mahindra 3PL in India, are waking up to these opportunities and may change the face of distribution—or even make current channels obsolete. Pharma companies will need to keep an ear to the ground and be ready to grasp new opportunities.

---

1   CSCMP – Global Perspectives – Brazil, 2007

Current state of distribution in key markets

Brazil

A typical pharmaceutical supply chain moves product from the manufacturing plant or port into a company-owned or 3PL-operated main warehouse. From here, goods typically flow through logistics operators, pharmacy chains or distributors, such as Panarello or Profarma, on their way to retail chains, hospitals and government distribution networks. Challenges in this market include complex tax laws that create complicated routes, high theft rates, and the need for road transport, which presents risks from overloading, long hours and excessive speed.

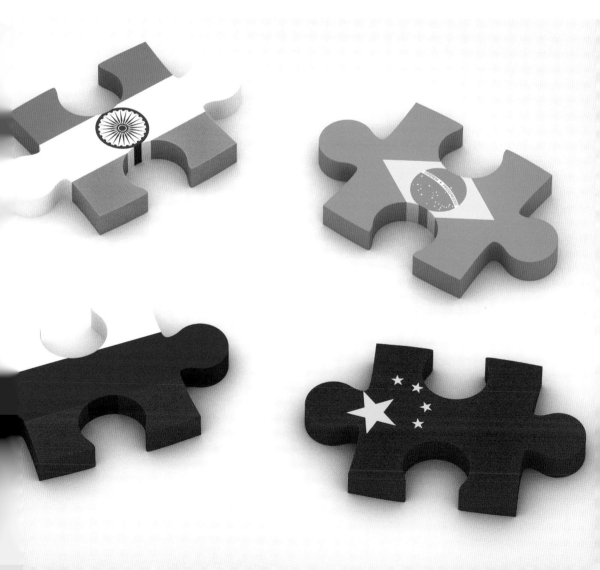

China

As the largest emerging market, China is seeing double-digit growth. Most major pharmacos focus their sales force on high-growth tier-1 markets with key account management and innovative services directed to hospitals.   Tier-2 and -3 markets are growing rapidly, too. The key to success there is cost-effective coverage. Manufacturers typically have a central warehouse and outsourced regional warehouses, with lower-tier warehouses in some markets. Dealers may be appointed to capture retail markets, but many companies go direct to hospitals. Key distribution challenges are local protectionism that can prevent 3PLs from operating across multiple provinces, supply chain security risks, fragmented logistics, and hard-to-reach rural markets.

India

Companies are beginning to tap India's huge growth potential, distributing 75% of their products through more than half a million retailers. The market is dominated by branded generics, and the typical route to market is from main to regional warehouses owned by the company. Carrying and sales agents work with stockists and dealers to reach the retail locations. Key challenges in this market are poor infrastructure, supply chain security risks, and a lack of temperature-controlled warehousing and transportation.

Russia

Ten players dominate pharmaceutical distribution in Russia, accounting for 85% of the market. The leading retailer in Russia, 36.6, has grown from revenues of $211 million in 2004 to more than $1 billion in 2008. It is the world's largest country, spanning 11 time zones and more than 17 million square kilometers of often rugged landscape that present unique challenges to transport. Russia's infrastructure, while extensive, has been in long decline due to lack of maintenance and modernization. Bureaucratic customs clearance, certification processes and order-specific import licenses pose challenges to timely delivery.

Five success factors and lessons learned from successful companies

Companies have used many approaches to penetrate tier-2 and -3 cities in emerging markets. While each nation-tier combination may have unique distribution challenges, the pharma industry could learn a lot from pioneers in its own and other industries. The following factors serve as a foundation to build compelling results in emerging markets.

1 Local understanding and customization

Local knowledge is critical to understanding market needs and cost-effective ways to reach customers and retailers. Replicating distribution strategies from more developed markets and other emerging markets have led to many false starts.

2 Supply chain talent

Rapid growth of distribution needs in emerging markets has resulted in a talent shortage. The lack of local expertise in this field highlights the need for companies to hire the best talent.

Jointown: Local understanding coupled with supply chain expertise

Jointown Pharmaceuticals in China is a joint venture that focuses on wholesale, logistics and distribution of pharmaceutical drugs and medical supplies. Its sales grew to RMB 18.9 billion in 2008, with online sales of RMB 1 billion, in the span of a few years. Since 2003, Jointown has made deliberate investments in talent, technology and infrastructure. It acquired the best available talent from places like Harvard, MIT, and NEC. It installed an order-to-cash online platform that makes it easy for its customers to make purchases.

Jointown has reached rural markets with a wide footprint. Ten subsidiaries and large-scale logistics centers, 30 regional distribution centers, and more than 100 branch distribution centers have allowed the company to cover 70% of municipalities and autonomous regions in China.

The next phase of expansion to 20 large-scale distribution centers, 100 regional DCs, 300 distribution branches and 5000 retail drug stores will allow it to cover most of China and capture a significant share of the Chinese pharmaceutical market.

3 High degree of ownership

Companies frequently own and operate distribution networks in emerging markets, in some cases with strategic partners, while in developed markets, a handful of strategic partnerships with distributors and wholesalers many be adequate. Retaining decision-making and ownership of end-to-end processes often helps companies provide better service for customers.

Many successful companies have vertically integrated distribution due to lack of reliable alternatives (especially in the cold chain), but this is being tested as foreign and domestic 3PL players expand their capabilities. When considering outsourcing in the distribution chain, companies must be careful not to underestimate the relationships they will need to build with local distributors or stockists, as they may control the channel to the point of sale.

Souza Cruz: Owning distribution end-to-end and investing in channel relationships

Souza Cruz, a subsidiary of British American Tobacco, is the unchallenged leader of the Brazilian cigarette market, with $3 billion in revenues and a 60% share. It is acknowledged as a model supplier by the COPPEAD business school in Rio. Its strength lies in direct service and its relationships with 240,000 POS locations. It has also invested in a large footprint, with a São Paulo distribution hub and five other integrated high-tech distribution centers. This is supplemented by 24 distribution centers and supported by more than 80 strategically placed supply stations, which allow it to cover the length and breadth of the country. Its fleet of 100 vehicles and 2000 sales and delivery staff control the last leg of transportation to retail locations. This allows the quick turnaround and high service levels critical to maintaining a high market share.

4 Commercial positioning

Product offering and route-to-market should be tailored to meet supply chain and customer needs. Consider greenfield development of a de-engineered product, with fewer features and more "value for the buck." For example, in many emerging markets, pharmacists are willing to cut blister packs in half or less as required by price-sensitive customers. Companies can win by tailoring packaging and pack sizes to meet market needs.

Frito-Lay: Taking charge of the distribution network and improving positioning of product offering

Frito-Lay entered India's highly fragmented snack food market in the 1990s. It tried to piggyback on parent Pepsi's distribution network, but the market failed to respond—local products continued to sell in higher volumes. Subsequently, the company created its own distribution network with super-stockists and about 800 distributors who could reach more than 400,000 retailers in all towns with more than a million people. It adapted products to local tastes and met with much greater success.

5 New and non-traditional models

Companies are trying new models to penetrate the market and make processes simpler, such as kiosks for rural reach and mobile technology to improve order-to-cash processes. Non-traditional distribution methods could also succeed in emerging markets. In India, for example, this could take the shape of a partnership with the Rural Health Mission. In addition, companies should also be willing to "unbundle" the business system, create ad hoc organizations to serve lower-income segments, or create tailored, lower-end businesses that run as separate units. These new organizations can be cheap and responsive, avoiding the parent company's traditional mindset and higher cost structures. This approach requires the development of a multicultural, multi-company governance system.

Mary Kay: Innovating to reach geographically dispersed customers despite infrastructure challenges

Mary Kay was founded in 1963 in Dallas, a market with well-developed transportation and logistics. How could the company expand and achieve success in a country like China, where distribution is less mature? With a strategy to replicate its business model of relying on Beauty Consultants (BCs), the question was, "How can we reach geographically dispersed BC's in a cost effective way?"

Now working with China Post, Mary Kay reaches more than 1000 cities in China cost-effectively and quickly—with tracking capabilities and a guaranteed lead time for deliveries of 1-3 days nationwide. In addition, 72 Order Pickup Points (OPP), have been set up across the country. Mary Kay covers the cost of delivery to OPPs, and BCs can either pick up products there or request delivery for the final leg at an additional cost.

Partly by ensuring an efficient distribution system, the business grew than 50% per year in 2007 and 2008. Today the company can deliver quickly to around 350,000 BCs in the in China, despite relatively few orders and low volumes per order (230k orders per month and less than 10 kg per order). The rapid response and reach have helped the company further expand its presence in a fast-growing market.

* * *

Emerging markets are known to have the potential for significant consumption growth. But companies should tailor their approaches carefully and look beyond top regions to consider opportunities—and challenges—in tier-2 and -3 regions.

Outpacing Change in Pharma Operations
December 2009

Authors

We welcome your thoughts and reactions to the topics and ideas in this book. Please contact our practice coordinator or any of the authors individually.

Knut Alicke (knut_alicke@mckinsey.com) is a senior expert in the Stuttgart office

Elissa Ashwood (elissa_ashwood@mckinsey.com) is a practice specialist in the Pittsburgh office

Vikas Bhadoria (vikas _bhadoria@mckinsey.com) is a principal in the Delhi office

Kai Biller (kai_f_biller@mckinsey.com) is an engagement manager in the Hamburg office

Sirish Chandrasekaran (sirish_chandrasekaran@mckinsey.com) is an engagement manager in the Silicon Valley office

Doane Chilcoat (doane_chilcoat@mckinsey.com) is an associate principal in the Los Angeles office

Sastry Chilukuri (sastry_chilukuri@mckinsey.com) is an engagement manager in the New Jersey office

Philipp Cremer (philipp_cremer@mckinsey.com) is an associate principal in the Berlin office

Peter De Boeck (peter_de_boeck@mckinsey.com) is a principal in the Brussels office

Aaron De Smet (aaron_de_smet@mckinsey.com) is a principal in the Houston office

Raymond De Vré (raymond_de_vre@mckinsey.com) is a principal in the Geneva office

Thibaut Dedeurwaerder (thibaut _dedeurwaerder@mckinsey.com) is an engagement manager in the Paris office

Kristoffer Dieter (kristoffer_dieter@mckinsey.com) is an engagement manager in the Orange County office

Thomas Ebel (thomas_ebel@mckinsey.com) is an associate principal in the Düsseldorf office

Lorenzo Formiconi (lorenzo_formiconi@mckinsey.com) is an engagement manager in the Frankfurt office

Ted Fuhr (ted_fuhr@mckinsey.com) is an engagement manager in the New Jersey office

Katy George (katy_george@mckinsey.com) is a director in the New Jersey office

Andrew Gonce (andrew_gonce@mckinsey.com) is an engagement manager in the Atlanta office

Michael Gordon (michael_gordon@mckinsey.com) is a knowledge expert in the New Jersey office

Jochen Großpietsch (jochen_grosspietsch@mckinsey.com) is a principal in the Barcelona office

Maia Hansen (maia_hansen@mckinsey.com) is a principal in the Cleveland office

Michele Holcomb (michele_holcomb@mckinsey.com) is a principal in the New Jersey office

Amit Jain (amit_jain@mckinsey.com) is an associate principal in the Silicon Valley office

David Keeling (david_keeling@mckinsey.com) is a director in the Chicago office

Martin Lösch (martin_loesch@mckinsey.com) is a principal in the Stuttgart office

Eric McCafferty (eric_mccafferty@mckinsey.com) is an associate principal in the Philadelphia office

Monica McGurk (monica_mcgurk@mckinsey.com) is a principal in the Atlanta office

Martin Møller (martin_moller@mckinsey.com) is a principal in the Copenhagen office

Chris Musso (chris_musso@mckinsey.com) is an associate principal in the Cleveland office

Janice Pai (janice_pai@mckinsey.com) is an engagement manager in the New Jersey office

Chris Paulson (chris_paulson@mckinsey.com) is an engagement manager in the Orange County office

Ric Phillips (ric_phillips@mckinsey.com) is a principal in the Chicago office

Sanjay Ramaswamy (sanjay_ramaswamy@mckinsey.com) is a principal in the New Jersey office

Sue Ringus (sue_ringus@mckinsey.com) is an engagement manager in the Pittsburgh office

Paul Rutten (paul_rutten@mckinsey.com) is an associate principal in the Amsterdam office

Nick Santhanam (nick_santhanam@mckinsey.com) is a principal in the Silicon Valley office

Frank Scholz (frank_scholz@mckinsey.com) is a principal in the Chicago office

Ulf Schrader (ulf_schrader@mckinsey.com) is a principal in the Hamburg office

Jatan Shah (jatan_shah@mckinsey.com) is an engagement manager in the Orange County office

Ketan Shah (ketan_shah@mckinsey.com) is an associate principal in the Chicago office

Jean-Philippe Talmon (jean-philippe_talmon@mckinsey.com) is an associate principal in the Geneva office

Vanya Telpis (vanya_telpis@mckinsey.com) is a senior knowlegde expert in the New Jersey office

Jonathan Tilley (jonathan_tilley@mckinsey.com) is a senior expert in the Orange County office

Marc Vinson (marc_vinson@mckinsey.com) is a practice manager in the Cleveland office

Marco Ziegler (marco_ziegler@mckinsey.com) is a principal in the Zurich office

McKinsey & Company is a global consultancy firm that helps leading corporations and organizations to make distinctive, lasting, and substantial improvements to their performance. The firm's 8,000 consultants around the world advise companies on strategic, operational, organizational, and technological issues across industries. McKinsey is a global leader in operations consulting with a network of over 2,500 practitioners. In the past four years, we have completed more than 4,200 operations engagements, spanning all major sectors.

Introducing the Operations Extranet

McKinsey's Operations Extranet is a global platform dedicated to exploring the latest developments in manufacturing, product development, supply chain management, procurement, and other operations topics.

We invite you to apply and enjoy access to an exclusive, online global community of operations professionals. Members can participate in conversations with peers at leading institutions to test and shape opinions, grapple with shared operational challenges, and broaden their professional networks. Members also receive exclusive articles, commentary, and analysis from experts in McKinsey's operations practice.

To apply, follow this link: http://operations-extranet.mckinsey.com

McKinsey's Pharmaceutical and Medical Products Operations practice focuses on issues specific to this industry. The practice's 180 members serve clients on lean manufacturing, supply chain, quality and compliance, technical development, outsourcing and offshoring, change management and capability building, strategic sourcing, and other topics.

For more information, please contact the practice coordinator:

Vanya Telpis
600 Campus Drive
Florham Park, NJ 07932
phone: +1(973) 549-6620
email: Vanya_Telpis@mckinsey.com

McKinsey offices

Chicago
21 South Clark Street,
Suite 2900
Chicago, IL 60603-2900
United States
Tel: +1 (312) 551-3500

Delhi
Plot No. 4 Echelon Institutional Area
Sector 32
Gurgaon Haryana 122001
India
Tel: +91 (124) 6611000

Hamburg
Am Sandtorkai 77
20457 Hamburg
Germany
Tel: +49 (40) 361210

New Jersey
600 Campus Drive
Florham Park, NJ 07932-1046
United States
Tel: +1 (973) 549 6600

Orange County
131 Innovation Drive,
Suite 200
Irvine, CA 92617
United States
Tel: +1 (949) 737-7400

Stuttgart
Birkenwaldstraße 149
70191 Stuttgart
Germany
Tel: +49 (711) 25535

Switzerland
Hotelstraße
CH-8060 Zürich-Flughafen
Switzerland
Tel: +41 (44) 876 8000
——
Avenue Louis-Castaï 18
CH-1209 Genève
Switzerland
Tel: +41 (22) 744 2000